初中英语教师职业发展需求
基于云南省多语民族地区的实证研究

Professional Development Needs of Secondary School English Teacher: An Empirical Study Based on Multilingual Ethnic Areas of Yunnan Province

钟 维◎著

科学出版社
北 京

内 容 简 介

相较于大城市里的教师而言,工作在多语民族地区的英语教师长期以来一直面对不同的困境,而这些困境恰恰成为其专业发展需求的社会动因。在职英语教师培训通常以三种方式展开:①针对新课标或政策的专题性短期培训;②专家入校系统培训;③自主展开的学习。前两种多为学校导向,而后者是个人导向。

本书以2010—2013年参与云南某高校的"国培计划"部分受训者作为被试,针对多语民族地区初中英语教师职业发展的需求展开实证研究。全书共分三个部分九个章节。第一部分即第一章,整体介绍研究背景、意义和研究的核心问题。第二部分为第二至第五章,分别介绍了建构主义学习理论、成人学习动机理论、教师信念理论,其中教师信念包括班杜拉的交互决定模型、教师工作效能和语言学习态度理论。第三部分为第六至第九章,分别从定量和定性研究的数据出发,分析并解读了多语民族地区初中英语教师的职业发展需求,重点探讨其自我效能以及语言学习态度和培训动机之间的内在关系。

本书适合高年级本科生、研究生以及从事与教育技术、英语教育等相关的科研人员阅读。

图书在版编目(CIP)数据

初中英语教师职业发展需求:基于云南省多语民族地区的实证研究 = Professional Development Needs of Secondary School English Teacher: An Empirical Study Based on Multilingual Ethnic Areas of Yunnan Province:英文 / 钟维著. —北京:科学出版社,2019.11
ISBN 978-7-03-055979-1
Ⅰ. ①初⋯ Ⅱ. ①钟⋯ Ⅲ. ①英语-中学教师-师资培养-研究-云南-英文 Ⅳ. ①G633.412
中国版本图书馆 CIP 数据核字(2017)第 312898 号

责任编辑:杜长清 / 责任校对:王晓茜
责任印制:李 彤 / 封面设计:润一文化

科学出版社 出版
北京东黄城根北街 16 号
邮政编码:100717
http://www.sciencep.com

北京建宏印刷有限公司 印刷
科学出版社发行 各地新华书店经销
*
2019 年 11 月第 一 版　开本:720×1000　1/16
2019 年 11 月第一次印刷　印张:14 1/4
字数:320 000
定价:89.00 元
(如有印装质量问题,我社负责调换)

Explanation of the Abbreviations

(Alphabetic Order)

AC	attitudes to the target language culture
AEC	attitudes to English culture
AEL	attitudes to English language
AES	attitudes to English speakers
AL	attitudes to the target language
AMC	attitudes to ethnic minority language culture
AML	attitudes to ethnic minority languages
AMS	attitudes to ethnic minority language speakers
APU	attitudes to particular uses of the target language
AS	attitudes to the target language speakers
ASV	attitudes to the social value of the target language
CPGPRC	the Central People's Government of the People's Republic of China
ELA	English learning attitudes
ELT	English language teaching
EPS	Education Participation Scale
ET	English teachers
ETE	English teacher efficacy
FT	family togetherness
GALL	general attitudes to language learning
GELA	general English learning attitudes
GLLA	general language learning attitudes
GMLA	general ethnic minority language learning attitudes
GTE	general teacher efficacy

HERC	Higher Educational Research Center
MOE	Ministry of Education of the People's Republic of China
MOF	Ministry of Finance of the People's Republic of China
NBSC	National Bureau Statistic Council
NECS	New English Curriculum Standards
NET	non-English teachers
NETE	non-English teacher efficacy
NTP	National Training Plan
PCD	participation course development
PD	program director
PU	particular use of the target language
PUE	particular use of English
PUM	particular use of ethnic minority languages
SCNPC	Standing Committee of National People's Congress
SLA	second language acquisition
SS	social stimulation
SVE	social value of English
SVM	social value of ethnic minority languages
TE	Teacher Efficacy
TES	Teacher Efficacy Scale

注：本书缩写词的写法大部分取自相应英文实词首字母，部分缩写词使用了核心词的缩写形式（如教师语言态度部分），部分缩写词使用了官方统一用语。

Contents

Explanation of the Abbreviations

Part 1　Background of the Research

Chapter 1　Introduction ······· 4
  1.1　National Training Plan ······· 4
  1.2　English Language Education Policy in China: Ideology Changes from Political-Oriented to Utilitarian-Oriented ······· 8
    1.2.1　Political-oriented English education: the 1860s to the mid-1970s ······ 8
    1.2.2　Economic-oriented English education: 1978 to 2000 ······· 9
    1.2.3　Instrumental English education: expansion after 2001 ······· 10
  1.3　Problems of English Education in Multilingual Ethnic Minority Areas of Yunnan ······· 12
    1.3.1　Language barriers in multilingual areas ······· 15
    1.3.2　English teachers' poor teaching quality ······· 16
  1.4　Significance of the Research ······· 18
  1.5　Research Questions ······· 19
  1.6　Research Rational ······· 20

Part 2　Theoretical Framework of the Research

Chapter 2　Key Concepts on Teacher Professional Development ······· 28
  2.1　Teaching as a Profession ······· 28
  2.2　Professional Teachers in Western Terms and *Shide* in Chinese Context ···· 31
    2.2.1　Professional teachers in Western terms ······· 31

  2.2.2 *Shide*: old Confucian requirements··33
 2.3 Stage of Teacher Professionalism in Current China···························36
 2.4 Teacher Knowledge Base ··45
Chapter 3 Social Constructed Cognitive Process ·······························47
 3.1 Constructivist Learning Theory ··47
  3.1.1 The "novice" and the "expert" in constructivist learning process ····47
  3.1.2 Vygotsky's dialectical constructivism ·································48
  3.1.3 Instructional scaffolding ··49
  3.1.4 Organizational context ···50
 3.2 Constructivist Learning Theory and In-service Teachers' Training··········50
Chapter 4 Motivation and Adults' Education Participation ················52
 4.1 From Maslow to Herzberg ··52
 4.2 Roger Boshier's EPS··54
Chapter 5 Teacher Beliefs ··57
 5.1 Bandura's Model of Reciprocal Determinism··································57
 5.2 Teacher Efficacy and Its Influencing Factors ·································59
 5.3 Attitudes in Language Learning···62

Part 3 Major Findings

**Chapter 6 Language Learning Attitudes of Secondary School
     English Teachers in Multilingual Areas** ·······························67
 6.1 Distribution and Strength of ELA··69
  6.1.1 General English learning attitudes ····································70
  6.1.2 Five English learning attitudinal dimensions ························71
  6.1.3 Spearman rank correlation analysis of ELA ·························73
 6.2 Distribution and Strength of Ethnic Minority Language
   Learning Attitudes··73
  6.2.1 General learning attitudes towards ethnic minority languages ······73
  6.2.2 Five ethnic minority language learning attitudinal dimensions ·····74
  6.2.3 Spearman rank correlation analysis of the ethnic minority
     language learning attitudes ··76

6.3	Strength and Correlation of Language Learning Attitudes ·················· 76

- 6.3.1 Strength and correlation of AC ···································· 76
- 6.3.2 Strength and correlation of AS ···································· 78
- 6.3.3 Strength and correlation of AL ···································· 80
- 6.3.4 Strength and correlation of attitudes to social value of the target language ··· 81
- 6.3.5 Strength and correlation of attitudes to the particular uses of the target language (PU) ·· 82

6.4 Teachers' General Attitudes to Language Learning ··················· 83
- 6.4.1 "English is a cultural carrier." ···································· 83
- 6.4.2 "English has more social values than ethnic minority languages."····· 85

Chapter 7 Teacher Efficacy of Secondary School English Teachers in Multilingual Areas ··· 88

7.1 ETE Strength ·· 89

7.2 Teacher Efficacy Strength and the Demographic Features ············ 90
- 7.2.1 Age ·· 90
- 7.2.2 Teaching years ·· 91
- 7.2.3 Teaching subjects ·· 93
- 7.2.4 Professional titles ·· 94
- 7.2.5 Ethnicity ·· 95

7.3 Difficulties for Teaching English in Rural Areas ····················· 95
- 7.3.1 "I don't know how I can motivate my students to learn English." ····· 96
- 7.3.2 "The principal always assigned me to do other things not related to my teaching." ·· 99
- 7.3.3 "Family guidance is so poor that parents barely have positive influences on students." ·································· 100

7.4 The language Barrier for Teaching English in Multilingual Areas ········ 104
- 7.4.1 "This is a multilingual area and you don't need to learn English to survive." ·· 105
- 7.4.2 "English can only be taught in Chinese, but I have many students who cannot speak Chinese." ·························· 108
- 7.4.3 "I don't know their languages and I can only teach in Chinese." ···· 110

7.5 Beliefs on Professional Teacher and Teaching Profession 112
    7.5.1 "If I care more about the students, they would gradually believe in us." 113
    7.5.2 "Sometimes I like being a teacher but sometimes I don't." 114
    7.5.3 "Being a teacher doesn't mean teaching knowledge only, and it also means educating students to be responsible for society." 115
    7.5.4 "We are the lowest of the society but doing the hardest job." 115

Chapter 8 Education Participation Motivation of Secondary School English Teachers in Multilingual Areas 119
  8.1 Exploratory Factor Analysis 120
  8.2 Strength of Educational Participation 123
  8.3 Differences of EPS Strength of English Teachers Among Various Demographic Groups 124
    8.3.1 Teaching years 124
    8.3.2 Age 127
    8.3.3 Professional titles 129
    8.3.4 Ethnicity 130
  8.4 Correlations Between ELA and EPS of English Teachers 131
  8.5 Correlations Between TE and EPS of English Teachers 133
  8.6 Differences of EPS Between High and Low GTE English Teachers 134
  8.7 Reflections on In-service Training 136
    8.7.1 "Long program is better than short one." 136
    8.7.2 "Some techniques are impractical for us." 138
    8.7.3 "Government should send young teachers to learn more, not just experienced teachers." 141

Chapter 9 Teachers' Professional Development Needs 143
  9.1 Three Major Findings 144
    9.1.1 AEL contributes most to the motivation in in-service training 144
    9.1.2 AES has a considerable effect on the motivation for professional advancement and cognitive interests 145

    9.1.3 Instrumental attitudes to English lead to pragmatic needs in teacher training ································· 146
9.2 Need One: Specific Language Support for Teachers Who Cannot Speak Ethnic Minority Languages ································· 149
9.3 Need Two: English Content Knowledge Training ························ 150
9.4 Need Three: Specific PCK Knowledge Suitable to Ethnic Minority Context ································· 152
9.5 Need Four: A Lifelong Support System ································· 155
9.6 Implications of In-Service Training for Teachers from Ethnic Minority Areas ································· 156
    9.6.1 Creating a PCD system ································· 157
    9.6.2 Building up an online community including trainees, trainers and experts ································· 157
    9.6.3 Developing bilingual or trilingual language supporting courses for ethnic minority language speakers ···················· 158
    9.6.4 Scaffolding teachers with cultural knowledge in language teaching ································· 159

Bibliography ································· 160
Appendix 1 **Questionnaire in English** ································· 175
Appendix 2 **Questionnaire in Chinese** ································· 179
Appendix 3 **Interview Questions (English)** ································· 183
Appendix 4 **Reliability and Factor Analysis of Language Learning Attitude** ··· 185
Appendix 5 **Reliability Analysis of Chinese Teacher Self-Efficacy** ············· 191
Appendix 6 **Factor Analysis of Chinese Teacher Self-Efficacy** ················ 193
Appendix 7 **Reliability Analysis of Modified EPS (Chinese)** ·················· 195
Appendix 8 **Exploratory Factor Analysis of EPS (Yunnan)** ···················· 198
Appendix 9 **General Profile of the Interviewees** ································· 202
Epilogue ································· 213

Part 1   Background of the Research

Professional Development Needs of Secondary School English Teacher: An Empirical Study Based on Multilingual Ethnic Areas of Yunnan Province

Secondary school English teachers from rural areas in China, especially ethnic minority areas, are facing different impediments compared to those from urban areas. These are obstacles which imply special professional development needs. Currently in these areas, in-service professional development for teachers is conducted through three forms: 1) short-term training on specific themes of new educational policies, such as training on New English Curriculum Standards (NECS); 2) in-school training given by some experts, such as scholars who do research on English teaching from universities; and 3) self-learning by teachers (Zhong & Gan, 2007; Zhong, 2008). The first two are usually school-initiated and the last one is generally initiated by individuals. Thus, in this research, NTP taken as a case of an in-service training program, is used to study the professional development needs of secondary school English teachers from ethnic minority areas. All the subjects and interviewees were selected from the trainees and trainers, and this research also includes a program director (PD) participating in an NTP program from 2012 to 2014 in one university of Yunnan Province. Adapted from social cognitive learning and social constructivist theories, a quantitative research was conducted to test subjects' (trainees') teacher efficacy, education participation motivations and language learning attitudes (towards English and ethnic minority languages) for two purposes. One was to get a general picture about the strength of trainees' teacher efficacy, the major motivational orientations for them to participate in the training, and the representations of their language learning attitudes; the other was to test whether English teachers in ethnic minority areas would confront different professional development needs in contrast to non-English teachers, in that their teacher efficacy, education participation motivations and language learning attitudes were different to those of non-English teachers. In addition, interviews with twelve trainees, two trainers and one PD were conducted to offer qualitative data. It was expected that the results from quantitative and qualitative researches could lead to some discussions about what the teachers' professional development needs would be, especially for English teachers in ethnic minority areas of China.

Chapter 1 as the introduction chapter firstly provides the background of this research, including a brief introduction to NTP, a short review of the ideological changes in English language education policies in China, and a detailed description of the specific problems of English education in multilingual ethnic minority areas of Yunnan. Moreover, this chapter explains the significance and structures of the research.

Chapter 1   Introduction

1.1   National Training Plan

As an essential part of teacher professional development, teacher education, in terms of both pre-service and in-service training, has gradually drawn more and more attention from scholars and the public in China. Influenced by the concepts of lifelong education, different levels of government-issued policies and projects have been promoted to enhance the quality of primary and secondary school teachers' education (Wang, 2009). In the summer of 2010, the Ministry of Education (MOE) and the Ministry of Finance (MOF) co-issued NTP. At the beginning, NTP included two projects: Primary and Secondary Teacher Training Modeling Project (PSTTMP) (2010-2012) and Primary and Secondary Leading Teacher Training Project in Central and Western Rural Areas of China (here in after as the Project). The central government thought highly of the function of NTP. In the first part of the Announcement on Implementing National Primary and by the Ministry of Education and the Ministry of Finance (MOE & MOF, 2010), it clearly stated the purposes of this national program:

> Primary and secondary school teacher training is local government's duty and responsibility, and it should be implemented mainly by local authorities. Central government's implementation of NTP is aiming at playing a role in demonstrating, "offering fuel in a snowy winter" and promoting reform. Through implementing NTP, a batch of "seed teachers" will be trained so as to fulfill their backbone function in carrying forward education for all-round development and teacher training. NTP will develop

high-quality teacher training resources, and innovate teacher training modes and methods, for the sake of carrying a nation-wide primary and secondary teacher training into a new stage. NTP focuses on supporting rural teacher training in central and western areas, guiding and encouraging local government, improving teacher training system and intensifying rural teacher training, in order to significantly improve rural teachers' quality. NTP will foster teacher education reform, and push forward tertiary teachers colleges and universities serving the basic education. (author's translation)

As claimed at the beginning of this official document, teacher training is part of local government's duties and responsibilities, and the central government's intrusion should be merely understood as playing the role for demonstrating, which can be taken as providing the model of teacher training. More ironically, the Chinese idiom "offering fuel in a snowy winter", which means showing good intention, was originally emphasized in parentheses in this official document. The use of parentheses leads to ambiguous meanings. For one part it can be deemed as emphasizing the original good intention. For the other, it can be interpreted as expressing the view that teacher training programs run by the local government in the past years were so weak in proficiency that the central government was not satisfied with its consequence and the serious educational inequity between urban and rural areas. Whether this is a criticism of local government's act of omission from central government, or central government really wants to grant this reward to central and western areas, it could not be denied that implementing NTP is an important action for improving primary and secondary teachers' quality, especially rural teachers' quality. It has significance in fostering equal development of compulsory education, promoting basic education reform and improving education quality (MOE & MOF, 2010).

In this official document, not only the purposes of initiating NTP are stated, but also the main problems of teacher professional development in rural China are pointed out, such as the shortage of financial support, lack of well-directed and systematic guidance, and insufficient academic resources (Wang, 2011; Wang & Li, 2009; Zhang et al., 2007; Zhu, 2006). Financial constraint has been consistently argued as one of the major reasons of the poor performance of rural education. According to some studies (Bao, 2006; Wang, 2011; Wang & Zhao, 2011; Zhu, Y. C., 2006), the gap of educational expenditure between urban and rural cities is addressed as an important reflection of educational inequity. Teacher quality, however, is addressed as the "chief criminal" for low efficiency in rural areas. The existence of insufficient full-time teachers and unqualified teachers is the chief reason for students' poor academic achievements in entrance examinations (Wang, 2011; Wang & Li, 2009; Zeng, 2012; Zhang et al., 2007). Nevertheless, as the saying goes, "the world does not hate for no reason", and this unsatisfactory situation is the result of a series of integrated causes which can be traced to the divergence between policies and practices (Feng, 2009, 2011).

As one part of the southwestern areas in China, Yunnan Province also benefits from NTP through the Project. The Project includes a three-month "replaced-training" program during which rural teachers were sent to teachers' colleges or universities to have their training, and simultaneously, teachers' colleges or universities sent pre-service students to replace those trainees' positions in rural schools as their internship. However, problems regarding administration and implementation had gradually been revealed since the beginning of the Project (Zhong, 2011). The first problem was relevant to curriculum development. Each university would apply to host different subjects from the educational bureau of local government, such as Chinese, English, and mathematics. Proposals about curriculum design of the training programs were required for the application process. Owing to the limited time, host universities tended to take for granted the content and form of the training. Consequently, these proposals were based on the literature and individual experience, not the analysis of the actual needs. The second problem was pertinent to information about trainees. Local educational departments would make their decisions on the eligibility of trainees and send the name list to host universities in 1-3 months before the beginning of each program. The name list contained little demographic information about the trainees so that except for name and gender, host universities barely knew any other educational background information about their trainees, which meant it was impossible for curriculum designers to conduct a needs analysis before the actual training. The third problem was pertained to selection of trainees. Many local authorities did not have specific detailed requirements for eligibility; on the contrary, the decision was made only on the number of trainees in each school, and it was the principals' decision as to who would be sent for the training. Meanwhile, due to the poor outcomes of previous teacher training programs, some of the trainees who were sent there could not function as the "seed teachers" who would train their colleagues afterwards and work as models in local areas. Contrary to the expectation, some of the trainees were "having nothing to do at school" or sent to "take a short break before retirement" (Duan, 2011: 3). In 2010, the first year of NTP, few host universities, local educational bureaus and departments knew what they should do next. "The whole process of the Project was like 'crossing the river by feeling for stones'. We could only passively react to each problem as it came out." (Zhong, 2011: 5)

As one of the trainers and curriculum developers in NTP hosted by one teachers university in Yunnan, I witnessed both the problems and improvements of the NTP programs in Yunnan from 2010 to 2014. Since the training in 2010, the weaknesses in teaching and learning English were revealed among these trainees through the classroom discussions. Their strong mother tongue accent merges into their Chinglish (Chinese English); their poor English vocabulary results in the "dumb English" phenomenon; the lack of confidence and necessary disciplinary knowledge leads to teaching English through Mandarin; they cherish the opportunities of the training but are reluctant to make efforts in the training and/or changes in their teaching after they return to the workplaces (Zhong, 2011). In face of their eagerness and helplessness, I questioned myself deeply beneath my heart: What could I do for these teachers from rural areas of Yunnan? Thus, it has become my first concern to do research about their ELA and motivations to participate in teacher training programs. Meanwhile, their difficulties as qualified English teachers in rural and ethnic minority areas of China were the concerns as well. For instance, would it be more difficult for them to teach English to ethnic minority students? Would ethnic minority teachers have more difficulties in teaching English? In this case, before exploring the aforementioned questions in depth, a quick review of English education policy in China, especially in Yunnan, is needed. In the meantime, the realities, mostly the specific problems, of teaching English in Yunnan will be introduced.

1.2 English Language Education Policy in China: Ideology Changes from Political-Oriented to Utilitarian-Oriented

1.2.1 Political-oriented English education: the 1860s to the mid-1970s

In China, English education officially began in 1862 with the establishment of the School of Combined Learning (Guo, 2001). It was the first English training institution in China, and its establishment marked the beginning of English education and also of foreign language education (Deng, 2004). However, there was neither a consistent English language policy nor a well-designed plan for English language education at that time. Even after the founding of the People's Republic of China (PRC), the changes of English language policy were mainly motivated by the prevailing political agenda of the time for about three decades (Feng, 2009). In 1954, in order to relieve pressure on students, MOE stopped foreign language education in schools and issued Announcement on "Declaration of Not Providing Foreign Language Course in Junior Secondary School". In 1959, MOE issued Announcement on Strengthening and Opening Foreign Language Course in Secondary Schools, which defined a specific ratio of different foreign languages. "One third of the schools in whole China should teach Russian, and the other two thirds teach English and other foreign languages." (Education History Research Project of Curriculum and Textbook Research Institute, 2008) In the early 1960s, China's break with the Soviet Union and its establishment of diplomatic and economic relations with many Third World countries made it increasingly necessary to adopt a new policy towards English. In 1963, MOE designed and launched the Full-time "Secondary School English Education Syllabus" (Draft) which contained the highest level of teaching requirements, the most teaching content and the largest amount of teaching hours after the establishment of the PRC. English was officially stipulated as the first foreign language in secondary schools. In 1964, Guideline of Foreign Language Education Seven Year Plan was launched (Qun, 1991: 67). It nominated English as the dominant foreign language in China and also encouraged a balance in training speakers of different foreign languages (Tong, 2011). This was the first time China had officially raised the concept of foreign language, indicating a great change in English language policy in China (Chang, 2006).

However, efforts were interrupted by the ten-year "Cultural Revolution". English was viewed as the language of the enemy, and in the first half of the decade, virtually all English teaching programs were abolished in the school system (Liu, 1993). "Although English reappeared in the secondary curriculums in the early 1970s, English instruction existed only in name: Virtually no teaching or learning was going on." (Hu, 2005: 5) Consequently, when China embarked on the modernization drive in 1978, there was a serious shortage of English-proficient personnel (HERC, 1993).

1.2.2 Economic-oriented English education: 1978 to 2000

Owing to the Reform and Opening-up Policy launched in 1978, with the new national modernization program, English language education figured prominently in the drive for modernization (Adamson & Morris, 1997). "English has been increasingly taken as essential for its (China's) 'Four Modernizations' ambition, aiming to modernize agriculture, industry, national defence and science and technology" (Feng, 2009: 86, insertion by the author). In 1978, MOE issued the first unified primary and secondary curriculum and the accompanying draft English syllabus in the era of modernization (Hu, 2005). Due to the lack of necessary resources in many schools, the curriculum also made allowances for the introduction of foreign language education at grade one in poorly equipped junior secondary schools (HERC, 1993). Nevertheless, at the first National Conference on Secondary Foreign Language Education, it was acknowledged that English language teaching (ELT) efforts made since 1978 largely failed and the quality of secondary ELT was deplorably low (Hu, 2005). In 1982, MOE required English to be taught as the main foreign language in some key secondary schools, and thus a small number of prestigious schools were set up as pivotal sites of educational excellence (Hu, 2001: 250). In 1992, Nine-year Compulsory Education Full-time Junior Secondary English Syllabus (Pilot) was launched. It represented the start of nationwide English education in junior secondary schools. The reason for pushing English education was to support the opening-up of the country in the globalized world.

Currently, the development of scientific technology marked with information technology has changed rapidly over time. The social life informatization and economic globalization make foreign languages, especially English, become an important instrument for opening-up and communication between China and other countries. Learning and mastering a foreign language are the basic requirements for every citizen in the 21st century (MOE, 1992) (author's translation).

This opening paragraph of the syllabus indicated that the economy-oriented English education policy had been successfully transformed into a utilitarian policy. The instrumental function of English had also been planted in the public's minds, including all English teachers.

1.2.3 Instrumental English education: expansion after 2001

In 2001, following the Basic Education Curriculum Reform Outline (Trail) (MOE, 2001a), another official document was issued by MOE, which suggested English should be taught from the third grade in the primary schools across the whole China (MOE, 2001b). The necessity of teaching English in primary schools drew great attention. Some English educators in China pointed out the non-adaptability of this policy in rural schools. Shortage of teachers and teaching materials were the main causes mentioned (Liu, 2001; Hu, 2001; Hu, 2007a). In responding to the questions, a government official explained that this decision was made based on the linguistic research advocating that an earlier start in the second language (L2) learning would be more beneficial. The official from MOE commented as follows:

Some researchers have studied how children learn foreign languages. Experience shows that the optimal age to learn a foreign language is around eight; students who start to learn a foreign language at this age threshold can learn it more efficiently, without getting confused between the target language and their native language (Li, 2001, cf. Hu, G. W., 2007: 375) (author's translation).

Another push in this expanding of nationwide English education was from the former Vice Premier Li Lanqing who was in charge of education at that time (Hu, G.

W., 2007). In 2000, Li Lanqing visited Zhejiang Province and commented that "an economically developed province such as Zhejiang should significantly improve ELT…in cities where conditions permit, English could be uniformly introduced in the third grade or even in lower grades" (Zheng, 2001, cf. Hu, G. W., 2007: 364). In his *Education for 1.3 Billion*, Li (2005: 349) echoed his intention about the early introduction of English in schools. He stated that "I believe the starting year of foreign language studies should be unified for schools in the same city…we need uniformity and standardization, rather than each place doing things in its own way". "Uniformity" and "standardization" could only be implemented through a top-down policy in China (Lu, 2003; Hu, G. W., 2007; Pan, 2011). Hence, in 2001, NECR (National English Curriculum Requirements) was launched.

Whatever reasons triggered this policy, it represents the popularization of English education in China. With this governmental push, English, the same as Chinese, exists in the whole education curriculum system in China from the primary level to the tertiary level. New English Curriculum Standards at Compulsory Education Stage states:

> The informatization of social life and economic globalization has increased the importance of English. As one of the most important carriers of information, English has become the most widely used language in various sectors of human life. (cf. Pan, 2011: 249)

Similarly, New English Curriculum Standards at Senior High Education Stage states at the beginning:

> Language is the most important tool for human beings to think and to communicate; it is also the pre-requisite for people's social activities and it is significant for people's all-around development. With the globalization of social and economic activities, foreign language competence has already become a basic requirement for people around the world. Therefore, learning and mastering foreign languages, especially English, is of critical importance. (cf. Pan, 2011: 249)

In the tertiary level, College English Curriculum Standards (Non-English) also specifies the importance of English to China's social and economic development as follows:

With a view to keeping up with the new developments of higher education in China, deepening teaching reform, improving teaching quality, and meeting the needs of the country and society for qualified personnel in the new era, College English Curriculum Requirements have been drawn up to provide colleges and universities with the guidelines for English instruction to non-English major students. (cf. Pan, 2011: 252)

These three NECSs clearly pointed out the utilitarian-oriented intention of the government. With the accelerating process of globalization in the last three decades of the 20th century, China has shifted the orientation of English education policy from political to economic development facilitators (Hu, 2005).

1.3 Problems of English Education in Multilingual Ethnic Minority Areas of Yunnan

In 2001, MOE (2001a) promulgated the Basic Education Curriculum Reform Outline (Trail). The curriculum reform is at the heart of education reform (Gu, 2001; Wang & Zhao, 2011). The official launch of the curriculum reform not only spurred the development of rural education but also caused many problems (Wang & Zhao, 2011). Insufficient educational resources caused by shortage of funding, and the inadequate quality of policy-making which underestimates the problems of teachers are the two major reasons for the poor performance of English education in central and western China (Hu, 2001; Hu, G. W., 2007; Wang, 2011; Wang & Li, 2009; Zhang et al., 2007; Zhu, 2006). "Both the policy documents and the unprecedentedly high status of English in prosperous societies have clearly impacted powerfully on minority groups in China." (Feng, 2009: 91)

China is a unified country with multi-nationalities. Besides the Han nationality, there are 55 other ethnic minorities with an aggregate population of 113 million that accounts for about 8.49% of the total (NBSC, 2011). Though ethnic minorities represent a relatively low proportion, the critical areas where they inhabit have socio-political and economic significance.

Firstly, they (ethnic minorities) occupy 62% of China's total land areas.

Secondly, over 90% of the border region of China is occupied by national minorities. And finally, by far the greatest portion, sometimes even the whole of forestry resources, mining resources, precious medical resources, tropical crops and bases of animal husbandry industries, are located in national minority regions. (Postiglione, 1992: 308)

Consequently, since the founding of the PRC in 1949, education for ethnic minorities has received high attention and has become an important component of China's educational policy initiatives (Yuan, 2007).

Before 1949, most of the regions inhabited by ethnic minorities had been comparatively backward socially and economically. For example, in some regions feudalism and the remnants of a slave society were still evident. In other regions, traditional indigenous education was still strong. Modern education, as it is known today, was not in existence (Yuan, 2007). Hence, after 1949, Chinese government defined the constitutional ways in which ethnic minorities should be assisted. In the Constitution, the Law of the People's Republic of China on Regional National Autonomy, and the Compulsory Education Law of People's Republic of China, clauses for supporting and helping ethnic minorities to develop education have been clearly stipulated. Administrative organizations were specially set up in the educational departments both at the central and local levels. Funds were earmarked as special project subsidies to meet the new expenditure needs of ethnic education as determined by the characteristics of ethnicity and locality. Hansen (2010: xiii) argued:

> The central and provincial governments in China have suggested and implemented various methods to increase school attendance and accomplish basic compulsory education among the ethnic minorities, such as establishment of special (mostly boarding) minority schools, experiments with bilingual education, introduction of locally edited teaching materials, and easier access for non-Han students to higher education.

Despite these policy initiatives and financial support, it has been difficult to overcome the barriers of geographical isolation and overall poor economic conditions, so education in most parts of the ethnic minority areas in China is relatively weak. Yunnan Province, the focus of this research, is provided as an example.

Generally speaking, the situation of ethnic minority and bilingual education in Yunnan is similar to that of the whole country. However, Yunnan has its own characteristics. As Hansen (2010: 19) mentioned, "since the beginning of the reform period, the central government has granted financial support to Yunnan as a border province with an underdeveloped economy, and a part of these funds is still earmarked for minority education." The standing committee of the National People's Congress (CPGPRC, 2011) claimed that in 2012, 73 out of 127 counties and cities in Yunnan were national "poor counties", and 43 of them were "ethnic minority autonomous counties". "Although minorities account for only one third of the provincial population, they represent two thirds of the twelve million people officially declared poor." (Hansen, 2010: 19) Because of the unique topography and highly-scattered pattern of inhabitation, there is an imbalance in the development of politics, economy and education among all ethnic groups, and thus advancement of education has been made extremely difficult. There are 127 counties in the province, of which 40 counties failed to institute the nine-year compulsory education and 23 counties did not eradicate adult illiteracy. All of these counties are centerd in poverty-stricken ethnic minority areas. Compared with the national average level of education in China, basic education in Yunnan has lagged behind for at least 10 years (PGYNP, 2002).

As mentioned before, from the official encouragement of long-term planning and a balance of training speakers of different foreign languages in 1979 to the suggestion that English be taught from the third grade in the primary schools in 2001, English is gradually becoming one of the three most important required subjects (the other two being Chinese and mathematics) offered in primary and secondary schools all over China, including rural areas in Yunnan. As one of the western China provinces, Yunnan has many drawbacks in terms of the slow development of economy, society and culture, as well as the weakness of the foundation of education (Research Center for Development, Shanghai Education Science Institute, 2002). With respect to English education, language barriers caused by multilingual context, and teachers' quality are the "two big mountains" blocking the way.

1.3.1 Language barriers in multilingual areas

The multilingual context in most ethnic minority areas in Yunnan makes English teaching and learning even harder. Located in the southwest part of China, bordered by Vietnam, Laos and Burma, Yunnan is viewed as the most multilingual province in China. Beside the dominant Han group, 52 ethnic minority groups inhabit the province and 25 of them have inhabited there for generations. The total population of all 52 ethnic minority groups is approximately 15.3 million, comprising 33.37% of the population of the province according to the 2010 national census (SBYP, 2011). Most of the minorities are living along the border areas or in the mountainous areas of the province where educational opportunities are of a low standard. Geographical, historical and cultural factors have caused each group to develop unique social and economic characteristics (Yuan, 2007). According to Yang et al. (1995), in the 1980s, the Provincial Government Institution, the Minority Nationality Language and Literature Executive Committee of Yunnan, proposed the implementation of 11 trial bilingual programs in the ethnic minority areas where Chinese was not spoken (cf. Yuan, 2007). Chinese (in the form of Mandarin) was not only taught as an L2 but also used as the language of instruction throughout the academic year. At the same time, English was also introduced into secondary schools in those areas as a regular and compulsory subject in the same way as in the centralized Han educational system. In some areas, English has been taught as the third language (L3) to students speaking Chinese only when some ethnic minority students are poor in Mandarin.

Language barriers for students and between students and teachers led to the poor English education quality in these areas. According to a comparative study of compulsory education qualities in rural schools in western China and in urban cities, Wang and Li (2009) claimed that mean scores in English at junior high schools in villages, towns and local cities are universally lower than in provincial capital junior high schools. Among the three, the quality of English education in villages is the lowest. Moreover, students from village high schools have the lowest English score in basic grammar and composition ability, also in vocabulary and reading comprehension. According to their study, the biggest gap between rural and urban students in their English proficiency was in sentence transformation. Consequently, the drop-out rate in village high schools is the highest at 38.6% contrasted with 16.9% of town junior high schools, 17.1% of local city junior high schools, and 2.1% of provincial capital junior high schools (Wang & Li, 2009: 80). Also, the statistics concerning illiteracy and the level of education of minority people points to a generally lower level of education compared to that of the Han and in relation to the Chinese national standard.

1.3.2　English teachers' poor teaching quality

A Chinese saying goes that "to feed the kid without teaching, is the father's fault; to teach without severity is the teacher's laziness". This saying vividly elaborates the responsibility of parents in education and of school education in China. Parents should educate the kids, but once the kids are sent to schools, it is teacher's responsibility to teach them well. Hence, teachers have always been the first to be blamed and criticized for the poor performance of students. "There is no one who cannot be taught well, but only the one who doesn't know how to teach." "There are no weak students, only unqualified teachers." These blaming statements can be heard here and there when the issue of educational quality is raised in China. Teachers shoulder more pressure for this burden. However, is it really teachers' fault? Who is the actual "evil" backstage manipulator? To answer this question, we have to dig into the reality of teacher quality first.

1. Serious shortage of full-time teachers

In 2002, the average student-teacher ratio was 19.29∶1 in regular secondary schools, with a total 3.467,7 million full-time teachers (MOE, 2003). In 2006, the ratio decreased to 17.15∶1 in regular secondary schools, with the total 3.475 million full-time teachers (MOE, 2007). Specifically, the ratio in rural junior secondary schools decreased from 20.16∶1 in 2002 (Zhang et al., 2007) to 17.7∶1 in 2006 (Zeng, 2012). After a decade of efforts from Chinese central and local governments, in 2011, the average student-teacher ratio was 14.38:1 in regular junior secondary schools, with the total 3.524,5 million full-time teachers (MOE, 2012). The figure seems satisfactory at the national level, but the data in Yunnan were far from enough. In 2007, the student-teacher ratio in regular junior secondary schools was 18.26∶1 with 106,323 full-time teachers and 1,251 part-time teachers; meanwhile, the ratio in vocational junior secondary schools was 40∶1 with 414 full-time teachers and 19 part-time teachers (the Education Bureau of Yunnan Province, 2008b).

2. Educational background of teachers

Teachers Law of the People's Republic of China (hereinafter Teachers Law, by SCNPC, 1993, Order No. 15) stated:

> To obtain qualifications for a teacher in a secondary school, or a teacher for general knowledge courses and specialized courses in a primary vocational school, one shall be a graduate of a specialized higher normal school, or other colleges or universities with two or three years' schooling or upwards. (selected from Article 11)

Data showed that in 1993, only 63.84% teachers in junior secondary schools reached the requirement of the Teachers Law (1993). After about two decades' efforts, in 2011, 98.91% teachers satisfied the degree requirements (MOE, 2012). However, Zeng (2012) pointed out that in 2006, among the total 534,872 English teachers in regular junior secondary schools, the rate of qualified academic credentials is 97.8%. This figure is lower than the national rate of qualified academic credentials (98.87%) (MOE, 2007) in the same year. Moreover, in 2006, the rate of qualified academic credentials of teachers from rural junior secondary shools is 94.8%, lower than that of the national rate by 4.07% (MOE, 2007).

3. Non-English academic background of English teachers

Li (2011) told a story in her article of a 32-year-old backbone teacher Ms. Kong who studied four years of Chinese literature in university but failed to continue her job in rural junior secondary schools.

> Because of her bachelor's degree, Ms. Kong was assigned as an English teacher to teach three classes, and due to her prudence, she was assigned as accountant while teaching. Last year, the local government required each school to set up one office for psychological consultation, and then she was assigned as the director of psychological consultation office. (Li, 2011) (author's translation)

Frankly, such "graft flower to tree" method is actually against administrators' and teachers' wills. However, this phenomenon is common in rural areas of China. More than one third of rural schools suffered the shortage of full-time teachers for all subjects, especially the shortage of full-time teachers for music, physical educaion, art, computer science and English (Gu & Tan, 2004, cf. Zhang et al., 2007: 480). Hence, the only solution for school principals is reassigning teachers to teach other subjects. Teachers are working under serious pressure and resistance; more importantly, a lack of academic knowledge makes their teaching problematic. Like most non-English major English teachers mentioned: "Enjoy learning English is one thing, and to teach English is another thing." They don't believe in themselves that they can teach English well even though most of them strongly agree that learning English is important for students. Maintaining discipline or the order of the class is the only thing they can do and be able to do well.

1.4 Significance of the Research

As a university teacher who has taught English education courses for more than eight years, I have been experiencing and suffering from the weaknesses and problems which exist in English teacher education in Yunnan. The most important one is the lack of needs analysis. Under the top-down policy, curriculum developers in teacher training programs usually had little freedom to design the curriculum based on trainees' real needs. Usually, the central government and local governments would provide some guidelines based on experts who had experiences of training teachers but not the exact ones who were from the target areas. Thus, there were gaps between trainees' real needs and government's requirements, which caused confusion and trouble to program developers; consequently, such teacher training programs might not really provide solutions to trainees who were expecting new methods to solve difficulties and problems in their teaching. This research project aimed at presenting part of the picture of rural secondary English teachers' expectations, doubts, and difficulties in their professional development. Through the research of the secondary school English teachers from rural areas of Yunnan who joined NTP from 2012 to

2014 in one university in Yunnan, this research explored topics regarding trainees' attitudes to English teaching, strength of their teacher efficacy and their motivation orientations in NTP.

This research would help teacher training program developers and policy-makers to gain a deeper and clearer understanding of the professional development needs of English teachers who are working in rural and ethnic minority areas. Meanwhile, it would provide some primary data to scholars for deeper studies on the situations and problems of English teacher professional development in the multilingual context of China.

1.5 Research Questions

The present research is essentially a primary one which sets out to survey the relationships between attitudes towards language learning (Chinese Mandarin, English and ethnic minority languages), teacher efficacy, and education participation orientation from both social cognitive psychological and social constructive linguistic perspectives. The purpose of the research is to find out the professional development needs of English teachers who are working in ethnic minority areas of China, Yunnan Province in particular. Quantitative data (questionnaire) will try to explore three general questions and 12 specific questions:

(1) To what extent do English teachers' language learning attitudes affect their motivation in NTP?

    a. What are the strengths of teachers' ELA?

    b. What are the strengths of teachers' ethnic minority languages learning attitudes?

    c. What are the attitudinal differences between English and non-English teachers to English learning?

    d. What are the attitudinal differences between ethnic minority and Han teachers to English learning?

    e. Do ELA influence English teachers' motivation in NTP?

    f. If so, to what extent and in what aspects can ELA motivate English teachers to pursue in-service training?

(2) To what extent does teacher efficacy affect English teachers' motivation in NTP?
- a. What is the strength of ethnic-minority-area teachers' efficacy?
- b. Do demographic factors (age, teaching years, teaching subjects, professional titles and ethnicities) affect the strength of teacher efficacy?
- c. Does teacher efficacy influence English teachers' motivation in NTP?
- d. If so, what are the differences in NTP training motivation between English teachers at a high level of teacher efficacy and those at a low level?

(3) What are the strengths and patterns of English teachers' motivation in NTP?
- a. What are the strengths of English teachers' motivation in NTP?
- b. Do demographic factors (age, teaching years, professional titles and ethnicities) affect the strength of motivation in NTP?

Qualitative data (interviewing) focus on language learning attitudes and in-service training expectations firstly to explore the reasons for the quantitative data results, and secondly to respond to the fundamental research question of this research: What are the needs of professional development for English teachers in ethnic minority areas?

1.6 Research Rational

Educational research, as Gall et al. (1996: 3) defined, is the "systematic collection and analysis of information in order to develop valid, generalizable descriptions, predictions, interventions, and explanations relating to various aspects of education". However, Gay (1996) remarks that the major difference between educational research and other scientific research is the nature of the phenomena which involves consciousness, context and culture (including language). It is very difficult to explain, predict, and control situations involving human beings. As Yuan (2007) pointed out, the process of crossing these major potential blocks to acquire accurate information is a serious concern for every educational researcher.

Consistent with some L2 research (Ellis, 1994; Gardner, 1985, 2000, 2006; Dörnyei & Clément, 2001; Yuan, 2007), the survey methodology conducted in this research aims at testing teachers' attitudes to L2 learning (Chinese, English and ethnic minority languages). Meanwhile, same as some teacher professional development researches (Schwarzer & Hallum, 2008; Schwarzer, Schmitz & Tang, 2000), this research gauges teacher efficacy of secondary school teachers (English and non-English) from rural or ethnic minority areas of Yunnan Province; also measures their education participation orientation or motivation towards NTP. Consequently, it tends to explore the relationship between these factors in order to present secondary school teachers' professional development needs.

This research combines statistical data from questionnaire and descriptive data from interviews to explore the research questions. Through employing one anonymous questionnaire (referring to Appendix 1 in English and Appendix 2 in Chinese), it was expected that quantitative data would be collected effectively and efficiently from teachers who participated in NTP at one teachers' university in Yunnan from 2012 to 2014. Interviews conducted with a subset of subjects intend to obtain data on teachers' attitudes towards language education (Chinese, English and ethnic minority languages), the difficulties of teaching English in ethnic minority areas, and trainees' beliefs on teaching career. The qualitative study attempts to probe certain issues more deeply and look for explanations that the quantitative data may fail to account for.

Figure 1.1 illustrates the elements of the research design.

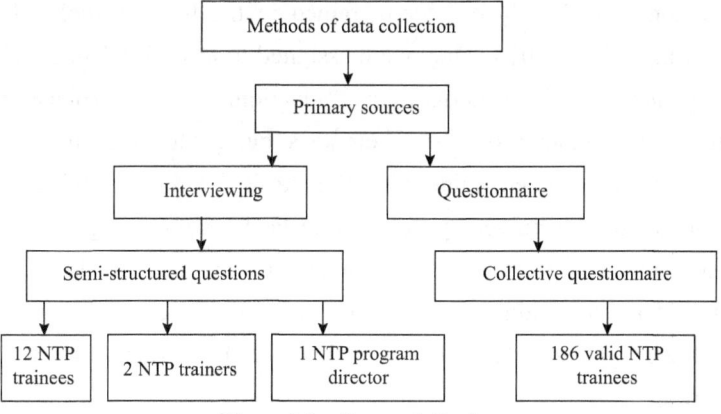

Figure 1.1   Research Design

The sampling of this research is not probable in nature, which means the probability of selecting a subject is unknown (Charles & Mertler, 2004: 151). Quantitative study was proposed to investigate the trainees who participated in the "Primary and Secondary Schools Leading Teacher Training Project in Central and

Western Rural Areas of China" (one of the two projects in NTP) at one teacher's university in Yunnan from 2012 to 2014. However, it was impossible for the researcher, within the constraints of time and finance, to collect information from all the teachers trained in the whole. It was a convenience and purposive sampling approach on the basis of the demographic variables regarding teaching subject (English and non-English), ethnicity (ethnic minorities and Han people), location of working place (ethnic minority areas), roles in NTP (trainers, trainees and program director), and their proximity to the researcher. Convenience sampling means the selecting of subjects based on their availability to the researcher; and purposive sampling indicates the selection of particularly informative or useful subjects (McMillan, 2003). The investigation was carried out in three schools of a university: the School of Foreign Languages and Literature, the School of Mathematics and Science, and the School of Chinese Literature. These three schools were responsible for the training of English, Chinese and mathematics teachers respectively in NTP. It was proposed that 200 questionnaires would be distributed to 100 English teachers and 100 Non-English teachers.

The interviewees (referring to Appendix 9), who are in-service teacher trainees of English and non-English subjects, were trained in the three schools of the chosen university during 2012 to 2014. They were assigned to teach English or other subjects in primary, junior or senior schools after graduation. Their workplaces were ethnic minority areas of Yunnan Province. Their ages ranged from 22 to 50. They were volunteer trainees or assigned trainees for this particular three-month program. They gathered together to the university for face-to-face instruction given by university teachers, and most importantly they assembled to take this training only for three months while two undergraduates were taking their positions in their home schools to teach their students. Hence, the reasons for choosing these trainees to be interviewees were as follows:

(1) They were teaching in ethnic minority areas of Yunnan Province where education level was poor.

(2) They were assumed to be the group of people who needed training most and were trained with the expectation of becoming "seed teachers" who should train other colleagues after they finished the training. They would provide information on both

English teaching and students' learning.

(3) Some of them could speak ethnic minority languages or they were ethnic minorities. They would offer their own English learning experiences and their teachers' English teaching methods.

With the help of the monitors at each school, I managed to check the trainees' name lists in the university and selected those who were teaching in the ethnic minority regions. I determined that 12 of them were likely prospects. For each of them, I got their verbal permission face to face or through telephone and scheduled the date and location for the interview. All the prospective subjects consented to be interviewed and agreed in written forms to allow interviews to be audio recorded. In December 2012, Li Rui, my colleague at the university, conducted four interviews because I was doing my visiting scholar program in the USA. He asked all the questions one after another based on the suggested Interview Questions (referring to Appendix 3) and e-mailed me the audio records. In November 2013, I conducted the other eight interviews during the periods of NTP.

At the same time, it was decided to choose the teacher trainers and program director from NTP. The recruiting principles for the interviewees were as follows:

(1) They had previously graduated from tertiary teachers' colleges with honours degrees;

(2) They had learned English as English education majors for four years in colleges;

(3) They had received master's degree in Applied Linguistics;

(4) They were teaching English Teaching Skills in universities;

(5) They had been working for more than 10 years;

(6) They had been a teacher trainer for more than five years and had taught in NTP for twice or more than twice;

(7) They taught in ethnic minority regions and had some knowledge about NTP trainees;

(8) They agreed in written form to allow interviews to be audio recorded.

Being one of the teacher trainers of NTP from 2010 to 2014, I was familiar with all the trainers at the School of Foreign Languages and Literature in the university that was responsible for the NTP program. Only two teacher trainers satisfied the recruiting principles. The program director was the same person from 2010 to 2014. Afterwards, in July 2012, I chatted with the two teacher trainers face to face respectively for their permission for the interview; then e-mailed them the general topics which might be asked about in the interview. We arranged the location and time for the interview. The interviews were conducted in 5th August, 2012, and 14th August, 2012, during the periods of summer break. Then, in June 2014, the program director was finally able to receive the interview.

The data gathering procedure had two major parts. Interview questions were prepared for 12 teacher trainees, 2 teacher trainers and 1 program director (referring to Appendix 9 for personal profiles). The questionnaire was designed for the 200 trainees in NTP to complete in the university in December 2012 and 2013 respectively when the training was taken. The medium of the interview and questionnaire is Chinese (with English as reference); the interviewees were allowed to use English when they felt comfortable in speaking English; otherwise much of the data would be filtered through their very limited English ability levels.

Questionnaire sheets were distributed four times when NTP was taken in 2012 and 2013. About 60 answered questionnaire sheets were collected from two classes in their classrooms immediately after they finished the classes in 2012. As for others, the trainees took the questionnaire sheets back to the dormitory and returned the answered sheets the following day or the day after to their monitors. About 50 were distributed in 2012, and about 100 in 2013. Approximately 200 questionnaire sheets were distributed, and 190 were returned, among which 4 sheets were not fully answered; thus the valid answered sheets were 186.

All of quantitative data were entered in and analysed by SPSS 20.0. All the interviews were recorded and the transcripts were provided based on the recordings. Dedoose was used as coding software to analyse the interviewing transcripts.

The interview transcriptions were analysed under the umbrella of qualitative research which concerned respondents' accounts as narratives or stories that related to the research purposes. All the interview information was read through and meaningful themes in five areas were arrived at: 1) attitudes to English language (AEL), 2) attitudes to ethnic minority language, 3) difficulties for teaching English, 4) experiences on teacher professional development, and 5) teacher beliefs on teaching profession, ethnic minority students and being an English teacher.

Firstly, the meaningless or irrelevant information in the transcription was not considered. Secondly, the remaining materials were reduced in accordance with the above five themes. Thirdly, the "reduced" information was narrowed down until I could extract some useful content out of it which served the focus of this research. Fourthly, the translated versions were refined to some extent to reach the required research standards but were faithful to the interviewees' original meanings.

The collected questionnaire data were analysed by non-parametric analysis aided by SPSS 20.0. Non-parametric analysis is a statistic method that "not involving any assumptions as to the form or parameters of a frequency distribution" (Oxford Dictionaries, 2013). In other words, different from parametric analysis which strictly requires parametrised distribution of the data, non-parametric analysis is a distribution-free method, which do not rely on assumptions that the data are drawn from a given probability distribution, such as normal distribution (Wikipedia, 2013). Hence, even the subjects do not have equal population, non-parametric analysis allows the researcher to test the differences and coefficient. At the same time, non-parametric statistics use data that are often ordinal, meaning it does not rely on numbers, but rather on a ranking or order of sorts.

Owing to the wider applicability and simplicity, non-parametric statistics are usually used for studying population and preferences, such as online purchase reviews receiving one to five stars. Hence, it is a much safer statistic method for researchers to explain the results of the data; however, due to the reliance on fewer assumptions, non-parametric methods are more robust. In other words, in the cases where parametric test will be appropriate, non-parametric tests have less power.

As the demographic information of the subjects (referring to Appendix 9) shows, the unequal or non-parametric population of samples requires non-parametric analysis method for the discussion.

In the whole Part 3, all the findings were from the data collected and analyzed from the above methods. Discussions in each chapter are based on the quantitative and qualitative results.

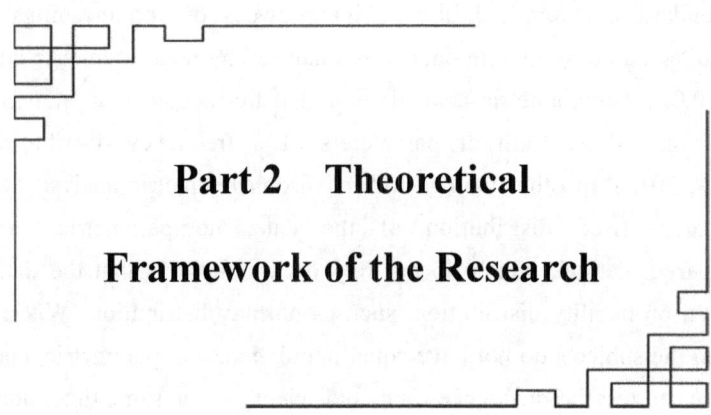

Part 2 Theoretical Framework of the Research

Part 2　Theoretical Framework of the Research

In this part, terms regarding teacher professionalism and teacher professionalization are firstly explained in Chapter 2 to narrow the focus of this research on teacher professionalism. Then, requirements of being a professional teacher in Western countries and that according to Chinese *Shide* are discussed. On the basis of Goodson's (2000) and Hargreaves's (2000) studies, the review explores the current stage of teacher professionalism in China. Finally, the concept of teacher knowledge base is introduced.

In Chapter 3, the review focuses on the main conceptions of the constructivist learning theory. Firstly, several conceptions of constructivism, such as the "novice" and the "expert", Vygotsky's dialectical constructivism, instructional scaffolding, and organizational context, are introduced to provide a theoretical background. Then, the second part specifically explores the connections between in-service teacher training and above-mentioned concepts in constructivist learning theory, as part of the theoretical rationale of this research.

In Chapter 4, Chapter 5 and Chapter 6, the review focuses on cognitive learning theories regrading adults' learning motivation and teacher beliefs. Adults' education participation orientation theories or learning motivation theories are firstly reviewed. Boshier's EPS, the measurement of in-service training motivation used in this research, is introduced based on Houle's (1961) typology. Then concepts regarding teachers' beliefs, especially teacher efficacy and language learning attitudes are discussed. Bandura's (1986, 1993, 1997) Model of Reciprocal Determinism is the theoretical base of teacher efficacy.

Chapter 2 Key Concepts on Teacher Professional Development

Regarding teacher professional development, a question usually to be raised is, "Are teachers professionals?" From the technical point of view, if teachers are not professionals, there will not be a thing called teacher professional development. Most Chinese people believe that everyone, such as their parents, friends, or even the strangers, can be teachers. As the well-known Confucius' saying goes, "Even when walking in a party of no more than three I can always be certain of learning from those I am with." (Confucius, 1998: 87) However, to be able to learn something from others is different from learning something academic from someone in a professional way. As far as I am concerned, before continuing to explore in what ways teachers are professionals, another significant question needing to be clarified is "Is teaching a profession?"

2.1 Teaching as a Profession

The question whether teachers are professionals has led to another debate during the last two decades of the 20th century: "Is teaching a profession?" In order to answer this question, it is necessary to define "profession" first. Through the changing historical, political and social contexts, the concept of profession has been used in different senses. A profession is "a paid occupation, especially one that involves prolonged training and a formal qualification" (Oxford Dictionaries, 2014); it is "an occupation based upon specialized intellectual study and training…" (Stinnett, 1962: 2, cf. Hart & Marshall, 1992: 3-4), and "an occupation requiring expert knowledge that justified a monopoly of services granted by government licensing" (Spring, 1985: 47, cf. Hart & Marshall, 1992: 4). Various definitions as it has, it seems inevitable that specific training is necessary for a profession; however, Western and Chinese scholars indicated other criteria to define profession. The Hong Kong scholar Zheng (1987) proposed eight characteristics: 1) significant social function, 2) complicated skills, 3) solving new problems, 4) ethical rules for self-regulation, 5) prolonged learning or training, 6) professional autonomy, 7) working union or organization, and 8) comparatively higher social status. Hart and Marshall (1992) suggested five fundamental aspects of a profession: 1) specific body of knowledge, 2) ideal of service, 3) ethical codes, 4) autonomy and 5) distinctive culture. Ye (2001), a leading scholar in the studies of teacher professional development field from China, emphasized three distinguishing features: 1) disciplinary base, 2) social responsibilities, and 3) professional autonomy. At the same time, Nunan (2001) elaborated four criteria in order to judge whether language teaching is a profession: 1) advanced education and training, 2) standards of practice and certification, 3) disciplinary base, and 4) advocacy or influence.

Critiques claiming teaching is a semi-profession (Lortie, 1969, 1975) or a middle-status profession (Zhong, 2001) are rooted in the fact that despite numerous reforms and efforts made by schools and educational departments, teaching still lacks many of the key characteristics associated with profession (Ingersoll & Merrill, 2012). Nevertheless, the imperfect or not fully professionalized situation of teaching as a profession might cry out for the professional development needs of teachers in order to reach their final goal—becoming professional teachers.

In fact, arguments about the nature of teaching as a profession evoke differences between two directions of teacher professional development, namely, teacher professionalism and teacher professionalization.

Teacher professionalism and teacher professionalization are generally a pair of mutually complementary but also contradictory concepts. Englund (1996: 76) suggested viewing teacher professionalism as a pedagogical concept, concerned with "internal quality of teaching as a profession"; while teacher professionalization as a sociological concept, related to the "authority and status of the (teaching) profession". Hargreaves (2000) further explained that these two aspects were usually revealed when asking teachers what it meant to be professional. One concerns more the quality of what teachers do and the standards which guide them, which is teacher professionalism; the other refers to how teachers feel about themselves through other people's eyes, i.e. teachers' social status, which is teacher professionalization. Goodson (2000: 182) regarded teacher professionalization activities as "promoting the material and ideal interests of teachers", such as increasing the salary or social status, while teacher professionalism activities are more about the "intricate definition and character of practice and profession of teaching". Thus, it is widely accepted that professionalism concerns more the skills and standards of being a professional teacher, but professionalization refers to the social status of being a professional teacher (Englund, 1996; Goodson, 2000; Hargreaves, 2000; Hargreaves & Goodson, 1996; Wise, 1989; Ye, 2001). This terminology has been adopted in the present research.

These two concepts are complementary in that improving the skills and standards of teachers will improve their social status to some extent; for example, in China, the professors in universities have higher social status than the teachers in secondary schools, because they arguably reach higher academic or professional standards and skills, such as educational degrees and research abilities. However, these two concepts are not always in harmony with Goodson (2000: 182) said, "when global forces are pursuing stratification projects, harmony between the two is unlikely", because in this context "professionalization has to be set against professionalism". Taking the same example, it is unfair to say professors in universities are better than those in secondary schools in terms of being passionate about teaching, or caring for students' learning as part of the emotional dimension of being a teacher. "In teaching, stronger professionalization does not always mean greater professionalism." (Hargreaves, 2000: 152)

Hence, improving teachers' social status or their professionalization cannot directly result in strengthening teachers' teaching skills, or their professionalism, and vice versa. However, the level of teacher professionalization would determine the methods or manifestations of teacher professionalism. Meanwhile, the efforts made in improving teacher professionalism could have a positive influence on teacher professionalization.

The direct consequence of in-service training programs would be improving trainees' professionalism rather than the professionalization. Thus, this research only focused on English teachers' needs for development in professionalism, not the eagerness for improving their professionalization. Then, what will be the final goal for teacher professionalism development in China? Actually this question is asking "What do the requirements for being a professional teacher mean to Chinese people?" Answers to this question would provide guidance for curriculum development in teacher training projects to explore the official and social requirements or standards of professional teachers, and more importantly it might offer scholars some insights as a basis for possible improvements of teacher professionalism in China in future.

2.2 Professional Teachers in Western Terms and *Shide* in Chinese Context

It was the Teachers' Law that firstly characterised teachers as "professionals" in China. However, long before this legal document, Chinese intellectuals have kept seeking for the criteria of "master" since Confucius started his lifelong career as a master, the earliest form of the professional teacher. For Chinese people, "professional teacher" is an imported Western term appearing in recent years, and "master" is the concept which would more suitably show the professional characteristics of a teacher. Both terms allude to the requirements of teaching at a professional level; however, "master" connotes more sense of respect towards the person, which indeed represents a special requirement of the professional teachers in China, that is *Shide*, the teaching morality. In the following section, standards, requirements or characteristics for professional teachers are discussed within the Western terminology framework; at the same time, old Confucian requirements for the professional teachers are explored to depict the historical and cultural influences on teachers' personal beliefs about being teachers in China.

2.2.1 Professional teachers in Western terms

The terms "profession" and "professional" have the same etymological root "profess" in Latin. To be professional is to profess to be an expert in some skill or field of knowledge (Baggini, 2005). Actually, "professional" has various indications in its literal meaning and pragmatic usage. Its definition in the dictionary shows that it can be something "relating to a job that requires special education, training, or skill" or "done or given by a person who works in a particular profession" (Merriam-Webster, 2014). In daily life, "professional" is often synonymous with successful, highly qualified, and strictly standardized or coded behavior. Being professional could be understood as showing the characteristics of a certain profession.

When used in noun form, "professionals" are distinguished by the level of skill that completely sets them apart from amateurs, and the level of skill that enables them to be paid for their performance, such as athletes and musicians. The meaning of professional is actually traced from "profession". Hart and Marshall summarized five fundamental aspects of a profession as mentioned in Section 2.1; however, they also pointed out that,

> ...(w)hile such lists may be analytically helpful, their usefulness is limited. The nature of profession is such that they are fluid, evolving, and subject to change and interpretation. In this sense, it is erroneous to view certain behavior or traits as evidence in support of one aspect of professionalism (e.g. ideal of service), while ignoring the importance of these same traits to other aspects (e.g. code of ethics, distinctive culture, etc.). The lines between such aspects are not distinctive. (Hart & Marshall, 1992: 23)

Hence, taking Hart and Marshall's understanding, a professional teacher should not be simply understood in a general sense as someone who has specific teaching skill can conduct best practice and is paid to teach. A professional teacher should be understood in a more complex way. Researchers believe that, in defining characteristics of a professional teacher, it is important to separate the micro concept of teacher, namely the person who "represents the best in the profession and sets the highest standard for best practice" (M. Tichenor & J. Tichenor, 2005: 90), from the macro one, namely "the person who can teach". Wise (1989: 304-305) depicted professional teachers as those:

> ...[who] have a firm grasp of the subjects they teach and are true to the intellectual demands of their disciplines. They are able to analyze the needs of the students for whom they are responsible. They know the standards of

practice of their profession. They know that they are accountable for meeting the needs of their students.

This definition suggests that teaching at a professional level is part of a complex understanding. When seeking the standards, meanings or requirements of a professional teacher, various countries have had their own requirements for the diverse regional and historical conditions of where and when teachers have been working. With the development of history in China, forms of education have changed throughout the time as well as the social and public expectation for teachers.

2.2.2 *Shide*: old Confucian requirements

In ancient China, teachers were a small group of people at the beginning, and usually they were government officers (Zhang & Fang, 2004). "Studying at government" and "Government officer is the teacher" were staple channels and manifestations of education system at that time. Until the Spring and Autumn period (770 BC to 476 BC), teachers who were called "Shi" appeared, which represented education was separated from other governmental affairs and teachers became an independent group. "Shi" are "the first generation of intellectuals in China and the first group of teachers" (Guo, 1987: 4). However, "Shi" worked in various places and mostly part-time, so they should not be regarded as professionals. Confucius (551 BC to 479 BC), usually called the Master, was the first person who devoted his entire life to teaching and started the private education, which indeed shifted the situation of "studying at government" into "studying from various intellectuals". He made teaching become a lifelong occupation and he became the first professional teacher or master in China (Li & Wang, 2000). Based on his own experience, Confucius was also one of the first scholars seeking for requirements of being a master or a professional teacher. Among those requirements suggested by him, two most important ones were 1) teaching new things from reviewing old knowledge, and 2) teaching by personal conduct and verbal instruction.

> The Master said: "He who by reanimating the old can gain knowledge of the new is fit to be a teacher." (Confucius, 1998: 17)

The old is the base of the new, and the new will be the development of the old; and to learn with constant perseverance and application will help transferring knowledge into skills. "If he only keeps reviewing the old knowledge but doesn't acquire the new, he cannot be the teacher." (Zhu X., 2015: 28) For Confucian sages, teaching new things from reviewing old knowledge was not only a method of teaching, but also a standard for judging the capability of a teacher. It could be viewed as the origin or the first voice for teacher professionalism from Chinese intellectuals.

> The Master said: If the ruler himself is upright all will go well even though he does not give orders. But if he himself is not upright, even though he gives orders, they will not be obeyed. (Confucius, 1998: 163)

> The Master said: Once a man has contrived to put himself aright, he will find no difficulty at all in filling an government post. But if he cannot put himself aright, how can he hope to succeed in putting others right? (Confucius, 1998: 165)

Confucius emphasized the importance of "personal conduct". As he explained, for governing a country, if the leader could behave in an "upright" way, the country would be easy to administrate; however, if the leader could not be a good model for his citizens to follow, no matter what kind of orders he gave, it would be hard for him to govern. Confucius's words imply that in school education, teachers are the "leaders" and "governors" in the classroom; at the same time, they should be the models for their students to follow.

Extending Confucius' ideas, Xun Zi (313 BC-238 BC) claimed four "personal conducts" of masters. Firstly, teachers should have the dignity which would win others' respect; secondly, teachers should have sublime prestige and abundant teaching experience; thirdly, teachers should be capable to teach systematically and logically and should not break the laws; and fourthly, teachers should know elaborate theories and be able to explain those in detail. It is obvious that for Xun Zi, teachers' dignity and prestige were very significant requirements. However, the best way to earn the dignity and prestige was actually through their personal conducts. In Confucian requirements, if "teaching new knowledge through the old" was explained as a specific teaching skill, "teaching by personal conduct and verbal instruction" should be understood as a moral standard, i. e., *Shide* in today's concepts.

The first article which clearly stated teachers' responsibilities or roles was "On the Teacher" from Han Yu (768-824), a Confucian intellectual. The first sentence of the article stated that, teacher is the one who could propagate the doctrine, impart professional knowledge, and resolve doubts. The "doctrine" as referred to here indicates Confucian principles of being a good person and rules for governing the country. Hence, teachers' main job is guiding learners to become responsible leaders of the country, and in the meantime the contents of teaching are mainly about thoughts of governing the country, as stated in *Li Chi* (Dais, 2006).

> When a man of talents and virtue knows that difficulty (on the one hand) and the facility (on the other) in the attainment of learning, and knows (also) the good and the bad qualities (of his pupils), he can vary his methods of teaching. When he can vary his methods of teaching, he can be a master indeed. (*Li Chi*, Dais, 2006)

Here, knowing "the good and the bad qualities" was assumed as the basis for a teacher to "vary his methods of teaching", which consequently was a necessary condition for him to become a master and a professional teacher.

Throughout the history, based on their own teaching experiences and educational expectations, ancient Chinese intellectuals and sages conceived the unique Chinese education wisdom that gradually became a basis for the rules and standards to judge masters' performance. In other words, they were the standards of being a professional teacher in ancient China. Among all thoughts, Confucianism is the foundation of Chinese educational philosophy and it is still influential among Chinese people nowadays. Thus, Confucian requirements as I mentioned before settled the basic criteria framework of professional teachers in China. Based on Xun Zi, teachers should be the ones that 1) have dignity and sublime prestige, 2) have abundant teaching experience, 3) are capable to teach systematically and logically, and 4) know elaborate theories and are able to explain those in detail. "Dignity" and "sublime prestige" were emphasized first in that *Shide* was the fundamental requirement for being a professional teacher in ancient China.

> *Shide* is an inner spiritual quality that teachers gain through continuous teaching practice. It is the morality of the specialized quality of teachers' personalities... *Shide* is beneficial to teachers' professional and personal lives... The basic requirements of *Shide* are non-maleficence, honesty, fairness and beneficence to students. (Ye, 2001: 44)

As stated, *Shide* is the ethical code of the teaching profession for every teacher in China, and it is the "principle" that leads teachers to fulfill their jobs and achieve their accomplishments. Besides all the pedagogic and craft knowledge, *Shide* has always been regarded as a significant quality that teachers should have. However, in today's society, as well as *Shide*, there are also other requirements in the category of teacher professionalism. In order to study the professional development needs of secondary school English teachers in ethnic minority areas, it is essential to recognize the current stage of teacher professionalism in China.

2.3 Stage of Teacher Professionalism in Current China

As mentioned in Section 2.1, representations of teaching as a profession change over time. Teacher professionalism has also varied throughout history. The most influential studies about the development of teacher professionalism are Hargreaves's (2000) four stages of professionalism and Goodson's (2000) three stages, which are indeed, in many ways, in parallel with each other.

Based on studies in anglophone cultures, Hargreaves (2000) pointed out four stages of teacher professionalism: the pre-professional stage, the stage of the autonomous professionalism, the stage of the collegial professionalism, and the post-professional stage. From different scenarios, he summarized various characteristics of these four stages and most importantly the foci of professional learning. At the same time, he also pointed out that among the four stages, pre-professional images of teaching were still dominant in many Asian countries, including China. He further explained that the constraints of class sizes in which "students were processed in large batches and segregated into age-graded cohorts or classes" (Hargreaves, 2000: 154) might be the reason leading to its dominance; he also admitted the cultural aspect, like Confucian conceptions of teaching and authority within schools and families, is another important reason for its dominance. Although he didn't explain more about how the Confucian conceptions influence the management of education in Asian countries, he stated that the pre-professional images are influential. In the pre-professional stage,

> Teaching was seen as managerially demanding but technically simple, its principles and parameters were treated as unquestioned commonsense, one learned to be a teacher through practical apprenticeship, and one improved as a teacher by individual trial-and-error. The "good" teacher was the "true teacher" who "devoted herself to her craft", demonstrated loyalty and gained personal reward through service, "whatever the costs". (Hargreaves, 2000: 156)

Educational administrators who are taught in such pre-professional settings are inclined to draw on their own biographical and sentimental memories of schooling as children when they make decisions on educational policy today. For the public, those early impressions of schooling and experiences with teachers form their later perceptions of teaching and education. In the pre-professional view,

> Teachers are (at best) enthusiastic people, who know their subject matter, know how to "get it across", and can keep order in their classes. They learn to teach by watching others do it, first as a student, then as a student teacher. (Hargreaves, 2000: 157)

Thus, governments tend to cut the budget down, because in a pre-professional view, teachers need little training or in-service professional learning.

With the spread of teacher pre-service education and the growth of in-service education, teacher autonomy is gradually strengthened in the second stage, namely the stage of the autonomous professionalism (Hargreaves, 2000). To put it simply, in this stage, teachers have their own rights to choose the methods they assume to be the best for the students; however, in order to protect such right to special autonomy, the professionalism in this stage was strongly related to licencing. Teachers had to get various licences to improve their skills. Such "licenced autonomy" strategy "isolated teachers from one another, and it subordinated teachers' professional learning to academic agendas, which often had only tenuous connections to their practice" (Hargreaves, 2000: 161). Thus, owing to few supporting systems for teachers, the innovations or reforms triggered from professional autonomy resulted in one teacher's individual action. For instance, one teacher just finished training on NECS and he wanted to use more activities like group discussion in the English classroom, but the school regulation was against group discussion because that would be hard for teachers to control the class. At the same time, he was not able to persuade his headmaster to change the rule, so finally he had to conduct the experiment by himself. Usually, he had to face peer colleagues' critiques if his classroom was too mussy or his students cannot get high scores in the term examinations. Consequently, it made little successful implementation. In most of the time, teachers kept their old ways of teaching while new methods they learnt from in-service training would seldom be introduced into classroom practice.

> The benefits of in-service education seldom became integrated into classroom practice, as individual course-goers returned to schools of unenthusiatic and uncomprehending colleagues who had not shared the learning with them. (Hargreaves, 2000: 162)

In the third stage, namely collegial professionalism, collaboration between professionals is emphasized. From this stage, professionalism moves from an "old" form into a "new". The challenge is how to build strong professional communities in teaching. Moving on from this point of view, Hargreaves (2000) suggested the fourth stage, the post-professional stage, in which the fate of teacher professionalism is not fixed, but pulled to different directions, given the swiftness of various policies and cultures. One possible outcome would be teacher professionalism becoming diminished and ending with de-professionalization. Another possible outcome would be a broader, more flexible and more democratic teacher professionalism, on the condition that teachers and others are willing to work together for its realization.

In accordance with Hargreaves, Goodson (2000) proposed a three-stage teacher professionalism: classical, practical and principled professionalism. In classical professionalism, academicization is the main characteristic (Hargreaves & Goodson,

1996). The inevitable consequence is the cleft between educational study and practice and research (Goodson, 2000). Through the process of pursuing social status, the application for professional standards of practice speeds up the standardization of teaching. In both lower-level educational organizations like public schools and higher-level educational administrative departments, assessment tools are applied to evaluate teachers' performance. Various criteria will indicate diverse skills of teaching, abilities of researching and managing. Failure in one aspect might be fatal for the promotion in one teacher's career, which might lead to a stagnant situation. In this process, "teaching is being technicized but not professionalized" (Goodson, 2000: 182).

Under the effects of developing marketization in anglophone areas, a practical professionalism emerges. "Practical professionalism tries to accord dignity and status to the practical knowledge and judgement that people have of their own work." (Goodson, 2000: 184) In this stage, teachers' experience becomes a major source and representation of their expertise. However, their experience is shown through their practical knowledge or craft knowledge, which includes their situated knowledge on curriculum, subject matter, teaching strategies, and the classroom milieu. Goodson (2000) noticed that teachers' situated knowledge is obtained within certain context. For instance, teachers' teaching strategies for large classrooms might differ if the school regulations are different. Taking the same example of whether allowing group discussion as I mentioned before, if the school regulation strongly forbids mussy classrooms, it would be really hard for teachers to try group discussion in large classrooms; but if the school regulation just suggests that teachers should ensure that the class is under their control, some experienced teachers would try to use group discussion when it is applicable. In China, most urban schools recommend an easygoing learning environment for students; nevertheless, in rural schools strict restrictions are conducted. Hence, an experienced teacher from an urban school might not be able to handle the class in a rural school. Meanwhile, teachers' practical knowledge is obtained over a long period of time, rather than a short one. Accordingly, Goodson proposed a "principled professionalism" in which teachers will behave based on "principles" or moral codes which may ultimately endow teacher autonomy instead of the external technical regulations.

This kind of professionalism will focus on the caring concerns which should lie at the heart of professionalism, rather than on the contradictory and narrow concerns of professionalization.... Principled professionalism will return to the initial concerns which underpin the profession of teaching. Teaching is, above all, a moral and ethnical vocation, and a new professionalism needs to reinstate this as the guiding principle. (Goodson, 2000: 187-188)

The only difference between the two, as far as I am concerned, is the orientation of their concerns. Hargreaves' four-stage professionalism is more of an activity orientation but Goodson's three-stage professionalism is more in tune with philosophical concerns. Hargreaves (2000: 153) claimed that the four stages are "not universal", but are "relatively common across anglophone cultures". He also admitted that the four phases are discrete stages which many countries might experience differently in the current era, or many countries, professionalism development would follow different orders of stages. The distinction of the four is based on the methods with which teachers organize their teaching, the external forces that affect teachers' learning motivation and also the efforts made to improve teachers' teaching skills. However, Goodson traced back to the nature of teaching and roles that teachers play. In what condition could teacher autonomy be realized becomes his major concern. For him, only when autonomy was realized could teachers work according to their free will, unconstrained by external forces, like govermental policies. Thus, the moral codes of teachers, the "principles" to which Goodson referred, seem to be the only regulations or rules teachers should follow, and also it might be a possible solution to endow genuine teacher autonomy.

The current stage of teacher professional development in current China cannot be simply understood from Hargreaves's standpoint as in the pre-professional stage. Frankly, the description of the pre-professional stage scenarios actually used to be the real situations in ethnic minority areas of China about 20~30 years ago. When the PRC was established and after the ten-year "Cultural Revolution", the central government was short of money and needed lots of personnel to undertake the basic construction of the country. From my understanding, the stage of Chinese teacher professionalism has always been a principled one as Goodson suggested, but the current one also has the features of the four stages as Hargreaves (2000) proposed. Although there was a period in which education developed slowly and teachers' status was disparaged in China, the deep-set educational philosophy and ideology from 1,000 years of history have not changed fundamentally in Chinese society and for Chinese people. Teachers, no matter to which extent they are professionalized in Western terms, have always been an independent group who are performing under requirements of *Shide* in Chinese, the Chinese ethic codes for teachers, inherited from our ancestors. Nevertheless, I admit that owing to the top-down policy, teacher professionalism has always been greatly influenced by the governmental and publics' requirements.

Viewed from the history, the central government never stopped teacher education in China. As a matter of fact, even before the establishment of PRC, there were four debates on the issues regarding teacher education systems. The first was in 1904 focusing on the necessity of setting teachers schools, and whether to put it in Imperial University of Peking (the former of Peking University) or build it independently. In the same year, the debate ended with the enactment of "Kui Mao Educational System" by Qing government, which settled the modern teacher education system and represented that a new stage of teacher professionalism in China was officially started (Shan, 2010). In this new stage, teachers should require professional training before they start teaching, which means teaching became a licensed career. Moreover, national standards of teaching profession were gradually coming into existence under the development of curriculum. The second debate was in 1922 which focused on whether teachers schools should be attached to universities or secondary schools. The debate ended with settling teachers schools as teacher educational departments in the universities. The third debate was in 1932 regarding whether to maintain or cancel the teacher educational departments since most of the universities already had education departments which shared some similar functions with teacher educational departments. In 1938, the Teachers College of National Southwest Associated University (the former of Yunnan Normal University) was established which represented that the system of teachers colleges (the later normal universities) appeared in China. The fourth was in 1947 concerning whether teachers colleges should be within universities or set independently. Finally, in 1952, Government Administration

Council (the predecessor of State Council) issued the Decision on Reforming Educational System which settled the basic teacher education system in a legal form.

The abominable event causing the complexity of current teacher professionalism was the ten-year "Cultural Revolution" which almost stopped the development of education in China. However, it was in this period that teacher professionalization became popular in the world. In 1966, UNESCO held a special intergovernmental conference in Paris on the status of teachers and finally suggested that "teaching should be regarded as a profession: It is a form of public service which requires of teachers' expert knowledge and specialized skills, acquired and maintained through rigorous and continuing study" (UNESCO, 1966). It was not until the 1980s that teacher training was re-recognized by the government. Confronting the huge gap of teacher professional development between China and foreign countries, the MOE (1985) issued the Decision of the Reform of Education System of the Central Committee of the Communist Party of China, which stated that the focus of education reform should be put on solving the problems of primary and secondary school qualified teachers. Teacher was officially listed as a profession in National Standard Occupational Classification and Code in People's Republic of China in 1986 (Lu, 2010). Teachers Law was issued in 1993, and then Education Law of the People's Republic of China was issued in 1995. Later, Teacher Qualification Regulation and Teacher Qualification Certifying Transitional Agreement were published, which standardized and pushed forward the teacher professionalism development in China.

However, under the pressure of continuous education reform in China and criticism of quality of education, the more professionalized standard to teachers seems, the more confused teachers become. Teachers' confusion might be reflected in the definiton of "teacher" in Teachers Law:

> Teachers are professionals who exercise the functions of education and teaching and are charged with the duty of imparting knowledge and educating people, training builders and successors for the socialist cause and enhancing the quality of the nation. Teachers shall devote themselves to the educational cause of the people. (State Council, 1994) (author's translation)

These words sound more like expectations of governments, but not the essential quality of teaching as a profession or responsibilities of teachers, except for the last sentence. Teachers Law continues to state the six rights of teachers as followed:

1) to conduct educational and teaching activities and carry out reform and experiment in education and teaching; 2) to engage in scientific research and academic exchanges, join professional academic societies and fully express their views in academic activities; 3) to give guidance to students in their studies and development and evaluate students' conduct and academic achievements; 4) to obtain salaries and remunerations on schedule and enjoy the welfare benefits prescribed by the State and the leave with pay in winter and summer vacations; 5) to put forward opinions and suggestions regarding education, teaching, management of schools and the work of the administrative departments of education, and participate in the democratic management of schools through congresses of teachers, staff and workers, or through other forms; and 6) to take refresher courses or other forms of training. (State Council, 1994) (author's translation)

At the same time, it is followed with teachers' obligations:

1) to abide by the Constitution, laws and professional ethics, and be paragons of virtue and learning; 2) to implement the educational policies of the State, observe relevant rules and regulations, carry out schools' teaching plans, fulfill teaching contracts and accomplish educational and teaching tasks; 3) to conduct education among students in the basic principles defined in the Constitution, education in patriotism, national unity and the legal system, and education in ideology, morality, culture, science and technology, and organize and lead students to engage in beneficial social activities; 4) to concern themselves with all students, love them, respect their dignity and promote their all-round development in such aspects as morality, intelligence and physique; 5) to stop acts that are harmful to students and other acts that encroach upon students' legitimate rights and interests, criticize and combat the phenomena that impair the sound growth of students; and 6) to ceaselessly raise their ideological level and political consciousness and improve their professional competence in education and teaching. (State

Council, 1994) (author's translation)

Actually, the rights and obligations of teachers stated in the Teachers Law are the indirect or direct requirements for professional teachers in China. Teachers' rights seems like requirements for teachers' working environment, and indeed they requeste teachers to reform their teaching, do research, and take part in teacher training. Meanwhile, Item 3 in Article 7 of Teachers Law, "give guidance to students studies" and "evaluate students' performance", is basic work of teaching. If only mention it as a kind of "right" of teachers, it implies that teachers do not necessarily need to do that, which seemes ridiculous for a professional occupation. As a fundamental legal document for every decision regarding teachers, Teachers Law claimes more on what teachers should do but states little about what educational departments can do in order to achieve teachers' professional development.

In the postmodern scenario, international economic organizations strengthened the links between nations, which makes it much easier for teachers to cooperate or make contacts with international forces, such as foreign experts. In addition, electronic and digital revolution in communication makes e-learning or mobile learning available to everyone, including teachers. In this postmodern era, it is not difficult to imagine that traditional classrooms with blackboards, desks and chairs are changed into whiteboard, multimedia and video talks; students from single or same cultural background will change to faces with various colors; and the scenario of one teacher standing on the platform in the small classroom crammed with students will become the teacher sitting in a café shop or office and giving the lectures through the Internet to students from all over the world. If one teacher wants to teach in such postmodern way, sometimes he might need several technicians to make an online course become available. Thus, requirements for professional teachers will be more complicated than before. As the recent popular concept, TPACK (short for technology, pedagogy and content knowledge), in the field of teacher education suggests, teachers should master techonology, pedagogy and content knowledge simutanously. In some developed areas of China, like Shanghai, Beijing, and Guangzhou, this scenario is not an idealized dream but the reality; and the teacher professionalism is developing towards a postmodern stage as Hargreaves (2000) suggested. However, in ethnic minority areas, it is still far away from the reality that most English teachers are confronting. The needs of teacher professionalism in these areas would be different from those in the developed ones.

2.4 Teacher Knowledge Base

Considering curriculum development of in-service training program, a necessary concept often referred to is the "teacher knowledge base". Theories and framework of teacher knowledge base were initiated by Shulman (1986, 1987). Shulman's conception of the knowledge base for teaching has seven parts: 1) content knowledge, 2) general pedagogical knowledge, 3) curriculum knowledge, 4) pedagogical content knowledge, 5) knowledge of learners and their characteristics, 6) knowledge of educational contexts and 7) knowledge of educational goals, purposes, values, philosophy and history. Among them, Shulman focused specifically on pedagogical content knowledge (PCK), or "teachers' ability to present subject matter in ways that students can understand and appreciate" (Fradd & Lee, 1998: 762). Zou (2010) claimed that PCK could be viewed as a tool which differentiates teacher and non-teacher professions from the knowledge base. Similar to Shulman, Gagné (2008) proposed another teacher knowledge base frame which involves six aspects: 1) subject knowledge and beliefs about the subject; 2) knowledge of the learners and their development, learning, motivation and concepts of self; 3) pedagogy and curriculum, such as assessment, evaluation, planning instruction; 4) equity and diversity, such as social, political, and institutional contexts of schooling, gender and identity; 5) knowledge about self/teacher development; 6) educational philosophy, such as educational goals and values, educational history, legal rights and responsibilities. Both of these two frames by Shulman and Gagné include three general aspects: 1) content knowledge (CK); 2) arts and general knowledge of education; 3) PCK.

Regarding teaching English to speakers of other languages (TESOL), Fradd and Lee (1998) pointed out three aspects of teacher knowledge for the English for Speakers of other Language (ESOL) teachers: 1) knowledge of academic content, including knowledge of the language acquisition process, knowledge of subject area content, and knowledge of culture and pragmatic language use, 2) knowledge of pedagogy, including curriculum and instruction, assessment, and technology, and 3) knowledge of students, schools and communities, such as classroom context, school context and community context.

Shulman's theoretical framework has been supported by research across subject areas, including English (Grossman, 1990), mathematics (Ball, 1990) and social studies (Wilson & Wineburg, 1993). Thus, on the basis of Shulman's (1987) and Gagné's (2008) frameworks, Zou (2010) and his colleagues researched 11 teachers universities in China. The results indicated that for the three aspects, on average, PCK courses only account for 4% of the total curriculum, and some universities do not offer PCK courses; meanwhile, CK courses represent 65% of the total. It is obvious that in these universities, CK outweighs PCK. This would possibly be part of the reason that pre-service teacher training is sometimes regarded as inefficient in China. Owing to lack of studies on English teacher knowledge base and no specific description of English teacher quality or knowledge base, except content knowledge as a disciplinary requirement for English teaching, English teachers would merely follow the general requirements as other teachers do. *Shide* becomes a major element in Chinese teacher professionalism requirements, especially for in-service teachers.

Chapter 3   Social Constructed Cognitive Process

3.1   Constructivist Learning Theory

Constructivism is a comprehensive term with philosophical, learning, and teaching dimensions (Bruning et al., 2011); however, in general, it focuses on the learners' contribution to knowledge and learning through individual and social activities, especially the interactions between learners and teachers in specific cultural context (Bruning et al., 2011; Fosnot, 2008; Packer & Goicoechea, 2000). This first section explains some key conceptions within the span of constructivist learning theory, such as the "novice" and the "expert", Vygotsky's dialectical constructivism, instructional scaffolding, and organizational context. Then, the second section specifically explores the connections between in-service teacher training and the above-mentioned concepts in constructivist learning theory, which is part of the theoretical rationale of this research.

3.1.1   The "novice" and the "expert" in constructivist learning process

Constructivism originated from Piaget's (1955) studies about children's intellectual development. Vygotsky (1986) emphasized the influence of socio-cultural development on human psychology; and he further argued that in the constructivist learning process knowledge or meaning was constructed through dialogue or communication with others. Constructivism not only acknowledges the uniqueness (unique needs and backgrounds) and complexity of each learner, but actually encourages, utilizes and rewards it as an integral part of the learning process (Wertsch, 2008). Constructivism widely holds that learning is a process in which individuals actively learn and construct the knowledge in a collaborative way through the interaction with teachers and society; at the same time, learners cognize the knowledge on the basis of their own experience, and then they form new concepts with codes or norms which could only be understood within certain contexts or cultural backgrounds (Bruning et al., 2011; Fosnot, 2008; Gao et al., 2008; Piaget, 1955; Packer & Goicoechea, 2000; Qin & Bao, 2010; Vygotsky, 1986; Wertsch, 2008).

Thus, a constructivist learning process is more like decoding, during which ideas proceed from dialogues between a "novice" and an "expert" when the former internalizes the new concepts with the help from teachers (Zhang, 2008). With regard to English learning in China, the "expert" is usually the teacher and all the students are the "novices", and mother tongue, in most of the cases, is the tool or medium language used; however, English on the one hand is the new knowledge for learners to learn, and on the other hand, it would be the tool for learners to learn other knowledge or concepts. That is to say, English has two functions for Chinese learners, one is the content of language learning, and the other is the outcome or final purpose for language learning. Therefore, like Chinese idiom goes, "Teach a man how to fish rather than give him the fish". Hence, that an essential concept needs to be constructed in language learning is actually the strategy or the method on learning a language, rather than the knowledge about that language (Chamot et al., 1999; Rubin, 2001; Wenden, 2002; Zhang, 2000). Once the learners grasp the methods of learning a language, i.e., the coding technique of that language, they can learn the language all by themselves along their whole lifespan.

3.1.2 Vygotsky's dialectical constructivism

Moshman (1982; cf. Bruning et al., 2011) distinguished three types of constructivism, namely exogenous constructivism, endogenous constructivism and dialectical constructivism. A simple method to understand their relationship is through different viewpoints on the construction of knowledge. Exogenous constructivism emphasizes the external influence (physical reality, presented information, and social models) on knowledge construction, while endogenous constructivism focuses on the internal influence in which cognitive structures or knowledge are created from earlier ones rather than the information provided by the environment. Dialectical constructivism, as the word "dialectical" suggests, stands between the other two in that it "places the source of knowledge in the interactions between learners and their environments" (Bruning et al., 2011: 195). The collaborative peer teaching method (O'Donnell, 2006) is an instructional example of dialectical constructivism.

In fact, dialectical constructivism represents one of Vygotsky's most influential contributions to cognitive psychology theories. The essential idea of Vygotsky's theory is that higher mental functions have their origin in social life as learners interact with more experienced members of their community. In order to understand the cognitive development during this process, it is necessary to describe another powerful concept Vygotsky (1978) raised, the zone of proximal development (ZPD), also called "construction zone" by Newman et al. (1989; cf. Bruning et al., 2011). In ZPD, learners bring their experience or already formed knowledge, and adults or teachers bring a support structure. When they interact with each other, they share the values, beliefs and cultural knowledge together. During this cultural sharing process, in Vygotsky's view, cognition changes; in other words, the learners acquire the knowledge.

3.1.3 Instructional scaffolding

On the basis of ZPD, another topic raised for teachers in instruction is "scaffolding". In instructional scaffolding, the teacher would provide learners with selective help, and use the "support structure" to aid learners, such as directing attention, giving hints about possible strategies, or offering resources for questions, and to enable them to do or understand things or conceptions they could not do or perceive on their own. Then, when students become more competent, the support would be withdrawn gradually (Bruning et al., 2011: 198).

Taking learning Chinese for foreigners as an example, when foreign Chinese learner meets the word gao-da-shang, an abbreviation word using the first letters of three Chinese words, namely *gao duan* (high standard), *da qi* (decent), and *shang dang ci* (high quality), the teacher's instructional scaffolding is helping him to realize the first-letter abbreviation technique. Hence, if this learner has the same rule in his mother tongue which is his already formed knowledge, it will be easier for him to use his own experience to decode the meaning of this new word; nevertheless, if he has never encountered such word formation, it will be more difficult for him to remember the meaning of this word and the teacher needs other ways to scaffold.

3.1.4 Organizational context

In the whole constructivist learning theory, context or cultural environment plays a magnificent role. Not only it serves as the origin in which knowledge emerges, but also the ground in which cognition develops. For adults, totally unlike children, they are working and living in a more regulated "organizational context", which is typical for Chinese teachers. Smylie (1995) stressed that the organizational context is a significant stimulating drive for teachers' professional development needs and opportunities in that, firstly, teachers are mature adults who can learn throughout their whole life in any settings and circumstances, especially when problems occur, and secondly, schools, as the organizational context for teachers, are the starting point to foster the need to change through a positive system to promote the changing (Schunk, 1991; Wu, 2005).

3.2 Constructivist Learning Theory and In-service Teachers' Training

Although the study of constructivist learning theory focuses more on children, it could shed light on adult learners' training as well. Firstly, in-service teachers used to be language learners, and the previous coding technique they learnt from their teachers would be unconsciously passed on through their teaching to the students. Thus, teacher trainers who learn and research more about language education theories and policies could be considered as the "experts", and trainees, usually in-service teachers, are viewed as the "novice". Secondly, research studies (Ma, 2012; Zhang, 2004) in China show that ZPD is adaptable to college students as well, and instructional scaffolding is efficient in fostering students' English learning. I have reasons to believe that the combination of constructivist learning theory and some concepts (in-service training motivation and teacher belief) in cognitive psychology theories would enable me to explore the professional development needs of secondary school English teachers in ethnic minority areas. In order to make the theoretical rationale of this research clearer, I use Figure 3.1 to explain my thoughts in a more vivid way.

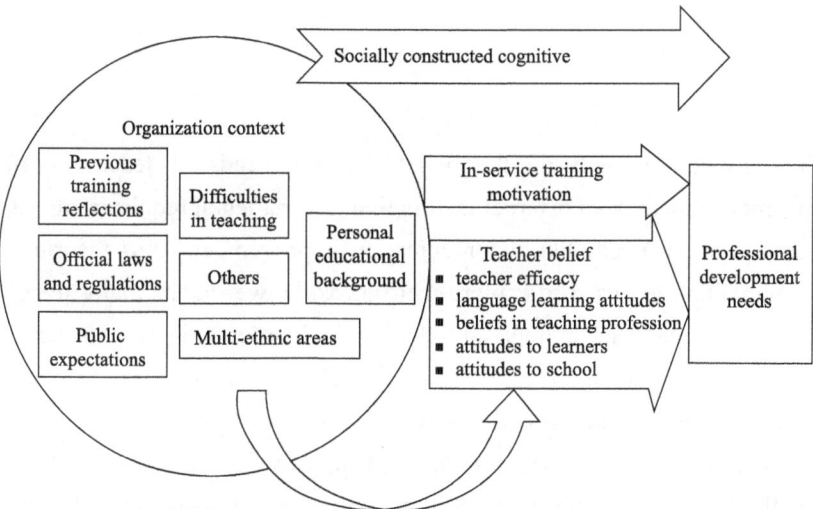

Figure 3.1   Framework for Theoretical Rationale

As Figure 3.1 shows, as far as I am concerned, the formation of professional development needs is a socially constructed cognitive process; there are cognitive psychological factors like in-service training motivation and teacher belief which directly indicate the needs; however, these factors are triggered by implicit factors that are closely related to organizational context. In the next chapter, conceptions concerning in-service training motivation and teacher belief, teacher efficacy and language learning attitudes in particular, are explored within the theories of cognitive psychology.

Chapter 4 Motivation and Adults' Education Participation

This research is built on the belief that the needs of teacher professional development originate from external factors like governmental requirements, as well as individuals' internal needs like communication improvement. Thus theories of adult training motivation are used to explore their needs. However, the major hypothesis in this book is that teachers' beliefs, attitudes to English learning and teacher efficacy, will influence their motivation to participate in NTP; hence, theories of teacher efficacy and language learning attitudes will also be explored.

As explained in the previous part, English teachers' professional development needs will be strongly influenced by the specific social and cultural expectations around the teaching profession. A motivational theory that admits the importance of social elements, such as learning environment, will be more suitable for this research. The basic premise of social cognitive learning theory is that an interrelation exists between an individual's cognitive process and the social environment where the learning happens (Alderman, 2004; Bandura, 1986, 1997). In other words, an individual's learning process is influenced either positively or negatively by the learning environment. From the perspective of social cognitive learning theories, this research tends to test the strength of English teachers' efficacy, the self-initiated in-service training motivation, and the relationship between the two. Thus, a review of these important conceptions is provided as in the following part.

4.1 From Maslow to Herzberg

Talking about adults' learning motivation theory, it is necessary to mention

Maslow's (1954) hierarchy of needs, not only for it has been one of the most widely discussed theories of motivation, but also in that it activated studies and researches on learning motivation theories. The basic hierarchy of needs indicates that human beings have desires influencing their behavior; only unsatisfied needs will affect behavior, and satisfied needs will not. Since needs are of various kinds, Maslow grouped them into five categories. Then the needs were arranged in order of their importance, from the basic to the complex, namely, physiological needs, safety and security, love, self-esteem and self-actualization. A person advances to the next level of needs only after the lower-level need is greatly satisfied. The further the progress is up the hierarchy, the more individuality, humanity and psychological health a person will develop.

Building on Maslow's theory and the force-field analysis of Lewin (1947), Miller (1967) provided the motivational force theory. From the work of Maslow, Miller hypothesized that adults from lower socio-economic classes would participate in education for job and basic-skill related reasons, whereas participants from higher social classes would seek education to satisfy achievement and self-realization needs. Moreover, Cross (1981) presumed a tendency that "members of the lower social classes will be interested primarily in education that meets survival needs, mostly job training and basic adult education, while the upper social classes will have fulfilled those needs and will seek education that leads to achievement and self-realization". This tendency was related to one's place in the life cycle as well: younger people would be more interested than older people in achieving economic security (Merriam & Caffarella, 1999). If these presumptions were correct, teachers with lower level of income would be more interested in participating in training for getting higher economic security. However, in-service training is part of teachers' professional development; economic security might be one reason for participation but there are other factors, such as working environment and recognition for achievement.

"Satisfiers-dissatisfiers" theory of motivation (Herzberg et al., 1959) concluded that some factors (such as pay, working condition, supervision, interpersonal relationships, company policy and administration) could cause employees' dissatisfaction, but even when the conditions complained about were corrected, they contributed very little to job satisfaction. Conversely, while the presence of other factors (such as achievement, recognition for achievement, intrinsic interest in the work, responsibility and advancement) produced satisfaction, their absence caused very little dissatisfaction. That is to say, changing economic-related factors has little effect on employees' satisfaction in their work, but their self-realization is the main factor of their job satisfaction. Regarding teachers, low income may cause them to be unsatisfied with the teaching career; nevertheless, the "satisfiers-dissatisfiers" theory suggests that in specific conditions, professional development needs outweigh economic security needs.

4.2 Roger Boshier's EPS

Talking about the five kinds of needs discussed in Maslow's hierarchy, there is a tendency of low-level ones (such as physiological needs, safety and security) to be external-oriented and high-level ones (such as love, self-esteem, self-actualization) to be internal-oriented. Hence, considering Herzberg's "satisfiers-dissatisfiers" theory, Maslow's hierarchy can be put in another way that when external needs are satisfied, people tend to pay more attention to internal ones. Teachers' motivation for in-service training or professional development, in this case, is more related to internal needs. To study this kind of needs, the focus should be on the relationship between learners' internal psychological factors and the external environment in which the learning appears. Houle's (1961) typology and Boshier's congruence model (Boshier, 1971, 1976, 1977, 1991) presented a social cognitive viewpoint for this research to test secondary school teachers' in-service training motivation.

In examining adults' motivation to learn, Houle (1961) conducted a very influential study. Through a study of 22 adult learners, he was able to identify three distinct groups of learners in terms of their motivation to learn: 1) Goal-oriented learners use learning to achieve very specific objectives, such as learning how to deal with stress or planning for retirement. They tend to be practical in outlook, turning to any readily available source for the information and instruction they need. 2) Activity-oriented learners value the activity itself. They pursue learning in order to escape boredom or to make social contacts. 3) Learning-oriented learners value learning for its own sake; they see learning as a way of staying mentally alert and tend to learn throughout most of their lives.

Following Houle's (1961) typology, from 1971 to 1991, Boshier made efforts to develop the EPS on account of his congruence model. Boshier believed that motivation for learning was a function of the interaction between internal psychological factors and external environmental factors. The discrepancy between participants' (students') self-concept and other aspects of the educational environment would directly result in the participation or dropout of adult education. Based on his test, Boshier found out that students with high incongruence scores were significantly more likely to drop out than the others (Cross, 1981). Hence, according to Boshier, it was important to provide suitable educational environments for students. At the same time, Boshier (1991) suggested that self-esteem of the individual, a kind of high-level need in Maslow's hierarchy, was important for educational participation. Those who evaluated themselves negatively were less likely to experience congruence with the educational environment.

As lifelong learners in their professional life, teachers will be continuously confronting various in-service training programs. As far as Boshier's congruence model is concerned, learners' motivations or orientations in participating in all kinds of training are deeply interrelated to their educational environment. Consequently, the strength of their motivation will be the basic and key factor to the final efficiency of the training program. In my research, Boshier's EPS was used to test trainees' educational participation strength and the results would in turn reveal the characteristic of the self-initiated motivational orientations of English teachers in ethnic minority areas of China.

The original EPS was published in 1971 by Boshier with 48 items and a 9-point scale which contained 8 subscales. In 1976, a modified version of the EPS was developed, including 40 items and a 4-point scale which contained 6 subscales (Boshier, 1976). Later on, O'Connor (1979, 1982) modified the original EPS by adding a 0 end point denoting no change, creating a 10-point scale. Also, O'Connor added 8 additional questions to bring the total number to 56 items and 6 subscales. Boshier (1991) developed the original scale (F-form) into a new one (A-form) with 42 items and a 4-point scale containing 7 subscales. Garst and Ried (1999) used the original EPS and created another modified version of EPS with 43 items and a 5-point scale which had 6 subscales.

As noted by Boshier (1991: 150), the first form of the EPS was widely used and "the availability of a large data base enabled researchers to create norms and investigate the durability of the factor structure across cultures". However, owing to the limits of the EPS-F(First)-form (Boshier, 1971), Boshier developed the EPS-A (Alternative)-form (Boshier, 1991). The EPS-A-form measures motivational orientations and consists of seven 6-items factors. The seven factors are communication improvement, social contact, educational preparation, professional advancement, family togetherness, social stimulation, and cognitive interest. EPS (English) has been translated into Chinese several times (Boshier et al., 2006). Because "back translation foregrounds isomorphism between words" and "word-for-word translation was not enough" (Boshier et al., 2006: 207), Boshier et al. (2006) deployed Chinese characters reflecting the deeper meanings of EPS items (e.g., friendship, sociability) for the EPS (Chinese), including 42 EPS items with 6 items for each factor arrayed on the same 4-point scale as the English version. However, factor analysis indicates that EPS (Chinese) and EPS (English) have many differences. For instance, factor loading for certain items are quite low in Chinese samples. Moreover, some items have repeated or overlapped meaning, such as "make friends" and "make new friends". Also, some items are aiming at all the population which is not suitable for teachers. For instance, items in Communication Improvement are about improving language ability, but not in relation to a specific language. Hence, to modify EPS for testing teachers is necessary. In this research, this book focuses on Chinese characters relating more to teachers, especially English teachers. It keeps items which have high factor loading both in EPS (English) and EPS (Chinese), and at the same time mingles some items which have similar meanings in Chinese concepts. It also specifies all the items in Communication Improvement into improving English ability. Meanwhile, considering the NTP is an in-service training program which does not provide degree or certificate for participants, the training does not have the function of "educational preparation" in the EPS. Hence, modified EPS (Chinese) (referring to Appendixes 1 and 2) contained 24 EPS items from 6 factors arrayed on the 4-point scale (from "no influence", "little influence", "moderate influence", to "much influence").

Chapter 5   Teacher Beliefs

Teachers' beliefs are an important factor that affects their attitudes and behavior in the classroom. These beliefs often involve assumptions about students, learning, teaching materials, and organization of the class (Kagan, 1992). Teachers' beliefs frequently affect student-teacher interactions and instructional planning (Ashton & Webb, 1986; Gibson & Dembo, 1984, cf. Bruning et al., 2011). Teachers' beliefs about teaching materials also shape their pedagogy in class (Cobb & Bowers, 1999; Chen & Chen, 2008; Hashweh, 1996; Qin, 2007). Generally, according to Schraw and Olafson (2002), beliefs about three classroom factors affect teachers' behavior most, namely course content, type of student receiving the instruction and teacher's own explicit beliefs about teaching. However, relatively little is known about the relationship between teachers' beliefs and their in-service training motivation.

Teachers' beliefs, teacher efficacy and teachers' attitudes to language learning can be understood as the representations of teaches' beliefs. Firstly, teacher efficacy is teachers' beliefs in personal capability related to teaching, which is a combination of teachers' beliefs about students and organization of the class; meanwhile, when language becomes the content of learning, attitudes to the target language will reveal teachers' beliefs in teaching materials and also their resolution in dealing with the materials. Thus, studying teacher efficacy and attitudes to language can help explore the effects of teachers' beliefs on training motivation.

5.1 Bandura's Model of Reciprocal Determinism

Alderman (2004) summarized that from a social cognitive perspective, motivation is related to three kinds of factors: 1) the personal factors (or cognitive factors), such as individual's beliefs about his ability; 2) the environmental factors, such as evaluation criteria used by the teacher and the social expectations on successful learning; 3) and the behavioral factors of the person regarding learning, such as reading loudly or reciting vocabulary. The three kinds of factors affect each other through the reciprocal interaction (referring to Figure 5.1). This reciprocal interaction is what Bandura called reciprocal determinism which implies that learning is the result of the three interacting variables. Personal factors involve learners' beliefs and attitudes that affect learning, such as self-efficacy judgements. Environmental factors involve the roles played by teachers, parents, peers and also the society. Factors involve learners' performance or actions responding to a given situation, for example, whether one works harder in response to a weak test score.

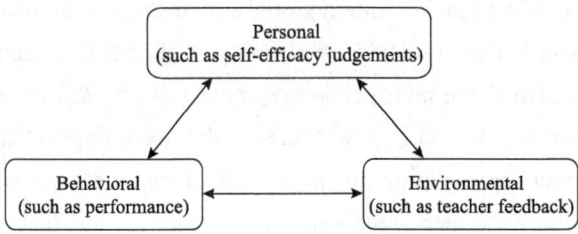

Figure 5.1 Bandura's Model of Reciprocal Determinism
(Bruning et al., 2011: 108)

The idea of Bandura's reciprocal determinism suggests that these three aspects interrelate to each other and affect each other. For example, personal factors will influence behavior and the interpretations of environmental factors. Bruning et al. (2011) explained that one way personal factors related to behavioral and environmental factors was through "mediated responses", and the situations about how events were interpreted cognitively before responding. Taking poor performance on a test as an example, it may elicit anxiety in one student but increase arduous working in another because they interpret this event in different ways.

In these two situations, self-efficacy is one of the important indexes that differentiate the two students' interpretations and also influence their performances. According to Bandura (1997), self-efficacy is the judgement of one's ability to perform a task within a specific domain. For example, poor score is the specific domain, the environment, and learners' upcoming performance is either working hard or feeling anxiety.

For Bandura (1986, 1993, 1997), an individual's judgement of self-efficacy varies along three dimensions related to performance, namely the task difficulty, the generality of one's self-efficacy, and the strength of one's efficacy judgements (Bruning et al., 2011). Learners with high efficacy may also feel reluctant to conduct difficult task. For instance, a freshman will feel it is challenging to take graduate class. The generality of one's self-efficacy indicates for some people who may have high self-efficacy in general statements like "I usually have confidence", but this does not mean they still have high efficacy in certain domains. For example, "I usually have confidence in running a marathon." The strength of one's efficacy judgements implies that high efficacy individuals will be more inclined to persist and maintain self-confidence than the individuals with low self-efficacy in confronting the same poor scores in one test.

For teachers, this reciprocal determinism exists as well. In the process of teacher professional development, learning is occuring while teaching is happening. As learners, teachers have different interpretations towards the same event, taking the same example given before. Meanwhile, teachers' past experiences of learning also affect their decisions on performance as teachers. Hence, teacher efficacy is an important index to differentiate motivation for in-service training and also teachers' behavior or performance in professional development.

5.2 Teacher Efficacy and Its Influencing Factors

Teacher efficacy refers to "the extent to which teachers believe that they have the capacity to affect student performance" (Ashton, 1984: 28). It refers to teacher's belief in his or her capability to enact the instruction needed in a given context to be successful (Tschannen-Moran et al., 1998). Teacher efficacy was first introduced in a Rand Corporation study (Armour et al., 1976; Alderman, 2004). The study concluded that a teacher's sense of self-efficacy was one of the best predictors of increased student achievement and the extent of teacher change.

Ashton and Webb (1986) continued self-efficacy research, and pointed out that teacher efficacy, similar to self-efficacy, has two components, namely general teaching efficacy and personal teaching efficacy. General teaching efficacy is constituted by teacher belief about what teachers can accomplish despite obstacles. Personal teaching efficacy is a judgement about the extent to which the teacher can affect students learning proficiency (Alderman, 2004).

Ashton and Webb (1986) indicated that a belief about the nature of intelligence strongly differentiates high-efficacy and low-efficacy teachers. Teachers with a high level of teacher efficacy are more likely to believe that all students can learn well and can feel responsible for their learning. Moreover, Pang and Sablan's (1998) study showed that teacher efficacy might differ in regard to students' cultures and ethnicities. For example, limited knowledge of African-American students and their culture contributes to the low efficacy of teachers. Beyond intelligence and students' cultures and ethnicities, beliefs about students' motivation also influence teachers' teaching practices (Rosenholtz, 1989).

Alderman (2004) highlighted three factors influencing teacher efficacy. School and classroom environmental characteristic is the first factor. Firstly, a supportive school climate is one factor that influences a high sense of teacher efficacy. Interdisciplinary teachers' team in an organization with common planning time has higher personal efficacy than teachers who are in single-disciplinary departmental team because the common planning time provides opportunity to collaborate and share problems with team members (Warren & Payne, 1997). Secondly, teacher efficacy is higher in schools where there is a high level of collegial support. Chester and Beaudin (1996) found that a collegial school culture is an important factor for new teachers in an urban district. Furthermore, students' ability level and the extent to which the teacher prepares to teach the students are conspicuous variables affecting the sense of efficacy (Ashton & Webb, 1986; Raudenbush et al., 1992; Soodak & Podell, 1998). If the teacher is able to keep students engaged in learning, the negative effects of tracking on efficacy can disappear (Alderman, 2004).

The second factor is teacher experience. Hoy and Woolfolk (1990) indicated that teacher efficacy tends to increase during pre-service training and student teaching when new skills are being learned and practiced. Also, pre-service teachers expose a higher efficacy belief about handling difficult motivation problems, whereas the experienced teachers reveal higher efficacy beliefs on planning and evaluation lessons (Benz et al., 1992).

The third factor is subject matter preparation. Ramey-Gassert and Shroyer (1992) found that many elementary teachers reported that they had inadequate backgrounds in science and consequently avoided teaching it when possible.

Influenced by foreign research, studies about English teacher efficacy (ETE) in China mainly focus on four aspects (Wang, 2013): ①the relationship between teacher efficacy and teacher instruction in classroom (Jiang, 2011; Liu, 2010); ② the relationship between working environment and teacher efficacy (Jiang, 2011; Liu, 2007; Lü, 2006; Peng, 2008); ③the correlation between teacher efficacy and teacher belief (Lin, 2008; Shi & Gao, 2010; Zhu, 2006); ④the correlation between teacher efficacy and teachers' demographic factors, such as gender, teaching year and professional title (Jiang, 2011; Shi, 2009; Teng & Wu, 2011; Wang, 2009; Wang & Huang, 2009). Similar to Gibson and Dembo (1984), Milner and Woolfolk-Hoy (2003), Woolfolk and Hoy (1990), Liu (2010) and Jiang (2011) claimed that teachers with high teacher efficacy will have stronger confidence, encourage more students to learn, and give more independence to students. Moreover, the location of schools, type of schools, management system of schools, and interpersonal relationships among teachers will influence teacher efficacy (Jiang, 2011; Liu, 2007; Lü, 2006; Peng, 2008). In other words, working environment has some effects on teacher efficacy, which is in accordance with the findings of Ross and Gray (2006), Tschannen-Moran and Hoy (2007) and Rubie-Davies et al. (2012).

To conclude, teacher efficacy relates to teachers' beliefs on their ability to affect students' behavior; and teachers with dissimilar (high or low) strength of teacher efficacy would represent teachers' belief on their ability to encourage and enforce students' learning, present various behavior in teaching, and consequently in their needs for professional development (Ashton, 1984; Alderman, 2004). Moreover, external factors (such as location of schools, type of schools, management system of schools, and interpersonal relationships between teachers) and internal factors (such as teachers' working experience, teachers' education background, and teachers' demographic features) will influence the strength of teacher efficacy. To what extent can teacher efficacy affect teachers' motivation for learning? In what aspects can teacher efficacy affect the strength of teachers' learning motivation? The answers to these two questions will resolve the fundamental argument on teachers' professional development needs. Beyond teachers' beliefs about their own ability, their attitudes to English learning might also influence teaching behavior and their motivation for professional development.

5.3 Attitudes in Language Learning

Kiesler et al. indicated (cf. Yuan, 2007: 10) that Thurstone pioneered the study of attitudes and made a great number of findings. Thurstone (cf. Lemon, 1973: 24-25) defined attitude as the intensity of positive or negative effect for or against a psychological object, and a psychological object was any symbol, person, phrase, slogan, or idea towards which people could differ as regards positive or negative effect. Thurstone theorized that the opinion about an object was not the same as the concept of the attitudes to an object; in that an opinion was simply a display of an attitude, and that an opinion could be employed to detect the underlying attitudinal predisposition. On the one hand, opinion was viewed as the expression of an overt belief about an affective reaction. On the other hand, attitude consisted of an affective reaction (Summers, 1969; Baker, 1992; Yuan, 2007).

According to Baker (1992), attitude was a hypothetical construct utilized to expound the orientation and persistence of human behavior. Attitude can be used to predict behavior but it is invisible and cannot be measured directly. Therefore, attitude is a relatively constant system of evaluative processes toward an object based on what individuals have learned in previous settings. Even though attitudes are relatively constant in individuals, attitudes have been learned. Because attitudes are learned, they may be changed through learning process (cf. Yuan, 2007: 11).

Referring to L2 learning, Ellis (1994: 198) states that,

> (L)earners manifest different attitudes toward 1) the target language, 2) target language speakers, 3) the target-language culture, 4) the social value of learning the L2, 5) particular uses of the target language, and 6) themselves as members of their own culture.

These attitudes to language are likely to reflect the particular social settings in which learners find themselves. Teachers used to be learners and their attitudes had an impact on the level of their language learning, which might ultimately influence their language teaching methods and professional development as well. In this research, Ellis' six dimensions of language learning attitudes for the following reasons are adopted. Firstly, either Chinese or ethnic minority languages are the L2 of the subjects in this research, and their attitudes to this L2 can be used to compare with their attitudes to English. Secondly, English is taught as a foreign language in China, so subjects' attitudes to English should be different to those who learn English as a second one.

Gardner and Lambert (1972) proposed "if individuals had a strong interest in another language community, or if they had an open appreciation and interest in other language groups in general, this could make them more open to learning in a second language" (cf. Gardner, 2006: 247). In his socio-psychological model of L2 learning (Gardner, 1985, 2000, 2006), same as Ellis (referring to Table 5.1), Gardner pointed out the importance of interest in foreign languages (not limited to target language but foreign languages in general) and attitudes toward the target group (target language speakers and target language culture). They are also in accordance with the instrumental orientation (social value and particular use) of language learning. However, Gardner (2006: 247) emphasized the significance of integrating into target culture by pointing out that individuals who are high in integrative orientation are "willing and able to take on features of another language group as part of their own behavioral repertoire". Gardner also stated that high integrative orientation doesn't mean individuals are willing to become a member of the target language culture, because orientation does not equal to identification in his theory. For Gardner, high integrativeness just means students are more open to the foreign culture and willing to do things with features of another language group, such as to communicate in another language. He explained that if individuals have strong awareness to their own ethnicity, their integrative orientation is low; if their sense of ethnicity is weak, their integrative orientation is high. The discrepancy here means that it is difficult to separate the definition of "integrative orientation" from "identification". According to social psychology study, cognition, evaluation and conation are three major correlated dimensions or representations of social identity (Blanz et al., 1998). Identification is greatly represented through the sense of ethnicity, or cognition to the ethnic group or social group. Gardner's integrativeness can be viewed as conation aspect of social identity. If a person has strong sense of ethnicity, in Gardner's theory, he will have low integrativeness; however, in social identity theories, strong sense of ethnicity means strong social identity to the ethnic group or social group. Thus, if one person has strong social identity to his own ethnic group, he has weak social identity to other groups, which indicates integrativeness actually has close relationship to identification. Hence, Ellis' "attitudes to themselves as members of their own culture" and Gardner's "integrative orientation" are two opposite but correlated aspects of social identity. One is cognition to personal ethnic group, and the other is conation to target language ethnic group.

Table 5.1 Attitudinal Dimensions Comparison Between Gardner and Ellis

	Gardner's Attitudes / Motivation Test Battery	Ellis' Language Learning Attitudes
Integrativeness	interest in target language	the target language
	attitudes toward the target group	target language speakers
		the target language culture
	integrative orientation	/
	/	themselves as members of their own culture
	interest in foreign languages in general	/
Motivation	attitudes towards language learning	/
	motivation intensity	/
	desire to learn the language	/
Attitudes towards language learning environment	teacher	/
	classroom	/
Instrumentality	instrumental orientation	the social value of learning the L2
		particular uses of the target language

The Attitude/Motivation Test Battery (AMTB) developed by Gardner (1985) to access various individual difference variables is based on socio-psychological model. The problem with AMTB is that it not only includes attitudes but also behavior. Gardner (1985, 2000, 2006) believed that highly motivated individuals not only have high attitudes but also study and use the language in their daily life as a manifestation of their motivation. However, Gardner's AMTB mixed attitude/motivation and motivated behavior, which makes it harder to "decide the exact nature of the underlying learner trait that the instrument targets" (Huang, 2008: 530). In this research, emphasis is on individuals' attitude to AL they are willing to learn, rather than their actual behavior in learning the language. Hence, this book chose five attitudes that are mentioned by Ellis' attitudinal theory and Gardner's socio-educational model to explore the language attitudes of secondary school teachers.

Twenty items (referring to Appendix 1) based on five attitudes (AL, AS, AC, ASV, APU) are designed to test teachers' attitude towards three languages, Chinese, English and ethnic minority languages. For those whose first language (L1) is Chinese, English and ethnic minority languages are considered as target languages. This group of teachers represent a large amount of the total proportion; however, most of them may not learn ethnic minority languages in their whole life. Correspondingly, for those participants whose L1 is one ethnic minority language, Chinese and English are the target languages.

Part 3 Major Findings

Chapter 6 Language Learning Attitudes of Secondary School English Teachers in Multilingual Areas

Twenty items of the five attitudinal dimensions—AL, AS, AC, ASV and APU (referring to Appendix 1)—are designed to test teachers' attitudes towards their L2 or third language (L3) learning. Owing to the fact that some subjects' mother tongues are not Chinese, they are asked to choose their attitudes to language learning from the following categories: Chinese, English, and ethnic minority languages. Subjects were asked to choose any language which fits the description, such as "I want to learn____ because it represents a civilized culture" (referring to Appendix 1). Hence, for those whose L2 is Chinese, they can choose Chinese and/or English; for those whose mother tongue is Chinese, they can choose English and/or ethnic minority languages. Each choice of the language is scored 1, and 0 for not chosen. If two languages are chosen, each can be scored 1 respectively. If none of the languages fits the description, subjects can leave it blank and the data are scored 0 in all categories.

Since English is not the mother tongue for all subjects, scores in English are used in the reliability test and exploratory factor analysis to test the structure and pattern of the items. With 20 items, Cronbach's alpha is 0.854 and Guttman Split-Half Coefficient is 0.762 (referring to Appendix 4). Reliability test shows that the items have high internal consistency, which is suitable for factor analysis.

Principal Component Analysis and Varimax with Kaiser Normalization are used in exploratory factor analysis. KMO is 0.856 and Bartlett's test also shows that data are significant for factor analysis. Using Eigenvalues 5 factors were extracted, and the total variance explained was 55.345. Considering Cronbach's alpha if item deleted, Communalities and the explanation of each factor, 4 items were deleted (referring to Appendix 4).

The final Teachers' Language Attitudinal Dimension contains 16 items (referring to Table 6.1), and the total variance explained was 59.799 (referring to Appendix 4). Five factors of the attitudes are AC, AS, AL, ASV and APU.

Table 6.1 Teachers' Language Attitudinal Dimension

No.	Items	Factors				
		AC	AS	AL	ASV	APU
12	I want to learn ___ because it represents a civilized culture.	√				
9	I want to learn ___ because it represents a great culture.	√				
2	I want to learn ___ because it has a long history.	√				
10	I want to learn ___ because it represents the culture I favor.	√				
6	I want to learn ___ because people who speak it are knowledgeable.		√			
7	I want to learn ___ because people who speak it have great fortune and are at a high status.		√			
8	I want to learn ___ because people who speak it are respectable.		√			
1	I want to learn ___ because I want to study it.				√	
4	I want to learn ___ because I like it.				√	
3	I want to learn ___ because it is beautiful.				√	
15	I want to learn ___ because it can let me communicate with people from different cultures.					√

Chapter 6 Language Learning Attitudes of Secondary School English Teachers in Multilingual Areas

Continued

No.	Items	Factors				
		AC	AS	AL	ASV	APU
20	I want to learn ___ because it can satisfy some of my personal needs.				√	
16	I want to learn ___ because it can make me knowledgeable.				√	
19	I want to learn ___ because my leaders arranged it.					√
17	I want to learn ___ because it can help me deal with my work better.					√
18	I want to learn ___ because it can help me improve my teaching proficiency.					√

Notes: ① √ indicates the item is loaded in that factor
② The order of the items is based on the rotated loadings of each item in the factors from high to low

6.1 Distribution and Strength of ELA

Guttman scaling (Guttman, 1944) is used to test the strength of attitudinal dimensions. Guttman scaling allows researchers to simply see a series of subjects' responses which belong to the same dimension in a simple "K+1" scales (K is the number of questions). Scoring each answer 1 (correct answer) or 0 (wrong answer) and then summing up all the answers in the same dimension can get the general results for this category. Consequently, it becomes easier for a comparative discussion when many possibilities exist.

Mean value is usually used to show the strength of a variable, but when the ranges of data (referring to Table 6.2) are different, standard scores are needed for comparison among various variables. Standard scores are usually called standard variables, Z-scores, Z-values or normal scores. In statistics, a standard score indicates by how many standard deviations (SD) an observation or datum is above or below the mean. Through converting all the raw scores into Z-scores, it becomes easier for researchers to tell the differences between two Z-scores or two variables when the ranges of data are different.

Table 6.2   Guttman Scaling of Language Learning Attitudes

Dimensions	AC	AS	AL	ASV	APU	GLLA
Ranges	4	3	3	3	3	16
"K+1" Scales	5	4	4	4	4	17

In statistics, the median is the middle value in a sorted distribution, sample or population. When there is an even number of observations, the median is the mean of the two central values. A median often used when there are a few extremes of the data that can greatly influence the mean and distort what may be considered typical (Weisstein, Statistical Median, n.d.). Usually, there are two kinds of distribution in descriptive analysis; normal or skewness. Normal or symmetrical distribution is also known as central tendency, the way in which the data tend to cluster around some value. On the contrary, skewness is a measure of the extent to which the variable inclines to one side of the mean. Skewness value can be negative, positive or undefined. Negative skew or the left-skewed means the tail on the left side is longer than that on the right side. Conversely, positive skew or the right-skewed means the tail on the right side is longer than that on the left side. Based on the Pearson second skew coefficient (Weisstein, Pearson's Skewness Coefficients, n.d.), if skewness value is between -1 to 1, a central tendency or normal distribution is shown. In this research, central tendency indicates participants' attitudes have great individual differences, and left-skewed distribution implies most participants have positive attitudes, and right-skewed distribution means a large number of participants have negative attitudes.

6.1.1 General English learning attitudes

Skewness value ($-1<-0.566<1$) indicates a normal distribution of GELA. Median value ($0.211>0$) shows that in average participants have positive attitudes to English learning (referring to Table 6.3); however, the distribution of data (referring to Figure 6.1) shows that many participants have negative attitudes (Z-score<0). Detailed analyses on five English learning attitudinal dimensions will reveal more findings.

Chapter 6 Language Learning Attitudes of Secondary School English Teachers in Multilingual Areas

Table 6.3 Descriptive Analysis of GELA

Item	Median	Range	Skewness	Percentile			N
				25th	50th	75th	
Z-score of GELA	0.211	4.242	−0.566	−0.5844	0.211	0.741	186

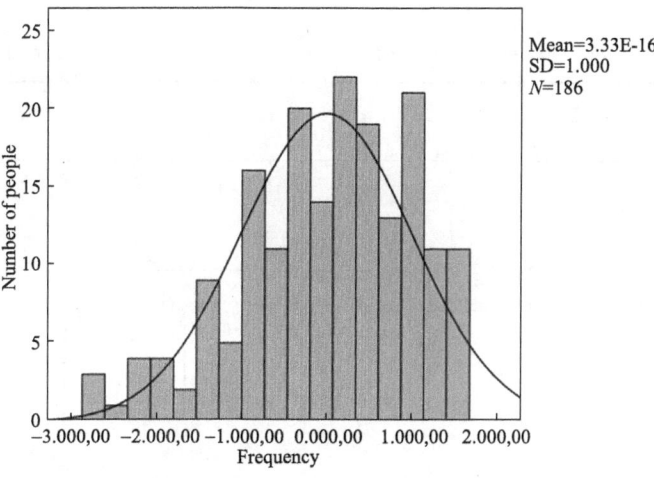

Figure 6.1 Histogram of GELA

6.1.2 Five English learning attitudinal dimensions

Descriptive analyses of five attitudinal dimensions imply more obvious differences. Skewness value suggests that attitudes to SVE and attitudes to PUE have left-skewed distribution, while the other three have normal distribution (referring to Table 6.4). As mentioned before, left-skewed distribution shows most participants have positive attitudes. Boxplot will imply more findings (referring to Figure 6.2).

Table 6.4 Descriptive Analysis of Five English Learning Attitudinal Dimensions

Items	Z-AEC	Z-AES	Z-AEL	Z-SVE	Z-PUE	N
Median	−0.443	0.025	0.098	0.628	0.744	186
Skewness	0.321	−0.639	−0.401	−1.56	−1.273	

		Z-AEC	Z-AES	Z-AEL	Z-SVE	Z-PUE	Continued N
Items							
Range		2.868	2.837	2.878	3.335	3.098	
Percentiles	25%	−1.160	−0.920	−0.861	−0.484	−0.289	186
	50%	−0.443	0.0254	0.098	0.628	0.744	
	75%	0.991	0.971	1.057	0.628	0.744	

Notes: Z=Z-score

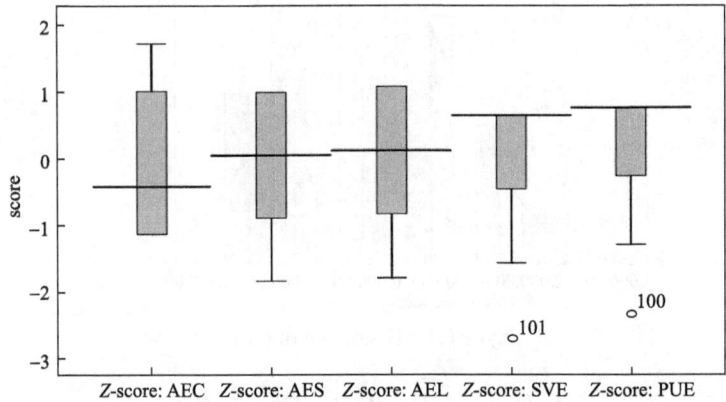

Figure 6.2 Boxplot of the Five English Learning Attitudinal Dimensions

Boxplot of five English learning attitudinal dimensions suggests the following findings. Firstly, in general, most participants have negative attitudes to learning English because of its splendid culture (Median=−0.443<0, referring to Z-AEC in Table 6.4) but positive attitudes to the other four dimensions. Secondly, the minimum value in AEC is the same as the 25th percentile value, which indicates 25% of the participants have similar negative AEC. Thirdly, the maximum values in AES and AEL are the same as their 75% percentile values, which implies 25% of the participants have similar positive attitudes to AES and AEL. Fourthly, though there is a single case at a low score, the median value and the maximum value of the majority are the same in SVE and PUE, which also indicates more participants have positive attitudes to SVE and PUE.

Chapter 6 Language Learning Attitudes of Secondary School English Teachers in Multilingual Areas

6.1.3 Spearman rank correlation analysis of ELA

Spearman's rho analysis or Spearman's rank correlation coefficient is a nonparametric measure of statistical dependence between two variables. Spearman's rho analysis (referring to Table 6.5) shows that all of the five dimensions of attitudes have significant positive correlation with general attitudes to English learning. However, among the five, AEC (γ_s=0.773) and AEL (γ_s=0.725) are more related to the general attitudes to English learning. This indicates that either positive or negative attitudes towards English culture and/or English language will increase or decrease their general attitudes towards English learning.

Table 6.5 Spearman Rank Correlation Analysis of English Learning Attitudes

Item		GELA	AEC	AES	AEL	SVE	PUE	N
Spearman's rho	γ_s		0.773**	0.687**	0.725**	0.601**	0.561**	186
	Sig. (2-tailed)		0.000	0.000	0.000	0.000	0.000	

** Correlation is significant at the 0.01 level (2-tailed)

6.2 Distribution and Strength of Ethnic Minority Language Learning Attitudes

One hundred and sixtyfour participants whose mother tongue is Chinese are taken as samples for discussion on distribution and strength of the ethnic minority language learning attitudes.

6.2.1 General learning attitudes towards ethnic minority languages

Skewness value ($-1<-0.967<1$) indicates a normal distribution of general ethnic minority language learning attitudes (GMLA). However, median value ($-0.060<0$) (referring to Table 6.6) implies that most participants have negative attitudes to ethnic minority language learning. Similar to GELA, the distribution of GMLA (referring to Figure 6.3) indicates large varieties between samples. Detailed analyses on five ethnic minority language learning attitudinal dimensions will provide more findings.

Table 6.6 Descriptive Analysis of GMLA

Item	Median	Range	Skewness	Percentile			N
				25th	50th	75th	
Z-score of GMLA	−0.060	4.221	0.967	−0.851	−0.060	0.469	164

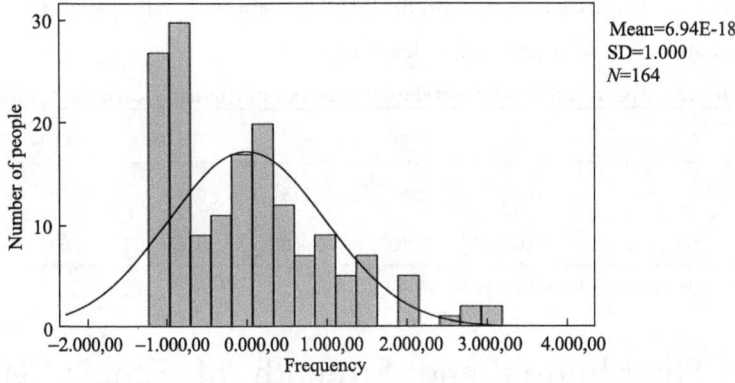

Figure 6.3 Histogram of GMLA

6.2.2 Five ethnic minority language learning attitudinal dimensions

Skewness value suggests that AMS and PUM have right-skewed distribution, which indicates most participants have negative attitudes; while the other three have normal distribution (referring to Table 6.7), which implies more individual different attitudes.

Table 6.7 Descriptive Analysis of Five Ethnic Minority Language Learning Attitudinal Dimensions

Items	Z-AMC	Z-AMS	Z-AML	Z-SVM	Z-PUM	N
Median	−0.161	−0.564	0.096	−0.082	−0.614	164
Skewness	0.776	1.795	0.704	0.549	1.628	

Chapter 6 Language Learning Attitudes of Secondary School English Teachers in Multilingual Areas

Continued

Items		Z-AMC	Z-AMS	Z-AML	Z-SVM	Z-PUM	N
Range		3.091	3.426	3.152	2.6974	3.513	
Percentiles	25	−0.933	−0.564	−0.955	−0.9814	−0.614	164
	50	−0.160	−0.564	0.096	−0.082	−0.614	
	75	0.613	0.578	1.147	0.817	0.557	

Notes: Z=Z-score

Different from the results in the five English learning attitudinal dimensions (referring to Figure 6.2), Boxplot of the five ethnic minority language learning attitudinal dimensions (referring to Figure 6.4) shows that, for most participants, except for the attitudes to ethnic minority languages (AML), their attitudes to other four dimensions are obviously negative. More importantly, although there is a single case of strong positive attitude, the distribution of AMS and PUM suggests more negative attitudes among the five with 50% participants having the same negative attitudes.

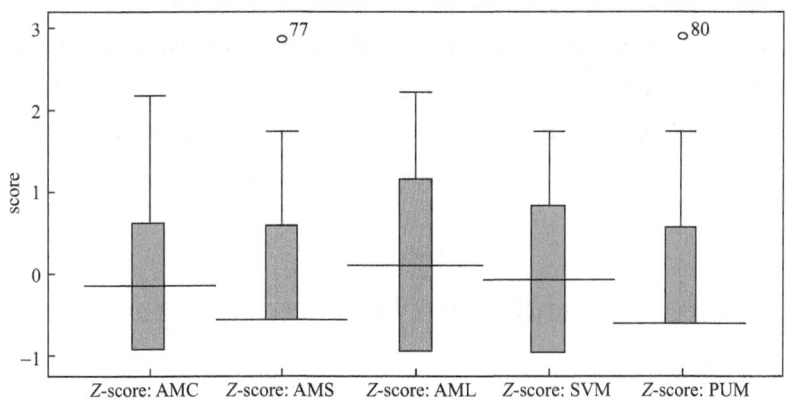

Figure 6.4 Boxplot of the Five Ethnic Minority Language Learning Attitudinal Dimensions

6.2.3 Spearman rank correlation analysis of the ethnic minority language learning attitudes

For 164 Chinese speakers, attitudes to ethnic minority culture (γ_s=0.814) and social value of ethnic minority languages (γ_s=0.823) are the main reasons for general attitudes to minority language learning (referring to Table 6.8). Particular use of the ethnic minority languages has comparatively low correlation with the general attitudes to ethnic minority language learning, but it still has considerably significant positive correlation (γ_s=0.491) to the general attitudes at level 0.05.

Table 6.8 Spearman Rank Correlation Analysis of the Ethnic Minority Language Learning Attitudes

Item		GMLA	AMC	AMS	AML	SVM	PUM	N
Spearman's rho	γ_s		0.814**	0.684**	0.694**	0.823**	0.491**	164
	Sig. (2-tailed)		0.000	0.000	0.000	0.000	0.000	

** Correlation is significant at the 0.01 level (2-tailed)

In general, teachers in ethnic minority areas have comparatively positive attitudes to English learning. Meanwhile, teachers whose mother tongue is Chinese have slightly negative attitudes to ethnic minority language learning. Most data indicate normal distribution while SVE and PUE show left-skewed distribution, and AMS and PUM show right-skewed distribution. All attitudinal factors have significant correlation with the general language learning attitudes, but among all of them AC plays a magnificent determinate role in teachers' general attitudes to target language learning.

6.3 Strength and Correlation of Language Learning Attitudes

6.3.1 Strength and correlation of AC

As mentioned in the previous part, Guttman scaling is used to test the strength of attitudinal dimensions. When "K+1" scale is conducted, there are 5 scales regarding the strength of AC (referring to Table 6.9). The mean value ranges from 0 to 4 for the AC and 0 to 1 for each item. The closer to each extreme the stronger tendency to negative (0) or positive attitudes the value indicates (4 or 1 respectively).

Table 6.9 shows that the mean value of AEC is closer to 0, which indicates negative attitudes. Among the four items which contribute to AEC, Item 2 is the lowest (Mean=0.230). It shows that a few subjects think "having a long history" may be their reason for learning a language. Meanwhile, Spearman's Rho analysis shows that Item 9 (γ_s=0.755) and Item 12 (γ_s=0.753) have higher relationship with the final AEC. It means whether English can represent "a culture with long history" (Item 9) and "a civilized culture" (Item 12) is the major reason leading to their general attitudes to the English culture.

Table 6.9 Strength and Spearman Rank Correlation of AEC

Dimensions		AEC	Items				N
			Item 2	Item 9	Item 10	Item 12	
Mean		1.618	0.230	0.420	0.470	0.490	
SD		1.395	0.423	0.496	0.500	0.501	
Range		4	1	1	1	1	186
Spearman's rho	γ_s		0.617**	0.755**	0.748**	0.753**	
	Sig. (2-tailed)		0.000	0.000	0.000	0.000	

** Correlation is significant at the 0.01 level (2-tailed)

Table 6.10 shows that among the 164 Chinese speakers, their average attitude to ethnic minority culture is 1.207, and both Item 2 and Item 10 have points below 0.3. They neither thought "(ethnic minority culture) having long history" (Item 2) might be one reason to learn ethnic minority languages, nor agreed that the target language culture would represent the culture they favor (Item 10). Spearman rank correlation analysis shows that Item 9 (γ_s=0.764), which indicates whether it represents a culture with long history, has the greatest relationship to their general AMC.

Table 6.10 Strength and Spearman Rank Correlation of AMC

Dimensions		AMC	Items				N
			Item 2	Item 9	Item 10	Item 12	
Mean		1.207	0.230	0.410	0.270	0.300	
SD		1.294	0.419	0.493	0.444	0.462	
Range		4	1	1	1	1	164
Spearman's rho	r_s		0.607**	0.764**	0.727**	0.666**	
	Sig. (2-tailed)		0.000	0.000	0.000	0.000	

** Correlation is significant at the 0.01 level (2-tailed)

It seems whether a language can represent a long history (Item 9) is the important cultural factor for participants to judge whether they will learn a new language. It may be because their knowledge about the five-thousand-year splendid Chinese history and exposure to Chinese culture makes them so proud of it; in the meantime, they have only learnt a little history of foreign culture which makes them lack the knowledge of English culture. The shortage of Western cultural knowledge is actually one of the major problems that result in their poor teaching proficiency. The data from interviews also support their need in learning English culture (see Section 6.4).

6.3.2 Strength and correlation of AS

Table 6.11 presents positive attitudes to English speakers (AES) (Mean=1.973>1.5). The value of Item 7 is the highest (Mean=0.750), which indicates most subjects believe that English speakers have high status and great fortune and that is one reason for them to learn English. However, Item 8 has the strongest relationship to the general AES (r_s=0.761). It implies that if the speaker is respectable (Item 8) he will be more likely to influence subjects' decisions on learning English.

Table 6.11 Strength and Spearman Rank Correlation of AES

Dimensions	AES	Items			N
		Item 6	Item 7	Item 8	
Mean	1.9731	0.630	0.750	0.590	186
SD	1.0575	0.483	0.436	0.493	

Chapter 6　Language Learning Attitudes of Secondary School English Teachers in Multilingual Areas

			Items			N
Dimensions	AES		Item 6	Item 7	Item 8	
Range		3	1	1	1	
Spearman's rho	γ_s		0.749**	0.697**	0.761**	186
	Sig. (2-tailed)		0.000	0.000	0.000	

** Correlation is significant at the 0.01 level (2-tailed)

Opposite to AES, Table 6.12 shows the value of Item 7 is the lowest (Mean=0.100), which implies most subjects believe ethnic minority language speakers do not have high status and great fortune. However, Item 8 still has the strongest relationship to the general AMS (γ_s=0.880).

Table 6.12　Strength and Spearman Rank Correlation of AMS

			Items			N
Dimensions	AMS		Item 6	Item 7	Item 8	
Mean	0.494		0.150	0.100	0.240	
SD	0.876		0.361	0.298	0.431	
Range		3	1	1	1	164
Spearman's rho	γ_s		0.706**	0.618**	0.880**	
	Sig. (2-tailed)		0.000	0.000	0.000	

** Correlation is significant at the 0.01 level (2-tailed)

In general, subjects have different AES and AMS. The major disagreement is on the status and fortune of the speaker. Subjects mostly believe English speakers have higher status and better fortune in contrast to those of ethnic minority language speakers. This peculiar result is likely because Western countries are substantially more prosperous than rural areas of Yunnan where ethnic minority groups mainly inhabit. It seems their beliefs about whether the group of people is respectable will be more likely to determine their decisions on learning the language. Dignity and prestige are actually a manifestation of *Shide* in China (referring to Section 2.2.2). If learning a language could make them become "respectable" people, they would be closer to being a professional teacher in terms of the Chinese concept.

6.3.3 Strength and correlation of AL

Table 6.13 shows that subjects have considerably positive AEL (Mean=1.898). Meanwhile, the three items (Item 1, Item 3 and Item 4) have similar high correlation to the final score of AEL. However, contrast to the high score in AEL, the Mean of teachers' AML is low (referring to Table 6.14), almost at 50% of AEL. Item 1, "I learn it because I want to study it", contributes more to the final score of AML than the other two items. Taking all the data into account, individuals' personal desire towards learning the language, "I learn because I want to learn", is probably the main reason or subjective indicator that shows "learning for learning's sake".

Table 6.13 Strength and Spearman Rank Correlation of AEL

Dimensions		AEL	Items			N
			Item 1	Item 3	Item 4	
Mean		1.898	0.610	0.580	0.720	
SD		1.043	0.490	0.496	0.453	
Range		3	1	1	1	186
Spearman's rho	r_s		0.737**	0.709**	0.716**	
	Sig. (2-tailed)		0.000	0.000	0.000	

** Correlation is significant at the 0.01 level (2-tailed)

Table 6.14 Strength and Spearman Rank Correlation of AML

Dimensions		AML	Items			N
			Item 1	Item 3	Item 4	
Mean		0.909	0.450	0.240	0.220	
SD		0.952	0.499	0.431	0.415	
Range		3	1	1	1	164
Spearman's rho	r_s		0.783**	0.647**	0.639**	
	Sig. (2-tailed)		0.000	0.000	0.000	

** Correlation is significant at the 0.01 level (2-tailed)

Chapter 6   Language Learning Attitudes of Secondary School English Teachers in Multilingual Areas

6.3.4 Strength and correlation of attitudes to social value of the target language

Subjects think highly of the social value of English (Mean=2.436), but their attitudes to social value of the ethnic minority languages (Mean=1.092) are opposite from that to English. Data also indicate that Item 20 has significant high correlation with the attitudes to the social value of the target language in both English (γ_s=0.766) and the ethnic minority languages (γ_s=0.776). It is likely that whether learning a language will satisfy personal needs is the most decisive social value of language learning. Meanwhile, learning a language to become knowledgeable (Item 16) is also a significant factor that determines teachers' attitudes to social value of the target language (referring to Table 6.15 and Table 6.16). However, communicating with people from different cultures (Item 15) is more important for subjects to learn ethnic minority languages than English.

Table 6.15   Strength and Spearman Rank Correlation of SVE

Dimensions		SVE	Items			N
			Item 15	Item 16	Item 20	
Mean		2.436	0.850	0.780	0.800	
SD		0.899	0.353	0.412	0.404	
Range		3	1	1	1	186
Spearman's rho	γ_s		0.650**	0.748**	0.766**	
	Sig. (2-tailed)		0.000	0.000	0.000	

** Correlation is significant at the 0.01 level (2-tailed)

Table 6.16   Strength and Spearman Rank Correlation of SVM

Dimensions		SVM	Items			N
			Item 15	Item 16	Item 20	
Mean		1.092	0.480	0.270	0.350	
SD		1.112	0.501	0.444	0.478	
Range		3	1	1	1	164
Spearman's rho	γ_s		0.821**	0.714**	0.776**	
	Sig. (2-tailed)		0.000	0.000	0.000	

** Correlation is significant at the 0.01 level (2-tailed)

6.3.5 Strength and correlation of attitudes to the particular uses of the target language (PU)

Similar to their attitudes to SVE, participants have positive PUE (referring to Table 6.17 and Table 6.18) (Mean=2.280), but their attitudes to SVE is stronger (Mean=2.436). Subjects have more positive attitudes to Item 17 (Mean=0.850), "learning English will help me deal with the work better"; but Item 19 has more correlation with general PUE (γ_s=0.826). Data implie that most participants agree that their leaders or administrators assign them to learn English. As mentioned in the Introduction part, some English teachers did not major in English. However, they are assigned to be English teachers by their school principals, which is a very common situation in most ethnic minority areas or rural areas which lack English teachers. Thus, they are usually the groups who need more in-service training. Since they didn't major in English, the need for English training is inevitable for them. Consequently, they might assume they are required to learn English because their leaders or principals ask them to do so.

Table 6.17 Strength and Spearman Rank Correlation of PUE

Dimensions		PUE	Items			N
			Item 17	Item 18	Item 19	
Mean		2.280	0.850	0.800	0.630	
SD		0.968	0.353	0.404	0.484	
Range		3	1	1	1	186
Spearman's rho	γ_s		0.642**	0.714**	0.826**	
	Sig. (2-tailed)		0.000	0.000	0.000	

** Correlation is significant at the 0.01 level (2-tailed)

Table 6.18 shows that participants' attitudes to PUM are negative. Different from PUE, it is likely whether learning ethnic minority languages can improve teaching proficiency (Item 18) is more correlated with PUM (γ_s=0.742).

Chapter 6　Language Learning Attitudes of Secondary School English Teachers in Multilingual Areas

Table 6.18　Strength and Spearman Correlation with PUM

Dimensions		PUM	Items			N
			Item 17	Item 18	Item 19	
Mean		0.5244	0.140	0.180	0.200	
SD		0.845	0.348	0.388	0.402	
Range		3	1	1	1	164
Spearman's rho	γ_s		0.681**	0.742**	0.694**	
	Sig. (2-tailed)		0.000	0.000	0.000	

** Correlation is significant at the 0.01 level (2-tailed)

In general, Item 19 (learning the language because leaders arranged it) has strong correlation with PUM (γ_s=0.694) and PUE (γ_s=0.826). As illustrated before, under the administrative system in China, following leaders' or administrators' orders is a common feature. It is not only a kind of Chinese culture, but also a way of interpersonal communication. Accomplishing administrators' orders always has effects on motivating individuals to do something. However, to what extent such orders can influence motivation still needs more analysis. In Chapter 9, this book will try to explain how administrators' orders can affect teachers' in-service training motivation.

6.4　Teachers' General Attitudes to Language Learning

6.4.1　"English is a cultural carrier."

The preference for English culture might motivate a person to become an English teacher, and the No. 4 teacher student interviewee, (TS4)[①] (referring to Appendix 9), is one example of this. He didn't major in English in college, but he changed to be an English teacher merely because he appreciated English culture.

> I enjoy being a teacher, especially an English teacher. I changed to be an English teacher because I love Chinese and American cultures, the different

---

① TS is used to refer to 12 teacher student interviewees.

ideologies (behind these two cultures). ①

Moreover, English teaching provides English teachers with more chances to experience English culture and to understand more clearly the role of language as a culture carrier, just as TS1 (referring to Appendix 9) stated.

> Language is the cultural carrier. Culture develops with the development of society. Teaching English makes me more sensitive to new culture. As an English teacher, I pay more attention to cultural development, such as some popular words or new expressions on Internet. Contrast to teachers teaching other subjects in school, we, English teachers, are always the first group who notices those changes. ②

TS1 becomes more sensitive to the cultural development in terms of new words or expressions after teaching English. However, her understanding of language as a cultural carrier is not only the result of English teaching, but also her working environment. Through working in ethnic minority areas, she learnt some ethnic minority languages for daily life. "Han people are the real 'minority' here. I can speak some simple words, but only limited to the ethnic minority groups." ③ Her openness to various languages makes her understand better the role of English.

Besides, the understanding of language as a cultural carrier leads teachers to hold an instrumental view of English. As TS3 (referring to Appendix 9) stated in the following, English is a medium or tool used to learn other knowledge.

> I think English is a carrier of culture. Chinese culture and Western culture have many differences in various aspects. Through it (English), you can learn many things, such as customs, geography, history, military and science of other countries. ④

---

① TS4-M2M. (2012, 12, 30). An interview with TS4-M2M. (R. Li, the interviewer & W. Zhong, the translator)
② TS1-H1F. (2012, 12, 28). An interview with TS1-H1F. (R. Li, the interviewer & W. Zhong, the translator)
③ TS1-H1F. (2012, 12, 28). An interview with TS1-H1F. (R. Li, the interviewer & W. Zhong, the translator)
④ TS3-H2M. (2012, 12, 30). An interview with TS3-H2M. (R. Li, the interviewer & W. Zhong, the translator)

Chapter 6 Language Learning Attitudes of Secondary School English Teachers in Multilingual Areas

Cultural carrier is a function shared by every language, but for teachers in ethnic minority areas, English as a cultural carrier works better than ethnic minority languages do. It seems that learning and teaching English strengthened teachers' AEC English culture; and simultaneously the fascinating English culture attracted teachers to learn and teach it.

6.4.2 "English has more social values than ethnic minority languages."

English teachers believe English learning enables them to communicate with speakers from other cultures, makes them more knowledgeable, and satisfies some of their personal needs.

PT1① (referring to Appendix 9) is satisfied with her English learning because she can communicate with foreigners, and watch movies or DVDs in English, and the most important is "I can teach my son now. I can teach him English at home. I think it's really good for him to learn English from his mother, in his daily life"②. PT2 (referring to Appendix 9) suggested English was a bridge for him to know more people.

> English helps me know more people, because people who know much about a language may think different from others······ Through some other programs we had cooperated with people from other countries and regions, such as Hong Kong of China and USA. In this way, it (English) gets me to learn about people from other countries. This is a good bridge (that connects me to others). ③

Different from PT1 and PT2 who are working in universities in big cities, TS4 is from an ethnic minority area. However, he still pointed out the social value of English. TS4④ stated three functions of learning English, namely, increasing knowledge, expanding one's vision and adapting to society. "English is integrated into our life,"

---

① PT is used to refer to two program trainer interviewees.
② PT1. (2012, 8, 14). An interview with PT1. (W. Zhong, the interviewer)
③ PT2. (2012, 8, 5). An interview with PT2. (W. Zhong, the interviewer & translator)
④ TS4-M2M. (2012, 12, 30). An interview with TS4-M2M. (R. Li, the interviewer & W. Zhong, the translator)

TS4 explained, "such as 'on' and 'off' on the TV remote controller, and the product description of CD player, they are all in simple English words." TS7[①] claimed she would tell her students the following to motivate them.

> Your parents are using chemical fertilizer at home. In the future, all kinds of fertilizer might come from foreign countries. If you don't learn English now, you couldn't read the instructions. Several years later, even if you have money, you still couldn't go to other countries because at the train station or airport, all instructions are in English.

It seems although ethnic minority languages are widely used in those areas, teachers still consider English is probably more influential. Their diverse attitudes to English and ethnic minority languages can also be traced by their attitudes to ethnic minority students and Han students.

In answering "What are the differences between Han students and ethnic minority students?", most teachers indicate ethnic minority students have lower ability than Han students, and ethnic minority students are reserved in the classroom and afraid of expressing their opinions in Chinese or English[②], but some also admit that ethnic minority students are extroverted and confident when using their mother tongue[③]. TS3 said that,

> Comparatively speaking, you cannot tell their differences in Grade one. However, ethnic minority students who live near the downtown areas are more influenced by Han culture, they still work hard in studies. For those who live far away from downtown areas, they are quite different from others.[④]

---

① TS7-H3F. (2012, 12, 30). An interview with TS7-M3F. (R. Li, the interviewer & W. Zhong, the translator)
② TT1. (2012, 8, 14). An interview with TS1-H1F. (R. Li, the interviewer & W. Zhong, the translator)
③ TS1-H1F. (2012, 12, 28). An interview with TS1-H1F. (R. Li, the interviewer & W. Zhong, the translator)
④ TS3-H2M. (2012, 12, 30). An interview with TS3-H2M. (R. Li, the interviewer & W. Zhong, the translator)

Chapter 6　Language Learning Attitudes of Secondary School English Teachers in Multilingual Areas

TS3 is a Han teacher. He unconsciously uses "Han culture" as a standard or benchmark to evaluate students' ability. His words indicate that if students cannot reach the "Han standard", they might have problems in learning or they might have lower abilities.

Being ethnic minority teachers, teachers may view their students totally from different positions. TS2 (referring to Appendix 9) expressed a serious problem that Han students more easily bullied ethnic minority students.

> Some Han students from nearby schools will gather as a gang and bully ethnic minority students. However, ethnic minority students are timid and honest, so they never fight back. ①

Except for ethnic minority students' characteristics, TS2 also pointed out that Han students had better learning habits and strategies, and they lived in a more civilized way than ethnic minority students. Contrasting with TS2, TS4 mentioned that

> Ethnic minorities are more optimistic than Han students. Han students will be more solitary because they cannot communicate in ethnic minority languages. ②

In general, though working in ethnic minority areas, teachers are better educated or more civilized than the other local residents and most of their students are from downtown areas where Han culture is dominant. Influenced by the mainstream culture, it might not be simple for teachers, English teachers in particular, to satisfy all students' needs, just like NTP studied in this research. Reflections from the interviewees expose some remarkable issues, usually neglected in the in-service teacher training programs.

---

① TS2-M1F. (2012, 12, 28). An interview with TS2-M1F. (R. Li, the interviewer & W. Zhong, the translator)
② TS4-M2M. (2012, 12, 28). An interview with TS4-M2M. (R. Li, the interviewer & W. Zhong, the translator)

Chapter 7 Teacher Efficacy of Secondary School English Teachers in Multilingual Areas

In this research, a modified Chinese Teacher Efficacy Scale (CTES, referring to Appendixes 1 & 2) is used to testify teacher efficacy in the Chinese context. Each of the ten items is rated by Likert four-scale response. Responses range from "not at all true" through "barely true" and "moderately true" to "exactly true", and are scored from 1 to 4 respectively. Hence, a high score means high teacher efficacy. Though Schwarzer et al. (1999) proposed that the "primary focus during the reduction was on optimizing the validity of the instrument rather than maximizing the internal consistency", result shows that the CTES still has high internal consistency (Cronbach's alpha=0.812) in the research.

One factor that Maximum Likelyhood factor analysis results indicate the CTES has high goodness-of-fit (referring to Appendix 6). However, Schwarzer et al. (1999) proposed that the original 27 items contained four aspects of job skills within the teaching profession, namely job accomplishment, skill development on the job, coping with job stress and social interaction with students, parents, and colleagues. In order to test whether the 10 items still meet the requirement of these four domains, in other words whether the 10 items will be naturally divided into four categories, Principal Component factor analysis is conducted. Nevertheless, result indicates three main factors existed in the ten-item scale. At the same time, some items are loaded in different factors simultaneously, which makes it hard to explain based on the original four domains. As far as I am concerned, why there is the uncertainty of the factors is that some items have overlapping meanings. As stated in Item 2, "I know that I can maintain a positive relationship with parents, even when tensions arise", for example, the first part of the sentence indicates "social interaction" but the second part implies "job stress". Thus, it is hard to say whether Item 2 only indicates the skill of "social interaction" or "coping with job stress". However, Bandura (2006: 311) suggested, "perceived efficacy should be measured against levels of task demands that represent gradations of challenges or impediments to successful performances". He believed that obstacles or challenges were important for the measurement of self-efficacy, because "if there are no obstacles to overcome, the activity is easily performable and everyone is highly efficacious" (Bandura, 2006: 311). "Job stress", in this sense, is a kind of obstacle that is unavoidable in teaching. Hence, one-factor structure can provide more findings than three-factor structure in this research.

7.1 ETE Strength

Mean value is computed to get the strength of TE. Missing value is substituted by series mean value. In the perfect normal distribution, mean value ranges from 1 to 4 and the median is 2.5. Taking 0.5 as the interval, there are 7 degrees of self-efficacy strength (referring to Table 7.1). The closer to each extreme, the higher or weaker self-efficacy the value indicates.

Table 7.1 Teacher Efficacy Strength Degree

Items	1	1.5	2	2.5	3	3.5	4
Degrees	extremely weak	comparatively weak	weak	strong		comparatively strong	extremely strong

Generally speaking, Table 7.2 shows that subjects have strong GTE strength (2.5<Mean=2.833<3). Skewness value indicates a normal distribution, which means most subjects have strong self-efficacy, and a few subjects have extremely strong or weak self-efficacy. Meanwhile, ET have slightly weaker teacher efficacy (Mean=2.815) than NET (Mean=2.897). Detailed differences analysis will provide more findings.

Table 7.2　Teacher Efficacy Strength

Items		N	Minimum	Maximum	Mean	SD	Skewness	
							Statistics	SE
Groups	GTE	186	1.36	4.00	2.833	0.452	−0.248	0.178
	ET	146	1.40	4.00	2.815	0.452	−0.230	0.201
	NET	39	1.90	3.80	2.897	0.460	−0.314	0.378

7.2　Teacher Efficacy Strength and the Demographic Features

Studies (Jiang, 2011; Rubie-Davies, Flint & McDonald, 2012; Shi, 2009; Teng & Wu, 2011; Wang, 2009; Wang & Huang, 2009) suggested that demographic features would influence ETE to some extent. In this research, demographic features like age, teaching years, teaching subjects (English and non-English), professional titles, and ethnicity were taken into considerations for differences analysis.

7.2.1　Age

Table 7.3 shows that subjects aged 21 to 30 have the lowest teacher efficacy and those aged 31 to 40 have the highest. However, it doesn't indicate significant differences of teacher efficacy among various age groups. Age seems not a reasonable demographic factor that can predict teacher efficacy. Another possible reason would be that ten-year interval is too long to show greater differences. Shorter interval like five-year might reveal more findings.

Table 7.3　Teacher efficacy Strength and Age

Items	Age	N	Mean rank	F	df	Asymp. sig. (2-tailed)
GTE	21-30	77	86.51	2.257	2	0.324

Chapter 7 Teacher Efficacy of Secondary School English Teachers in Multilingual Areas

Continued

Items	Age	N	Mean rank	F	df	Asymp. sig. (2-tailed)
GTE	31-40	73	99.12	2.257	2	0.324
	41-50	33	89.06			
Valid number		183				

7.2.2 Teaching years

Dissimilar to age, teaching years connect more to subjects' mastery experience. Although Kruskal Wallis Test doesn't show significant differences among groups, data show that teaching years directly determines the variety of GTE. Table 7.4 illustrates that though all the subjects indicate strong GTE, novice teachers (teachers with less than five-year working experience) have weaker efficacy than experienced ones. As working years increase, subjects would have more confidence in their job. Six to ten years seem like a golden period for teachers. In this period, they are gradually familiar with their job and feel more capable of handling the difficulties; they are young and have better education than teachers elder than them; they are still ambitious on professional development and fulfilling their life mission. However, after they work much longer to more than 10 years, they understand the complexity of teaching career better; they experience more of the frustration from work and realize their real capability of solving problems. For subjects with 11 to 20 years' working experience, their GTE weakened. For subjects who have worked more than 20 years, facing their coming retirement, with great imagination of retired life and a sense of final release from the job pressure, subjects have the weakest GTE.

Table 7.4 Teacher Efficacy Strength and Teaching Years

Dimensions	Teaching years	N	Mean rank	F	df	Asymp. sig. (2-tailed)
GTE	Less than 5 years	53	79.44	7.114	3	0.068
	6-10 years	44	100.33			

Continued

Dimensions		Teaching years	N	Mean rank	F	df	Asymp. sig. (2-tailed)
GTE		11-20 years	78	99.53			
		21-30 years	9	70.17			
Items	Item 9	Less than 5 years	53	84.01	11.004	3	0.011*
		6-10 years	44	101.97			
		11-20 years	78	96.80			
		21-30 years	9	49.83			
	Item 10	Less than 5 years	53	81.85	6.464	3	0.091
		6-10 years	44	102.14			
		11-20 years	78	95.80			
		21-30 years	9	70.39			
Valid number			185				

*$p<0.05$

This research is not a longitudinal one; hence I am not suggesting GTE will change as teaching years increase, though studies (Jiang, 2011; Shi, 2009; Teng & Wu, 2011; Wang, 2009) demonstrated that two factors were correlated. Teaching year is one index to differentiate mastery experience, the major resource of self-efficacy, however, there are also other indexes, such as the strength of effort teachers put in their teaching and professional development. In the meantime, GTE is regarding teachers' confidence of skills in various tasks; thus, when tasks change or the obstacles change, strength of GTE also varies, as the examples shown in Table 7.4. A significant group difference of subjects' efficacy to "motivate my students to participate in innovative projects" (Item 9) ($F=11.004$ (3), $p<0.05$) is shown, but no significant difference is presented on their efficacy to "carry out innovative projects, even when I am opposed by sceptical colleagues" (Item 10). Although these two tasks related to "innovative projects", for some subjects, their confidence in motivating students to participate in the projects is different from carrying out projects by themselves.

7.2.3 Teaching subjects

As described before (referring to Section 7.1 and Table 7.2), ET have weaker GTE than NET, however, is this difference significant? Among the ten teaching skills asked, are there some differences between ET and NET? Two-sample Mann-Whitney Test (referring to Table 7.5) indicates there isn't a significant difference between GTE of ET and NET, but the two items show significant differences between these two groups. Regarding the continuous increasing capability in helping to address students' needs as time goes by (Item 4), ET indicate weaker confidence at 29.89 points apart. However, ET have stronger belief in their positive influences on students' personal and academic development if they tried hard enough (Item 7). Data suggest that ET believe the possibility of increasing their own effort would change students' achievements; however, they do not think their capability improvement can change through time. Another way to understand this is that, for ET, personal efforts might account more for their professional development in helping their students than teaching year increasing does.

Table 7.5 Teacher Efficacy Strength and Teaching Subjects

Dimensions		Teaching subjects	N	Mean rank	Difference of mean rank	Asymp. sig. (2-tailed)
GTE		English	146	90.83	−10.3	0.285
		Non-English	39	101.13		
Items	Item 4	English	144	87.76	−29.89	0.021*
		Non-English	39	107.65		
	Item 7	English	146	98.74	27.24	0.002**
		Non-English	39	71.50		
Valid number			185			

*$p<0.05$, **$p<0.01$

7.2.4 Professional titles

Kruskal Wallis Test doesn't show significant differences of TE among subjects from different professional title groups. Generally speaking, the higher one's professional title is, the stronger teacher efficacy he would have; but the subjects with primary level and secondary level barely have any difference (referring to Table 7.6). The presumption for me is professional title which indicates different academic abilities of subjects could show substantially different TE; however results from the data repudiate my presumption. Though unbalanced sample population might influence the result (referring to Table 7.7), another possible reason might be the professional title for secondary school teachers in rural areas cannot show the fundamental academic abilities of subjects as a result of the drawbacks of teacher promotion system in rural areas of China, which I would explore more in the following three sections.

Table 7.6 Teacher Efficacy Strength and Professional Titles

Items	Professional titles	N	Mean rank	F	df	Asymp. sig. (2-tailed)
GTE	Advanced	11	96.18			
	Intermediate	120	88.76	0.241	2	0.887
	Primary	46	87.91			
Valid number		177				

Table 7.7 Demographic of Professional Titles and Teaching Years

Professional Titles	Teaching Years					Total
	Less than 5 years	6-10 years	11-20 years	21-30 years	More than 30 years	
Advanced	0	0	8	2	1	11
Intermediate	23	33	57	7	0	120
Primary	25	10	11	0	0	46
Total	48	43	76	9	1	177

7.2.5 Ethnicity

In general, ethnic minority subjects show higher TE than Han teachers at 4.63 points apart (referring to Table 7.8). Again, data results are against my presumption that ethnic minority teachers, who are usually viewed as the weaker group, would have weaker teacher efficacy. I cannot help asking, "Why Han teachers, who have larger population of teacher group and represent the mainstream, have weaker teacher efficacy than ethnic minority teachers?" A feasible answer would be their working environment is in ethnic minority areas, in which Han teachers are actually the "minority". Though they have larger population in micro-context (schools), they are culturally subordinated to ethnic minority groups in macro-context (the whole area). In the mean time, most of more capable Han teachers are working in big cities, which in contrast might imply that those who are working in rural or ethnic minority areas, especially those who have been working for years, are weaker in academic abilities. Thus, it might be reasonable that Han teachers are not confident enough about their teaching in this sense, and weaker teacher efficacy is shown.

Table 7.8 Teacher Efficacy Strength and Ethnicity

Item	Ethnicity	N	Mean rank	Difference of mean rank	Asymp. sig. (2-tailed)
GTE	Han	126	90.56	−4.63	0.582
	Ethnic minority	57	95.19		

7.3 Difficulties for Teaching English in Rural Areas

Teaching in secondary schools has never been an easy job for teachers in China. No matter in urban cities or in rural areas, they are worried about students' scores in each final test, because that relates to their reputation and also bonus at the end of a year. Apart from that, especially for teachers working in rural areas, they have to make sure all of their students will come to school again after the summer or winter break, because dropout rate will influence the ranking of the school; sometimes even worse, it might cause teachers lose jobs. As for English teachers, they may have further worries. "How can I motivate students to learn?" "Is there any better way to help my students remember new words?" "How can I improve my own English?" "How can I answer students' grammar questions if I am not sure about the answer?" Pre-service teachers are sometimes panic before their internships in ethnic minority areas; some in-service teachers are still short of confidence even if they have taught for many years (Zhong & Gan, 2007). The answers for "Are there any difficulties in your teaching?" from twelve interviewees reveal some of their obstacles in English teaching practice in ethnic minority areas. Beyond the language dilemma I mentioned in the first chapter, teachers are facing more complicated problems caused by the specific working context.

7.3.1 "I don't know how I can motivate my students to learn English."

In English as a Foreign Language (EFL) contexts, extrinsic motivation tends to have a stronger influence on students' English performance. However, in ethnic minority areas of Yunnan, teachers felt it was hard to motivate their students to learn English for some external reasons.

> Most of my students think English is useless, they have no place to use it. They usually ask me, "Master, where can we use English in future?"[①]

> They think learning English is useless. English is far away from their lives and they won't use it in future. They often fail to have the motive for English learning. No matter how hard I tried, they don't have the motivation to learn. They will only use English in the entrance examination for senior high schools, and they will only learn for passing the examinations. Some of them have never come to the downtown areas, let alone big cities like Kunming. English is far away from them. Even if they learn in the classroom, they won't review it again at home. It is too far away from them. They won't jump out of this county, they don't have the ability and their

---

① TS5-M3F. (2013, 11, 8). An interview with TS5-M3F. (W. Zhong, the interviewer & W. Zhong, the translator)

parents won't allow them to. After having graduated from secondary school, they have to go back, being cowmen or shepherds, just as their parents did.[①]

As TS4 and TS5 (referring to Appendix 9) stated, as a matter of fact, all of my interviewees mentioned that students' motivation is a major problem for English education in ethnic minority areas. TS4 emphasized three times that "English is too far away" from students.

In fact, in ethnic minority areas, some local people not only consider English learning is not useful, but also believe "Education per se is useless" (Yuan et al., 2013; Zhong, 2010; Zhong & Gan, 2007). "Working in big cities" "earning more money" "being away from the poverty" and "leaving the rural areas" have always been described as goals and beautiful images for students to pursue higher education. Their parents and themselves have been told to believe that degree or education can change their lives. Ten years ago, when there were not many people graduating from universities, this might have been true; however, the society is changing so fast that their dreams cannot so easily come true now. Owing to the contradiction between aggressively increasing enrolment in university and slow reform of tertiary education since 2000, an increasing number of students cannot find jobs in big cities with high salary. According to one government report, from 2001 to 2013, the number of students graduated from tertiary schools increased from 1.14 million to 7 million (Eol. Cn, 2013), which means some students could not find jobs after they graduated from universities. The phenomenon results in different reactions from parents and children in making their decisions on school education. For one thing, in big cities, parents send their children to various training programs to equip them for the serious competition; meanwhile the children know clearly that if they don't work hard, they will be more likely to lose a job. By contrast, in rural and poor areas, especially ethnic minority areas, parents would feel it reasonable that their children should start working earlier under the condition that they are not good at studying; besides, students believe that school education is not the only way out, as what TS3 and TS1 stated.

---

① TS4-M2M. (2012, 12, 30). An interview with TS4-M2M. (R. Li, the interviewer & W. Zhong, the translator)

They (students) think it is useless for them to learn at school. Their siblings couldn't find (satisfactory) jobs after (graduating from) college. Even for those who find one, the salaries are not so high as they desired. They may as well drop out the school and find a job in big cities with someone's parents or friends, at least they can earn money earlier.①

Students in my area don't have strong desire to further their study in universities or colleges. They just want to finish the compulsory education. It has been fiercely competitive in the job market these years. Many students can't find a job after graduation and this has big influence on other students. Even for some students from rich families, they may also drop out or be unwilling to learn. After graduating from secondary schools, most of the students started working. There is only one mountain between Nujiang (a city near the boarderline between China and Burma) and us, and it is quite easy going to Burma from Nujiang. Some will work in Nujiang, or directly work in Burma. Others will work in big cities if they have *Guanxi* (interpersonal relationships with others who could provide or have the possibility in finding job opportunities).②

I think in border areas like Ximeng (County), the ethnic minorities don't have strong recognition of education. For the whole society, family (members) pay little attention to education, so the dropout rate is really high.③

Motivating students to learn becomes a big issue for teachers and the government as well, which is not merely a teaching technique that teachers can use in the classroom, moreover it is a result of the much-complicated social phenomenon. If education cannot bring a better job, why should we spend much money on children in

---

① TS3-H2M. (2012, 12, 30). An interview with TS3-H2M. (R. Li, the interviewer & W. Zhong, the translator)

② TS1-H1F. (2012, 12, 28). An interview with TS1-H1F. (R. Li, the interviewer & W. Zhong, the translator)

③ TS9-M5F. (2013, 11, 16). An interview with TS9-M5F. (W. Zhong, the interviewer & W. Zhong, the translator)

pursuing education? In rural areas, parents holding this doubt are not just a few but many (Yuan, 2007). Some of them hope their children can join the family business, such as planting rubber trees, or become farmer-workers who are working as coolies in big cities. In such a circumstance, they can earn more money for a better life, rather than wasting a life without clear goals.

7.3.2 "The principal always assigned me to do other things not related to my teaching."

Due to the shortage of resources, teachers in ethnic minority areas tend to teach more than one subject, or they will be assigned to teach a subject which they are not good at. Ms. Kong, the example I gave in the introduction chapter, majored in Chinese Literature for four years of college education and ended up teaching English in secondary school. Beyond teaching, Ms. Kong was assigned as an accountant while teaching because of her prudence and was nominated as the director of psychological consultation office. Finally, she quit the job due to the pressure. Ms. Kong is not a single case. Frankly, teachers working in rural areas might be asked to do extra assignments not related to teaching. They might receive a call early in the morning to join a certain meeting representing their principal because the principal has to attend or host another more urgent meeting; they might be asked to join a dinner party with experts from big cities right after they finished 8 hours of teaching for the experts want to have some talks with school teachers and only have one day to stay in town; and they even might ride the motorcycle at the weekends to one student's home because the student didn't attend the school and one dropout means no bonus at the end of the semester, etc. They are like figurants playing an insignificant role in the show whose names even don't show in the list, but the only difference is teachers do not expect to do such work. TS2 struggled a lot each time the principal asked her for other assignments, such as participating in the training for teaching music.

> I don't like singing and I don't think I can teach music. I am not a music teacher at school either. I just don't know why the administrators assign me to do it. The principal always assigned me to do other things not related to

my teaching.①

TS2 mentioned this when she commented on her other in-service training experiences. It is no doubt that she barely remembered what she learnt from the training, because as an English teacher who doesn't love singing, the training seems like a torture to her. However, she is a very obedient teacher though she murmured the question to herself; she still followed the principal's words while struggling on her own.

The high dropout rate also brings extra work for the teachers.

> Our headmaster assigned us to different villages to enrol students. Three or four teachers form a group. We have to motivate students (to come back to school). For each village, we have to take notes on those dropout students' information and we will go to each family to persuade them. We will ask the reasons (why they quit school) like they don't want to learn or something happened in the family.②

TS6 (referring to Appendix 9) pointed out that for each semester, after the first school convention, they would be assigned to different places to persuade students to come back to school. However, though this is not an easy job, TS6's headmaster volunteered to go to the furthest village, which made her think that "our headmaster is pretty good"③.

7.3.3 "Family guidance is so poor that parents barely have positive influences on students."

> All the students have to live in school. Their dormitories are usually classrooms. When a lot of children are staying together, you cannot imagine

---

① TS2-M1F. (2012, 12, 28). An interview with TS2-M1F. (R. Li, the interviewer & W. Zhong, the translator)

② TS6-M4F. (2013, 11, 8). An interview with TS6-M4F. (W. Zhong, the interviewer & W. Zhong, the translator)

③ TS6-M4F. (2013, 11, 8). An interview with TS6-M4F. (W. Zhong, the interviewer & W. Zhong, the translator)

Chapter 7 Teacher Efficacy of Secondary School English Teachers in Multilingual Areas

there will be no conflict.[①]

> Our school is a boarding school. Students stayed longer with us than their parents. In my school, students went home every two weeks. But every time after they came back from home, we have to train them the school rules again. Going home has a negative influence. Parents wouldn't bother to ask about their studies or even lives. They only gave them the money. Each Sunday after they came back, we could find snacks everywhere.[②]

In big cities like Kunming, parents receive messages from teachers about their children's behaviors at school and the assignments every day through mobile phone; teachers can call to meet the parents whenever they want for a discussion about how parents can help improve education. Good communication between teachers and parents is constructed and parents understand very well that they should be responsible for their children's education. However, in rural areas, this image is usually like fairy tales only happening in movies or on TV. Most of schools in ethnic minority areas are boarding schools where students study and live in, so do teachers. As TS2 and TS4 mentioned above, problems are raised because of the boarding school management. For some schools don't have cooks or dining hall, teachers are the cooks and classrooms are the dining halls; furthermore, if the schools don't have special dorm supervisors, the teachers will be the dorm supervisors, then they will teach in the day and babysit the same group of children at night. These teachers who are working in boarding schools work day and night as teachers and also parents. Just as an ancient Chinese saying goes, "One day's teacher, a lifelong father."

For teachers who are not working in boarding schools, they also shoulder pressure from poor parents' guidance. In China, *stay-at-home children* or *left-over children* is a special term referring to children who have to live with grandparents or other relatives because their parents are both working in big cities. According to statistics (MOE, 2012), there were 22 million stay-at-home children in 2011, and 7.63 million of them

---

① TS2-M1F. (2012, 12, 28). An interview with TS2-M1F. (R. Li, the interviewer & W. Zhong, the translator)
② TS4-M2M. (2012, 12, 30). An interview with TS4-M2M. (R. Li, the interviewer & W. Zhong, the translator)

were in secondary schools. These students are the minority and vulnerable groups. Confronting them, teachers felt helpless.

> Their parents were busy earning money in big cities. For some students who have stronger self-regulative ability, they will learn as others do; but for those who cannot regulate themselves, they are hard to manage. They don't have the parents' pressure. If a teacher tries to talk to them, they are irritated because of adolescent rebellious issues. Their parents can only make some calls to check (ask about) their studies, but not often. Even if they called, they preferred to say "we will earn money for you". The children would lie to the parents too. We cannot watch (supervise) them in every minute.[①]

As TS3 stated, stay-at-home students are different from students in boarding schools. In China, there is neither Child Protective Services nor specific legal articles about the responsibilities of parents on children's education and the consequences if they violate them (Ge, 2014). In the meantime, Chinese tradition makes people believe that who stay with the kid should be responsible for the kid. From kindergarten to university, parents assume that school should be responsible for everything because their children are "at" school. Hence, in boarding schools, teachers are functioning as the guardians to make sure students would not leave school; however, for students who are staying at home with relatives, their relatives become the guardians.

As a matter of fact, in China, no matter whether in boarding schools or not, quite a large number of parents are absent in students' education from kindergarten to university. In secondary school, class usually starts at 7:30 in the morning and ends at 6:00 in the evening. In ethnic minority areas, most parents believe school is the place where their children receive education because they cannot teach nor have time to teach by themselves. However, it seems for teachers, educating the parents is more important than teaching the students, because students are afraid of their parents more than the teachers and teachers cannot punish students for their inappropriate behaviors but their parents can. After all, most Chinese people, parents or teachers, believe the

---

① TS3-H2M. (2012, 12, 30). An interview with TS3-H2M. (R. Li, the interviewer & W. Zhong, the translator)

Chapter 7   Teacher Efficacy of Secondary School English Teachers in Multilingual Areas

infallible law that "Spare the rod and spoil the child". It seems that parents are the first group of people whom teachers could and would blame, especially when parents are farmers who have received little education.

> In downtown areas, if parents received better education, they would urge their children to learn. Teachers can provide knowledge to students but cannot help to shape their values. Some parents will consistently say "study hard" to beat the ideas into the children's heads, the same as in developed areas where people are comparatively better educated. If the parents are businessmen, farmers ploughing every day, they will say "these days we are harvesting watermelons, come back home and help us". Then the children will go back to help the parents and gradually never come back. If we tell the parents the child has to come back to school, they will say "after the harvesting" in that they think education is useless. If it's not for free of charge, there will be fewer students. Most students who drop out are from remote and mountain areas, far away from downtown. Their parents would say "You'd better go back to study, at least you can get the subsidy and we can live better". I know a father. After three years' study, he told his son "Others come back home with a girlfriend, why don't you have one?" What he really meant is his son could neither learn well nor get a wife for marriage.[1]

TS3 believes that parents can influence the students' viewpoints of study and also their motivation, but at the same time he agrees that parents' viewpoints are defined by the social context and the government policies.

> If 40 of 60 students in my class will join the entrance examination for high school, it would be so great! Those 20 students who stick to the end of the school year are mainly an "economic strategy" for the family, because (they are studying for) the government subsidy. Schools require them to come back as well, because of annual inspection. Parents are one cause of the

---

[1] TS4-M2M. (2012, 12, 30). An interview with TS4-M2M. (R. Li, the interviewer & W. Zhong, the translator)

drop-out, but the influence from society is another. There used to be some students who entered the high school and finally made in the college, and they were from some downtown areas, not from mountainous areas.①

In China, three-year secondary school is part of the nine-year compulsory education, which means children have to finish the secondary school. Meanwhile, in mountainous areas, children, especially boys, are the major labor force for the family. Once the children are at school, the family might lose the main labor force. The poorer the family is, the more important their sons are. Hence, in order to encourage parents to send their children to school, the government guarantee they can learn for free and even get subsidy, which is usually called "Two Free One Subsidy" policy (CPGPRC, 2006). If children drop out from school, their family will lose the subsidy. The Central Government will invest money based on students' enrolment numbers each year. Hence, dropout rate becomes a crucial index for showing principals' administration and also determining whether a teacher can keep his job or not. This is also the reason why teachers will be assigned to persuade their students to come back to school as I mentioned in the previous part (referring to Section 7.3.2).

7.4 The language Barrier for Teaching English in Multilingual Areas

In ethnic minority areas, some English teachers are facing more problems owing to the language barrier (Hu, 2007a; Yuan, 2007; Zhong, 2010), because teachers' and students' use different mother tongues. English teaching becomes more difficult in these multilingual areas. On the one hand, English learning has little use in daily life except for taking the entrance examination. If English is not required for entrance examinations, few teachers will consider the necessity to learn English in ethnic minority areas (Yang, 2003; Zhong & Yuan, 2012). On the other hand, since Chinese is the only medium of instruction allowed to be used in secondary schools, some ethnic

---

① TS3-H2M. (2012, 12, 30). An interview with TS3-H2M. (R. Li, the interviewer & W. Zhong, the translator)

minority students, whose mother tongue is not Chinese, have some trouble in learning Chinese and more in learning English. If teachers cannot speak ethnic minority languages, they need a third party (usually bilingual students who can speak both Chinese and ethnic minority languages well) to be the interpreter in class. However, this group of bilingual students also have difficulties in English learning, and consequently their help is limited. Interviewees mentioned three aspects of their problems owing to the language barrier.

7.4.1 "This is a multilingual area and you don't need to learn English to survive."

Located in the southwest part of China, bordered by Vietnam, Laos and Burma, Yunnan is viewed as the most multilingual province in China. Besides the dominant Han group, 52 ethnic minorities inhabit the province and 25 of them have inhabited for generations (NBSC, 2012). The total population of all 52 ethnic minority groups is approximately 15.3 million, comprising 33.37% of the population of the province according to the 2010 national census (Yunnan Daily, 2011: 4). Most of the minorities live along the border areas or in the mountainous areas of the province where educational opportunities are few. Geographical, historical and cultural factors have caused each group to develop unique social and economic characteristics (Yuan, 2007). According to Yang and Li. (2010), in the 1980s, the Provincial Government Institution, the Minority Nationality Language and Literature Executive Committee of Yunnan, proposed the implementation of 11 trial bilingual programs in the ethnic minority areas where Chinese was not spoken (cf. Yuan, 2007). Chinese (in the form of Mandarin) was not only taught as a second language but used as a medium of instruction (MI) throughout the academic years in elementary schools. Meanwhile, English was also introduced into secondary schools in those areas as a regular and compulsory subject in the same way as in the centralized Han Chinese educational system. This phenomenon still exists today.

Among the twelve interviewees in this research, six claimed that they have more than one group of ethnic minority students in their classrooms.

The place I am working in is a downtown area, but it is a multi-ethnic minority area. My students are not only from downtown, but also near counties. Those who are from suburbs are all ethnic minorities, such as Lisu, Naxi, Tibetan. 90% of my students are from ethnic groups. Most of students speak ethnic minority languages, and they come to the downtown areas for their secondary schools. I have grown up in downtown areas. Language problem exists (for communication). Some of my students even cannot speak Chinese though they are in secondary school.[①]

I have many ethnic minority students, such as Tibetan, Lizu and Pumi. Right now I am teaching 52 students. Two are Pumi, most of them are Naxi, and some Han students also. Usually, 30 to 40 students in one class are ethnic minority students. They speak their ethnic minority languages from the day they were born.[②]

In my area, Han people are the minorities. Most people are Yi and Lisu. Though my county is a Bai Nationality Autonomous County, my town is co-inhabited by Yi and Lisu. Students speak their ethnic minority languages, even when they have discussions in classrooms. They learnt other groups' ethnic minority languages in elementary schools. Hence, after they entered the secondary school, they almost can say other ethnic minority languages. English is their third, fourth, or even fifth language. However, they don't like chatting in English, because no one will speak English to them. They prefer ethnic minority languages to English. This is a multi-ethnic co-inhabited area.[③]

In my current class I have 33 students. Fourteen of them are Han, and others are Jingpo and Dai… We speak Chinese in the classroom but ethnic minority students will complain in their own languages. If they dislike one

---

[①] TS1-H1F. (2012, 12, 28). An interview with TS1-H1F. (R. Li, the interviewer & W. Zhong, the translator)

[②] TS2-M1F. (2012, 12, 28). An interview with TS2-M1F. (R. Li, the interviewer & W. Zhong, the translator)

[③] TS4-M2M. (2012, 12, 30). An interview with TS4-M2M. (R. Li, the interviewer & W. Zhong, the translator)

teacher, they will blame or even curse the teacher in their own languages.①

My students are Wa, Lahu and Dai. Two thirds of them are Wa students... I'm Bai but I don't speak Wa. Students chat in Wa mostly but they will use Chinese or Mandarin to speak with teachers. I can only guess some of their words.②

We have Lisu, Naxi and Tibetan students. Students will chat in their own minority languages in daily life. Tibetans speak Tibetan and Lisus speak Lisu language... We have many ethnic minority students and some of them can't even understand Chinese. I only have to teach English very slowly. But in the English learning process, they speak little English. Sometimes they are reluctant to ask or answer questions in English.③

In their cases, the multilingual context is the main feature of their teaching environment. As TS4 stated, newcomers in these areas, not only students but also teachers, have to learn multiple languages, in that "you have to use other ethnic minority languages. If you meet a Lisu seller, you use Lisu; if you meet a Yi, you use Yi; otherwise, you cannot live"④. Han people living in these areas have to learn some ethnic minority languages, even though they have been inhabitants for generations, just like TS1. TS1 is a Han, but she learnt several kinds of ethnic minority languages from her friends when she was a child. Picking up new local language(s) from classmates or colleagues is usual and necessary in one's daily life and for professional development in such multilingual areas; however, the need for English in daily life is not strong. In China, English is a required course in the whole curriculum system from primary to tertiary level. As mentioned before, the important role of English is owing to the development of globalization; nevertheless, ethnic minority areas in Yunnan are

---

① TS6-M4F. (2013, 11, 8). An interview with TS6-M4F. (W. Zhong, the interviewer & W. Zhong, the translator)
② TS9-M5F. (2013, 11, 16). An interview with TS9-M5F. (W. Zhong, the interviewer & W. Zhong, the translator)
③ TS10-M6F. (2013, 11, 16). An interview with TS10-M6F. (W. Zhong, the translator)
④ TS3-H2M. (2012, 12, 30). An interview with TS3-H2M. (R. Li, the interviewer & W. Zhong, the translator)

usually poor remote and mountainous areas. Residents in those areas are still living in an undeveloped way and only a few of them have visited big cities. For some elderly ones, the downtown area of the county which will usually take them 10 hours to walk from home is the furthest place they have travelled to. Having lived there for generations in almost the same way, this group of people feel little needs to change, because their tribes still exist and family tradition should be kept. It comes to them that, learning English, more often than not, is something they care little about. For some students and even their teachers, taking the examination is the only application for English learning.

7.4.2 "English can only be taught in Chinese, but I have many students who cannot speak Chinese."

Most of the time, learners start to learn Chinese from primary school and English from secondary school. However, bilingual education (Chinese and one ethnic minority languages) is only offered in some primary schools which only enrol ethnic minority students according to the Implementing Regulations of Compulsory Education Law (State Council, 1992, Article 25). This is, however, not true in those schools with multi-nationality students. These learners need a complex language code-switching mechanism to help them learn English. They have to switch what they want to express from ethnic minority languages to Chinese, then from Chinese to English. Moreover, when they hear English, they have to switch from English to Chinese, and then from Chinese to their mother tongue. This phenomenon might disappear if learners' English proficiency increase to a certain level at which they could switch English automatically to ethnic minority languages, or if they are largely exposed to English in studies through ethnic minority languages. However, the situation is that they only learn and use English in classrooms from teachers who never teach or cannot teach English through ethnic minority languages, which reduces the chances of a direct link between English and ethnic minority languages. Unfortunately, for those who cannot learn Chinese well within six-year primary studies, they will start to learn English in some confusion.

Chapter 7 Teacher Efficacy of Secondary School English Teachers in Multilingual Areas

More importantly, English is taught through Chinese (Mandarin) according to the Implementing Regulations of Compulsory Education Law (State Council, 1992). The original official statement is:

> All schools in compulsory education level should implement the use of Mandarin in all kinds of educational activities. (author's translation, State Council, 1992, Article 24)

When reviewing his experience of learning English in secondary school and high school, TS4 stated that,

> All of my teachers in (secondary and high schools) are ethnic minorities, but they spoke in Chinese when they gave lectures. It was required that we had to speak Chinese in the classroom. Outside the classroom, we chatted either in Chinese or ethnic minority languages. Teachers used ethnic minority languages out of class too, but they used Chinese in the office. They were the models for us to follow.[①]

In his words, TS4 mentioned a widely accepted Confucian educational philosophy in China, "teaching by personal conduct and verbal instruction". As reviewed in Section 2.1.5, making oneself a model for students to follow is a significant characteristic for a professional teacher. Those who fail to do so are considered as incompetent teachers in Chinese culture.

In answering "Do you use ethnic minority language to teach in the classroom?", TS4 affirmatively answered "No". He explained that "In primary school, bilingual education is allowed; but in secondary school, Chinese (Mandarin) is required".

It seems administrators fulfilled the obligation of using Chinese; in the meantime, all the teachers also set themselves up as good examples for students to follow through using Chinese. In such circumstances, for those students whose Chinese is still poor in secondary school, English learning is much harder. Learning Chinese (Mandarin) well seems more necessary and useful. After all, speaking good Chinese will enable them to communicate better with more people around.

---

① TS4-M2M. (2012, 12, 30). An interview with TS4-M2M. (R. Li, the interviewer & W. Zhong, the translator)

7.4.3 "I don't know their languages and I can only teach in Chinese."

For those teachers who cannot speak ethnic minority languages, like TS3, teaching English in Chinese needs greater effort in organizing his teaching activities. However, a large classroom makes scaffolding more challenging especially when teachers lack the awareness and knowledge of ways in which scaffolding can be used.

TS3 works in a suburban area. His school is an ethnic boarding school to which some students, mostly ethnic minority students, travel a long way to study and live on campus. His school is one of the best in the area, and his students are much better than those from other schools in his opinion. He noticed that students from rural areas (mostly ethnic minority students) have difficulties in English learning, but he attributed this to students' Intelligence Quality (IQ). "They (students from rural areas) have some problems with IQ. They cannot catch up with others (students from urban areas)."[①] Moreover, he almost gave up helping the students who had weak progress in their study. He explained that,

> (These backward students might think) school doesn't want me go out and do something harmful, parents are worried if I made any troubles, so I had to stay in the classroom. Sometimes, these students will cause many problems such as not following the rules or regulations, playing the mobile phones, or sleeping. For them, I have to pacify them and tell them "It is all right if you don't understand, but you can make some friends at school or practicing calligraphy". I can only do this to them. My solution is very simple. I will directly tell him "I won't quarrel with you in these three years. You try your best to remember as much as possible. You can find some novels you like to read or I can recommend one to you. If you want to practice your handwriting in Chinese or in English, you can try. Or, you can find a journal to read". If he doesn't want to do any of these, I will tell him that as long as he does not influence other students' learning, he can do

---

① TS3-H2M. (2012, 12, 30). An interview with TS3-H2M. (R. Li, the interviewer & W. Zhong, the translator)

whatever he wants to do.①

TS3's words sound very helpless. In describing his difficulties in English teaching, he explained that the low employment rate makes the public believe that education is useless; he stated parents' poor guidance had negative effects on students' motivation; he complained his "nanny" role when students dropped out for working in other cities which ended in stopping his teaching to look for them; and he criticized the low income as a teacher. He strongly believes that "If a student wants to study, he can learn it well; if he doesn't want to, it's useless for you to say anything"②. However, another important reason might be that most of his students can speak Chinese and he cannot speak ethnic minority languages; hence, the only solutions for him is to devote more energy to the larger group and give up support for the smaller one. In answering "Do you realize ethnic minority students and Han students have language differences?", he simply replied,

> Yes, for those who live in mountainous areas, they have; but those who live near the downtown areas are more influenced by Han culture, they don't have.③

Because his school is in a downtown area and his students have higher scores in entrance examinations, TS3 assumes that his students are influenced by Han culture and he doesn't need to use special methods to solve the language barrier problems.

TS3 is not the only teacher who encounters this problem. TS6 also mentioned her helplessness.

> TS6: Some younger Jingpo kids are really slow in study. They can't understand Chinese at all. They even can't write their own names.
>
> Zhong: How do you deal with these kids?

---

① TS3-H2M. (2012, 12, 30). An interview with TS3-H2M. (R. Li, the interviewer & W. Zhong, the translator)

② TS3-H2M. (2012, 12, 30). An interview with TS3-H2M. (R. Li, the interviewer & W. Zhong, the translator)

③ TS3-H2M. (2012, 12, 30). An interview with TS3-H2M. (R. Li, the interviewer & W. Zhong, the translator)

TS6: Drag them.

Zhong: How can you drag, if they can't understand your words?

TS6: They would sit there in a daze and never handed in their homework. Sometimes I forced them. They would hand in the homework. Then, they would put the textbooks in the drawer at school, and left the school with nothing. If I become harsh, they would open the book. (Mostly) they just sleep in the classroom or do their own things… Sometimes I think they can't do anything and I think I don't have enough energy to deal with them. If students who are smart and hardworking, I will try my best to communicate with them.[①]

Different from TS3 and TS6, though also working in downtown school, TS1 paid more attention to the problem of the language barrier of ethnic minority students. TS1 claimed that "(I will) let a student who can speak Chinese better help those who have language barriers"[②].

7.5 Beliefs on Professional Teacher and Teaching Profession

Twelve participants in this research reflect various beliefs about the professional teacher and teaching profession. Some acknowledge the significance of student-centerd theory in that all the decisions should be made on the basis of students' needs; some concern more personal conduct and consequently would focus on individual acceptance by the public and their own reputation; some emphasize the importance of being knowledgeable as teachers and are more likely to pursue self-accomplishment.

---

① TS6-M4F. (2013, 11, 8). An interview with TS6-M4F. (W. Zhong, the interviewer & W. Zhong, the translator)

② TS1-H1F. (2012, 12, 28). An interview with TS1-H1F. (R. Li, the interviewer & W. Zhong, the translator)

Chapter 7 Teacher Efficacy of Secondary School English Teachers in Multilingual Areas

7.5.1 "If I care more about the students, they would gradually believe in us."

TS4 believes that teachers should stay more with students and communicate with them to understand their difficulties. The reason for doing this, as he explained, is merely building up a trustworthy relationship between teachers and students. "If I care more about them, they would gradually believe us."① He enjoyed the moment when he shared his knowledge with students, and the love of sharing could trace back to his high school English teacher. "He was so nice to us though we started learning English from high school."② His English teacher triggered his preference for English, and finally drove him to become an English teacher after four-year study in Chinese literature.

From his own case, TS4 has been convinced that teachers can influence students potentially, "especially in encouragement". Such belief is so strong that he considers the fundamental purpose for teacher professional development is being able to satisfy students' needs.

> Students lack the knowledge of learning strategies. They don't know how to learn, and then they can't learn it well, finally they don't want to learn. If a teacher doesn't develop his professional skills, he will stick to a narrow point of view and students won't favor that. If a teacher wants students to enjoy learning English, he has to make some changes. Only when a teacher has personal development can he change the teaching to satisfy various needs from students. We cannot improve merely through pre-service or in-service training. ③

TS4 suggested an important issue in teacher professional development, personal willingness for the change or development. For some teachers, they persist in their own

---

① TS4-M2M. (2012, 12, 30). An interview with TS4-M2M. (R. Li, the interviewer & W. Zhong, the translator)
② TS4-M2M. (2012, 12, 30). An interview with TS4-M2M. (R. Li, the interviewer & W. Zhong, the translator)
③ TS4-M2M. (2012, 12, 30). An interview with TS4-M2M. (R. Li, the interviewer & W. Zhong, the translator)

styles because they learnt English in the same way and it worked well; for others, change means starting everything over again and it may fail also. Hence, some teachers would prefer ignoring students' diverse needs because that would be easier for them to control the class and their teaching. However, TS4 is not this kind who fears failure. It is his concentration on students that makes him unsatisfied with the current situation and focus more on personal development. He not only knows the problems in English education, but also tries to seek for solution. He is clear about what he has and what he needs. He would be strongly motivated and gain a lot through his lifelong professional development.

7.5.2 "Sometimes I like being a teacher but sometimes I don't."

Half of the teachers in ethnic minority areas are exactly like TS2. They found teaching a stable job which is "not easy to look for". They felt excited at the beginning but felt bored when unexpected things happened and repeated.

> Sometimes I do like being a teacher but sometimes I don't… I enjoy teaching children but might feel frustrated as well. I would feel happy when my students got high scores in the examinations. The same applies to the compliment I obtained from students' parents.[①]

It is clear that different from TS4, rewards like parents' praise or students' score can bring her happiness. Her confidence in teaching, or teacher efficacy, will be strengthened if she receives more compliments like these; however, her statement of frustration indicates she still has a lot of frustrations. Teachers like TS2 know they have deficiency in teaching skills and cannot name exactly what aspects should be improved, because the deficiency is caused by the environment, the external reasons, not by themselves. TS2 assumes "reading more books" is a good solution to improve herself, but the reason is "we are in a backward area"[②]. These teachers will be more

---

① TS2-M1F. (2012, 12, 28). An interview with TS2-M1F. (R. Li, the interviewer & W. Zhong, the translator)

② TS2-M1F. (2012, 12, 28). An interview with TS2-M1F. (R. Li, the interviewer & W. Zhong, the translator)

prone to seek help from experts because they are in the subordinate positions. In TS2's example, she would go to the principal for solutions on the dropout issues, because the principal is her superior, and by doing this can she avoid making mistakes.

7.5.3 "Being a teacher doesn't mean teaching knowledge only, and it also means educating students to be responsible for society."

"Students in my working area don't enjoy learning, and we don't care about their scores either," TS1 explained, "but I felt happy when three years later some of them would say 'Madam, though we learnt little English from you, we learnt how we can be socially gregarious.'" Like TS1, most teachers, wherever in downtown or rural areas, agree that "being a teacher doesn't mean teaching knowledge only, and it also means educating students to be responsible people for society". In ethnic minority areas, English is seldom used in daily life and only a few students would further their studies in senior high school or college, not to mention English teachers' own English proficiency. It is challenging to strengthen the necessity of English education. Nevertheless, moral education is a lifelong lesson about becoming a noble person. Some teachers are working like "soul engineers", teaching doctrines of good behaviors and educating learners to be upright people. Exactly as the Russian educator Mikhail Ivanovitch Kalinin's (1875-1946) metaphor claimed, "Educators are the engineers of the human soul."

7.5.4 "We are the lowest of the society but doing the hardest job."

Although in his forties, TS3 still sounds like a disappointed dreamer. His decision about becoming a teacher was coincident with TS2's, for a stable job. "I wanted to be a teacher for merely thinking teaching is a pure profession and my parents hoped I would find a job with stable income first; however, after I became one I realized teaching was not the same as what I assumed."[①] He explained that some of his colleagues quit

---

① TS3-H2M. (2012, 12, 30). An interview with TS3-H2M. (R. Li, the interviewer & W. Zhong, the translator)

teaching and became businessmen or government officers, because "those who are teaching are not capable ones, but those who can teach best are promoted to become administrative leaders"①. It seems he indicates that the teachers who remain teaching in rural areas for years are actually not the best teachers or not the most capable ones; however, he is part of this group. Being a teacher for more than 20 years, in his logic, means that he belongs to the "less capable group", but he attributes his failure or unsuccessful career to external reasons, the government and family. He regrets being a teacher, but his age doesn't allow him to make changes. As he said, "If I were ten years younger, I would go out and have a try. I would never choose to be a teacher."②

Francis Bacon said "Knowledge is power" and Li Ka Shing, the founder of Li Ka Shing Foundation and the richest man in China, changed the saying to "Knowledge reshapes destiny". However, in ethnic minority areas, teachers like TS3 don't feel knowledge changes their lives, at least not in the way as they expected. TS3's experience tells him that becoming a teacher is not a wise decision for three reasons: low salary, weak social respect and slow promotion. He stated that teaching for 20 years, his salary has seldom changed and even "lower than those farmer workers working in big cities". For teachers whose professional titles are in primary level, they earn much less than they should. In his words, "It's better to clean the street or sell the eggs."③ Teachers can get bonus if their students get high scores in the entrance examination, but not every teacher can teach the graduating year which means not everyone can get the big bonus. "We teach three-year a round. Only when students' average score is the first in whole district can we have the bonus, possibly 2000 *yuan* or 3000 *yuan* (about 300 or 500 dollars). Most teachers just got 200 *yuan* (about 30 dollars), 500 *yuan* (80 dollars) or 1000 *yuan* (160 dollars). That was the maximum

---

① TS3-H2M. (2012, 12, 30). An interview with TS3-H2M. (R. Li, the interviewer & W. Zhong, the translator)

② TS3-H2M. (2012, 12, 30). An interview with TS3-H2M. (R. Li, the interviewer & W. Zhong, the translator)

③ TS3-H2M. (2012, 12, 30). An interview with TS3-H2M. (R. Li, the interviewer & W. Zhong, the translator)

Chapter 7 Teacher Efficacy of Secondary School English Teachers in Multilingual Areas

bonus we had for three years."[①] TS3's comparison with street cleaners and egg sellers might exaggerate the worse situation to some extent, but it is true that teachers do not have high salaries in the whole China. According to Wang's (2012) study, from 1990 to 1999, teachers' average income was ranked 1st to 3rd from the bottom among the 12 professions, mostly lower than the average income of the whole China. From 2000 to 2008 (Wang, 2012), teachers' avearage income became higher than the average income. Wang (2012) also pointed out that teachers' income differs from province to province. In Yunnan, according to data in 2008, teachers' average income was lower than the disposable income, meaning teachers' average salary was lower than other professions and the local government didn't spend money on enhancing teachers' living conditions. Teachers' income index, the ratio of teachers' average annual income and average GNP (Gross National Product), is used to show the role of teachers' income in certain economic development environment. From 1990 to 2008 secondary school teachers' income index changed from 1.03 to 1.37, much lower than the average point at 9.58 of other developing countries similar to China (Wang, 2012). Low teacher income index will demotivate teachers' work and consequently influence the education quality. More importantly, it results in a pseudo-respect to teacher profession.

> We are the lowest of the society but doing the hardest job… Our income is mainly based on government budget. If they allow us to start our own business, I believe we can earn as much as others do, like teachers in Kunming. If I could earn money like this, I would work harder for it. Teachers in Kunming can afford the house and car, while some teachers in rural areas just earn 1000 *yuan* (166 dollars) a month. I have worked so many years, but my salary is about 3000 *yuan* (about 500 dollars) a month. You even can't afford a marriage. Some college students usually cried for this.[②]

Like TS3 described, teachers are gradually demotivated if their salary can't bring

---

① TS3-H2M. (2012, 12, 30). An interview with TS3-H2M. (R. Li, the interviewer & W. Zhong, the translator).
② TS3-H2M. (2012, 12, 30). An interview with TS3-H2M. (R. Li, the interviewer & W. Zhong, the translator).

them a life worth their parents' financial investment and their own efforts. They are still striving for the lowest level of Hierachy of Needs (Maslow, 1970), physiological needs that aim at food, rest, water, oxygen, and anything the physical organism needs to survive. According to Maslow's needs hierachy (referring to Section 2.2.3), if the things that satisfy the lower level needs are swept away, we are no longer concerned about the maintenance of the higher level ones. In other words, when teachers like TS3 still focus on salary needs, higher needs like self-actualization is a fantasy for them.

Beyond the salary, TS3 pointed out another magnificent issue, the problems in promotion administration system. Promotion can increase a teacher's salary and also provide more opportunities for realizing the higher-level needs. However, if a promotion system is not based on achievements teachers made, it cannot motivate teachers to contribute diligent efforts. "My school doesn't consider one's achievements and age, but other reasons."[①] He thought those "hidden rules" are the reason that he couldn't get promotion.

Living and working in almost the same environment, these teachers showed different beliefs about the teaching profession and professional teachers. The belief is one cause for a teacher's actions or performances in English teaching which would be revealed after the in-service training (Wu, 2005); however, other decisive causes equally exist, one of which is the attitude to language learning, especially English learning.

---

① TS3-H2M. (2012, 12, 30). An interview with TS3-H2M. (R. Li, the interviewer & W. Zhong, the translator)

Chapter 8 Education Participation Motivation of Secondary School English Teachers in Multilingual Areas

Twenty-four items of modified EPS (Chinese) (referring to Appendixes 1 & 2) are adopted from Boshier et al.'s (2006) EPS (Chinese) and contain only six subscales (referring to Section 4.4 and Table 8.1) of the original seven. The six factors are communication improvement, social contact, cognitive interest, professional advancement, social stimulation and family togetherness. A four-point Likert scaling is used in correspondence with CTSE for further analysis. Items were coded as no influence=1, little influence=2, moderate influence=3, and much influence=4. Because each of the six factors contains 4 items, a minimum scale score is 4 (suggesting low influence) and maximum scale score is 16 (suggesting high influence).

EPS (Chinese) data were secured from 186 subjects participating in NTP. Reliability analysis (referring to Table 8.1) shows that the 24 items of modified EPS (Chinese) have high internal consistency (Cronbach's alpha=0.859). Five of the six sub-scales' Cronbach's alpha are over 0.60, but the Cronbach's alpha of Professional Advancement is 0.588.

Table 8.1 Reliability Test of Modified EPS (Chinese)

Dimensions	Modified EPS (Chinese)	Factors					
		CIm	SC	CIn	PA	SS	FT
Cronbach's Alpha	0.859	0.899	0.801	0.736	0.588	0.640	0.768
N of Items	24	4	4	4	4	4	4

Notes: CIm=communication improvement; SC=social contact; CIn=cognitive interest; PA=professional advancement

8.1 Exploratory Factor Analysis

I wondered about how well the modified EPS (Chinese) factor structure would withstand. In most tests using EPS, authors seldom change their scoring criteria every time when another language is used or new population are surveyed (Boshier et al., 2006: 211). However, because the standard EPS factor structure was derived from mostly Euro-American people, and items in one sub-factor, communicative improvement, is changed to meet special needs of English teachers, it seemed prudent to examine the English teacher factor structure before calculating scale scores and proceeding with further analysis, just like what Boshier et al. (2006) did with Shanghai samples.

In accordance with Boshier et al. (2006), Principal Component Analysis and Varimax with Kaiser Normalization were used to analyze the factor structure of modified EPS (Chinese). Commonalities of 24 items were extracted and a screen plot was examined. Different from Boshier et al. (2006), five factors were naturally extracted. However, regarding factor loadings, the main question is to what extent items would migrate to "their" factors (as previously identified in Shanghai). Hence, six-factor extraction was conducted. Of the six factors, the first explained 24.60% of variance after orthogonal rotation (Varimax with Kaiser Normalization), the second 18.09% and the third 7.14%. In all, six factors explained 64.78% (The data retains two decimal places and is consistent with the data in the appendix) of the variance (referring to Appendix 8).

Table 8.2 shows items and loadings for the England, Shanghai and Yunnan versions. Loadings on the English version were mostly derived from learners at the King Edward Campus of Vancouver Community College (Boshier, 1991). Loadings on Chinese-Shanghai version (hereinafter "Shanghai version") were derived from learners who enrolled in adult education classes at Shanghai Seniors University or Putou Spare-time University (Boshier et al., 2006). Results show that 20 of the 24 items cohered in the expected manner (referring to Table 8.2). On four of the six factors, the mean English-version loadings were higher than that in Yunnan, and one was the same as in Yunnan. At the same time, on two of the six factors, the mean Shanghai-version loadings were higher than that in Yunnan, and one was the same as in Yunnan. On each of the six factors in Yunnan, the mean loadings exceeded 0.30.

Chapter 8 Education Participation Motivation of Secondary School English Teachers in Multilingual Areas

Because all participants in this research are in-service teachers and 78.5% of them are English teachers, there was some incoherence. Each of the following factors contained items where loadings were below 0.40—professional advancement, social stimulation, and family togetherness. On professional advancement, one high loading (0.73) item from Shanghai almost failed to register (Item 14), and another reached only 0.11 (Item 15). However, most factors strongly resembled those from Shanghai. As Boshier et al. (2006) stated that owing to large numbers of older participants in Shanghai study population, the deviations from English version might have occurred. 100% in-service teacher samples in this study also repeated the population problem in Shanghai. As suggested by Boshier et al. (2006), a more diverse and larger study population is needed to test the final or definitive Chinese factor structure. Factor structure provided in Table 8.2 cannot be regarded as the final EPS (Chinese), but it can still reveal some findings.

Table 8.2 Factor Structure of EPS English, Shanghai and Yunnan

Abbreviated Items	EPS (English)	EPS (Shanghai)	EPS (Yunnan)
Communication Improvement (CIm)			
1. improve English	0.81	0.25	0.85
3. understand Western culture and customs	0.61	0.60	0.72
11. improve English reading and writing ability	0.69	0.42	0.86
17. speak English better	0.79	0.30	0.87
Mean loadings	0.73	0.40	0.83
Social Contact (SC)			
2. new friends	−0.81	0.71	0.67
8. friendly people	−0.53	0.53	0.58
20. make friends	−0.78	0.67	0.74
24. meet new people	0.99	−0.83	0.84
Mean loadings	0.78	0.69	0.71
Cognitive Interest (CIn)			
7. more knowledge	−0.60	0.71	0.61

	EPS (English)	EPS (Shanghai)	EPS (Yunnan)
Abbreviated Items			Continued
9. get something meaningful out of life	−0.57	0.47	0.60
12. expand mind	−0.63	0.58	0.73
18. joy of learning	−0.59	0.63	0.47
Mean loadings	0.60	0.60	0.60
Professional Advancement (PA)			
4. job status	−0.67	0.83	0.73
10. find a better job	−0.74	0.70	0.41
14. occupational goal	−0.63	0.73	0.02
15. increase job competence	−0.81	0.81	0.11
Mean loadings	0.71	0.77	0.32
Social Stimulation (SS)			
5. escape from complex relationship	0.54	0.51	0.78
21. overcome frustration in work	0.70	0.28	0.79
22. break the routine	0.63	0.24	0.32
23. avoid loneliness	0.65	0.50	0.43
Mean loadings	0.63	0.38	0.58
Family Togetherness (FT)			
6. others in the family	−0.56	0.54	0.26
13. talk with children	−0.82	0.80	0.67
16. answer children's questions	−0.83	0.80	0.81
19. keep up with children	−0.83	0.80	0.79
Mean loadings	0.76	0.74	0.63

8.2 Strength of Educational Participation

Because each of the six factors contains 4 items, a minimum scale score for each factor is 4 (suggesting low influence) and maximum scale score is 16 (suggesting high influence). Mean value of the six factors is computed to show the general strength of the educational participation. As Table 8.3 indicates, a minimum mean score is 4 (suggesting extremely weak educational participation strength) and a maximum mean score is 16 (suggesting extremely strong educational participation strength). The missing value is substituted by the series mean value. High standard deviation (SD) indicates large individual differences. Skewness value shows the distribution of the data. If skewness value is between −1 and 1, a normal distribution is shown. If skewness value is larger than 1, a right-skewed distribution is presented, which indicates most subjects have low scores.

Table 8.3 EPS Strength Degree

4	6	8	10	12	14	16
extremely weak/low	comparatively weak/low	weak/low	strong/high	comparatively strong/high	extremely strong/high	

The main focus of this research is on English teachers, so data used for the following studies are 146 English teacher subjects. Generally speaking, subjects have weak educational participation strength (Mean=9.692). Subjects are strongly motivated by communication improvement (Mean=13.250), cognitive interest (Mean=12.950) and professional advancement (Mean=11.650). However, they are weakly motivated by social contact (Mean=7.250), family togetherness (Mean=6.670) and social stimulation (Mean=6.390). Of the six motivational orientations, subjects are comparatively highly motivated by cognitive interest (Mean=12.950), same as samples in Shanghai and Vancouver (Boshier et al., 2006: 212). Distribution of social stimulation shows a right-skewed tendency, indicating most subjects are low motivated by social stimulation in their educational motivation in NTP (referring to Table 8.4).

Table 8.4 Descriptive Analysis of EPS Strength

Items	N	Mean	SD	Skewness Statistics	SD	Spearman's rho
General EPS	146	9.692	1.505	0.259	0.201	/
Communication improvement	146	13.250	2.316	−0.797	0.201	0.592**
Social contact	146	7.250	2.720	0.822	0.201	0.604**
Cognitive interest	146	12.950	2.293	−0.601	0.201	0.615**
Professional advancement	146	11.650	2.166	−0.026	0.201	0.729**
Social stimulation	146	6.390	2.226	1.132	0.201	0.507**
Family togetherness	146	6.670	2.508	0.897	0.201	0.599**
Valid N (listwise)	146					

**$p<0.01$

Spearman's rho coefficient test shows that professional advancement has the strongest correlation to the general EPS (γ_s=0.729, $p<0.01$). Cognitive interest (γ_s =0.615, $p<0.01$) and social contact (γ_s =0.604, $p<0.01$) have significant high correlation to the general EPS, while social stimulation has the weakest correlation to general EPS (γ_s =0.507, $p<0.01$).

8.3 Differences of EPS Strength of English Teachers Among Various Demographic Groups

Difference studies among various demographic groups will present quantitative findings on whether demographic features can influence subjects' EPS strength. General EPS strength is studied to provide a macro view and six factors of EPS are all studied at the same time to give a micro explanation.

8.3.1 Teaching years

Kruskal-Wallis test (referring to Table 8.5) shows that group differences of family togetherness among subjects with different teaching years are significant at 0.05 level.

Significant group differences of communication improvement also exist among groups with different teaching years at 0.01 level. However, no significant group difference is shown in general EPS.

Table 8.5 Teaching Years and Educational Participation Motivation

Items	Teaching years	N	Mean rank	Asymp. sig. (2-tailed)
General EPS	Less than 5 years	43	77.06	
	6-10 years	36	71.03	0.794
	Over 10 years	67	72.54	
Communication improvement	Less than 5 years	43	85.57	
	6-10 years	36	77.75	0.020*
	Over 10 years	67	63.47	
Social contact	Less than 5 years	43	73.59	
	6-10 years	36	66.14	0.430
	Over 10 years	67	77.40	
Cognitive interest	Less than 5 years	43	83.83	
	6-10 years	36	75.71	0.081
	Over 10 years	67	65.69	
Professional advancement	Less than 5 years	43	84.65	
	6-10 years	36	69.40	0.115
	Over 10 years	67	68.54	
Social stimulation	Less than 5 years	43	67.57	
	6-10 years	36	66.36	0.124
	Over 10 years	67	81.14	

Continued

Items	Teaching years	N	Mean rank	Asymp. sig. (2-tailed)
	Less than 5 years	43	54.95	
Family togetherness	6-10 years	36	77.64	0.002**
	Over 10 years	67	83.18	

*$p<0.05$, **$p<0.01$

It seems that subjects with less working experience tend to be motivated more by communication improvement, cognitive interest and professional advancement; in other words, they have stronger professional development needs. English communicative ability is an academic requirement for English teaching. Improving it can greatly help teachers' teaching proficiency and make them more confident in the classroom. Cognitive interest, the factor more relating to intrinsic motivation, is an innate drive that leads to learning. During the process of professional development, this intrinsic motive will result in continuous learning or lifelong learning. If improving English communication and cognitive interest are also shared by other English lovers, professional advancement clearly aims at professional development. Hence, stronger desire or intention in these three factors could indicate individual's professional development desire to some extent. As mentioned in previous part, teachers with over 10 years' working experience didn't receive formal English training when they started their teaching careers. For some, they were trained to be English teachers in short-training programs or through correspondence courses. For others, they might learn English but received little pedagogy education. Through years of teaching, they formed their own education philosophy and teaching methodology. "If English teachers really want to learn something (through the training), he should work really hard; because of this, many teachers do not want to come to such a training."[①] As noted by TS4 from the interview, teachers had little expectancy about their professional development because the longer they work, the stronger they tend to feel less confident and do not believe they could still improve after the short training. For these teachers, they came to the training

---

① TS4-M2M. (2012, 12, 30). An interview with TS4-M2M. (R. Li, the interviewer & W. Zhong, the translator)

Chapter 8   Education Participation Motivation of Secondary School English Teachers in Multilingual Areas

more for other reasons. Data suggest that subjects with more working experience more incline to study for social contact, social stimulation and family togetherness.

In the meantime, data indicate that social contact and social stimulation would be less likely to make subjects with less than 5 years' working experience and those with more than 10 years' join NTP. Human relationship is a kind of human capital in Chinese society. Good relationship with some important people, such as principals or department leaders, can sometimes bring more opportunities for promotion or chances to change one's teaching career. In-service training programs, like NTP, provide lectures, seminars or workshops by national experts. These chances are precious, especially for teachers in rural and ethnic minority areas. Subjects with less than 5 years' working experience just start their careers; thus they are probably still too young to realize the importance of human relationship. By contrast, subjects with more than 10 years' working experience might need these chances to broaden their social network and seek for more opportunities for academic cooperation or another change in their lives or their careers.

It is worth noticing that a significant difference is shown the longer subjects have worked, the more eager they would be to pursue training for family togetherness. Among the four items that contribute to family togetherness, three concern children (referring to Table 8.4). Subjects with longer working experience may be more likely to realize the gaps between their educational background and their children's; hence, they are more eager to join NTP to fix this problem within the family. It also might be because, as teachers, they understand the importance of family education, and consequently they would learn more for helping their children to learn.

8.3.2   Age

Kruskal-Wallis test (referring to Table 8.6) shows age does not make many differences of educational motivation orientation except for family togetherness. Data indicate that the elder subjects are more motivated by family reasons, such as talking with children, than the younger ones. This result is in accordance with previous idea that when individuals grow older, the generation gaps they are facing might become more serious if the aged don't update their knowledge or refresh their minds to keep up with the continuously changing society.

Table 8.6 Age and Educational Participation Motivation

Items	Ages	N	Mean rank	Asymp. sig. (2-tailed)
General EPS	21-30	63	71.40	
	31-40	57	73.90	0.946
	41-50	24	72.06	
Communication improvement	21-30	63	68.33	
	31-40	57	70.66	0.090
	41-50	24	87.81	
Social contact	21-30	63	68.33	
	31-40	57	70.66	0.132
	41-50	24	87.81	
Cognitive interest	21-30	63	76.81	
	31-40	57	70.24	0.509
	41-50	24	66.56	
Professional advancement	21-30	63	74.71	
	31-40	57	76.10	0.174
	41-50	24	58.17	
Social stimulation	21-30	63	63.64	
	31-40	57	80.05	0.073
	41-50	24	77.81	
Family togetherness	21-30	63	60.42	
	31-40	57	80.55	0.007**
	41-50	24	85.08	

**$p<0.01$

8.3.3 Professional titles

Similar to teacher efficacy, though small population of advanced-level subjects might influence the results, Kruskal-Wallis test (referring to Table 8.7) shows no significant difference of educational participation motivation among different professional title groups.

Table 8.7 Professional Titles and Educational Participation Motivation

Items	Professional titles	N	Mean rank	Asymp. sig. (2-tailed)
General EPS	Advanced	7	73.64	
	Intermediate	99	69.06	0.955
	Primary	32	69.97	
Communication improvement	Advanced	7	54.64	
	Intermediate	99	69.06	0.487
	Primary	32	74.12	
Social contact	Advanced	7	88.64	
	Intermediate	99	68.55	0.423
	Primary	32	68.25	
Cognitive interest	Advanced	7	67.36	
	Intermediate	99	70.86	0.810
	Primary	32	65.77	
Professional advancement	Advanced	7	54.29	
	Intermediate	99	69.68	0.551
	Primary	32	72.27	
Social stimulation	Advanced	7	66.50	
	Intermediate	99	69.02	0.928
	Primary	32	71.64	

				Continued
Items	Professional titles	N	Mean rank	Asymp. sig. (2-tailed)
Family togetherness	Advanced	7	84.86	0.562
	Intermediate	99	69.05	
	Primary	32	67.53	

8.3.4 Ethnicity

Again, Mann-Whitney test (referring to Table 8.8) doesn't suggest significant difference of educational participation motivation among Han and ethnic minority subjects. Generally speaking, however, Han groups show weaker motivation than ethnic minority groups.

Table 8.8 Ethnicity and Educational Participation Motivation

Items	Ethnicities	N	Mean rank	Difference of mean rank	Asymp. sig. (2-tailed)
General EPS	Han	98	72.36	−0.43	0.954
	Ethnic minorities	46	72.79		
Communication improvement	Han	98	72.92	1.32	0.857
	Ethnic minorities	46	71.60		
Social contact	Han	98	72.31	−0.59	0.936
	Ethnic minorities	46	72.90		
Cognitive interest	Han	98	74.83	7.29	0.324
	Ethnic minorities	46	67.54		
Professional advancement	Han	98	69.27	−10.12	0.170
	Ethnic minorities	46	79.39		

Chapter 8 Education Participation Motivation of Secondary School English Teachers in Multilingual Areas

Continued

Items	Ethnicities	N	Mean rank	Difference of mean rank	Asymp. sig. (2-tailed)
Social stimulation	Han	98	72.36	−0.43	0.953
	Ethnic minorities	46	72.79		
Family togetherness	Han	98	69.28	−10.09	0.170
	Ethnic minorities	46	79.37		

8.4 Correlations Between ELA and EPS of English Teachers

Studies in SLA have gradually accepted that attitudes play an important role in forming individual's English learning motivation (Dörnyei & Clément, 2001; Ellis, 1994; Gardner, 1985, 2006). English learning motivation is theoretically constructed on the general learning motivation theories, which means English teachers' ELA which influence English learning motivation, will consequently affect their in-service training motivation. However, to what extent and in which ways can ELA make the influence? Correlation matrix between ELA and EPS can provide a general view of their relationships.

Spearman's rho analysis (referring to Table 8.9) shows that at the primary level GELA does not have a significant correlation with general educational participation strength, but GELA has stronger positive relationship to communication improvement (γ_s=0.204, $p<0.05$) and cognitive interest (γ_s =0.204, $p<0.05$).

Considering the secondary level, some dimensions of ELA can influence English teachers' educational participation strength to some extent. First of all, among the five dimensions of ELA, AEL is the most important factor that determines English teachers' in-service training motivation (γ_s=0.286, $p<0.01$). Meanwhile, it positively affects teachers' communication improvement needs (γ_s=0.278, p<0.01), cognitive interests needs (γ_s=0.290, p<0.01), and professional advancement needs (γ_s=0.265, p<0.01). AES is another factor that has positive influence on professional advancement needs (γ_s=0.186, p<0.05). SVE, on the other hand, has a significant negative relationship to social contact (SC) needs (γ_s=−0.180, p<0.05).

It is likely that learning English cannot bring English teachers stronger motivation for social needs. Table 8.9 indicates that GELA have negative relationship with SC, SS and FT needs. AEC, AES, and SVE all contribute to these negative influences.

Table 8.9 Correlation Between ELA and EPS

Spearman's rho		GEPS	Factors					
			CIm	SC	CIn	PA	SS	FT
GELA	Correlation coefficient	0.110	0.204*	−0.002	0.204*	0.112	−0.046	−0.026
	Sig (2-tailed)	0.187	0.013	0.983	0.013	0.179	0.581	0.759
AEC	Correlation coefficient	0.025	0.135	−0.037	0.108	−0.059	−0.021	−0.030
	Sig (2-tailed)	0.763	0.105	0.661	0.195	0.482	0.802	0.723
AES	Correlation coefficient	0.083	0.145	−0.013	0.176*	0.186*	−0.090	−0.075
	Sig (2-tailed)	0.317	0.081	0.878	0.034	0.024	0.278	0.367
AEL	Correlation coefficient	0.286**	0.278**	0.156	0.290**	0.265**	0.027	0.095
	Sig (2-tailed)	0.000	0.001	0.060	0.000	0.001	0.749	0.254
SVE	Correlation coefficient	−0.014	0.043	−0.180*	0.155	0.090	−0.108	−0.032
	Sig (2-tailed)	0.863	0.610	0.030	0.062	0.281	0.195	0.704

Chapter 8 Education Participation Motivation of Secondary School English Teachers in Multilingual Areas

Continued

Spearman's rho		GEPS	Factors					
			CIm	SC	CIn	PA	SS	FT
PUE	Correlation coefficient	0.003	0.026	0.024	−0.075	−0.065	0.006	0.026
	Sig (2-tailed)	0.972	0.756	0.772	0.370	0.435	0.939	0.758
N				146				

Notes: CIm=Communication Improvement; SC=Social Contact; CIn=Cognitive Interest; PA=Professional Advancement; GEPS=General EPS

*$p<0.05$(2-tailed), ** $p<0.01$(2-tailed)

8.5 Correlations Between TE and EPS of English Teachers

Perceived self-efficacy, according to social cognitive theory (Bandura, 1986, 1993, 1997), is one's belief or sense in his or her ability to succeed in specific situations, such as self-efficacy in using computers. It can play a major role in determining the ways and efforts that one approaches goals, tasks, and challenges (Luszczynska & Schwarzer, 2005). TE is the belief that teacher holds about his or her ability to be successful in teaching. Hence, it not only influences their teaching careers, but also affects their motivation for professional development. In-service training has been widely used in China as a required professional development method to improve teachers' ability (Guan, 2005; Yuan, 2005; Zhong, 2008), but the element of compulsion increases reluctance when programs are not well designed or the curriculum is not developed based on needs analysis (Zhong, 2008). In such circumstances, to what extent can TE influence their training motivation? Among the six aspects of EPS, which one does TE impact most? For teachers with obviously high or low TE how are their learning motivations different? Answers to these questions will enable us to understand better about the needs of ET and in turn to look for helpful and effective solutions to their professional development.

Spearman's rho analysis (Table 8.10) shows that GTE has a significant positive correlation to general EPS (γ_s=0.221, p<0.01). The main contributors are cognitive interest (γ_s=0.291, p<0.01) and professional development (γ_s=0.236, p<0.01). The only negative correlation is to social stimulation (γ_s=−0.097, p<0.01).

Table 8.10 Correlations Between TE and EPS

		GEPS	Factors					
Spearman's rho			CIm	SC	CIn	PA	SS	FT
GTE	Correlation coefficient	0.221**	0.130	0.106	0.291**	0.236**	−0.097	0.158
	Sig (2-tailed)	0.007	0.119	0.204	0.000	0.004	0.245	0.058
	N			146				

Notes: CIm=Communication Improvement, SC=Social Contact; CIn=Cognitive Interest; PA=Professional Advancement; GEPS=General EPS
** p<0.01(2-tailed)

It is likely that the strength of GTE will have a positive influence on teachers' educational participation motivation, especially their cognitive interest and desire for professional development, but negative influence on social stimulation. Is it true that with low or high efficacy teachers will have different educational participation motivation? Difference analysis between the high GTE group and the low GTE group is needed to find out more findings on the tendency.

8.6 Differences of EPS Between High and Low GTE English Teachers

Of the 146 ET, GTE score at 2.4 and 3.1 are used as the grouping value for low and high GTE groups respectively (24% of the total number). Mann-Whitney and Wilcoxon analysis (referring to Table 8.11) shows that ET with low or high GTE have a significant difference in general educational participation strength with 12.16 points apart (p<0.01). Low GTE subjects have obviously weaker educational participation strength than high ones; while high GTE subjects have stronger desire to study for their cognitive interest, professional development and family togetherness.

Table 8.11 Differences of EPS Between High and Low GTE English Teachers

Items	TSE group	N	Mean rank	Difference of mean rank	Asymp. sig. (2-tailed)
Communication improvement	Low	30	29.47	−6.56	0.157
	High	35	36.03		
Social contact	Low	30	30.13	−5.33	0.253
	High	35	35.46		
Cognitive interest	Low	30	25.18	−14.52	0.002**
	High	35	39.70		
Professional advancement	Low	30	27.87	−9.53	0.041*
	High	35	37.40		
Social stimulation	Low	30	35.55	4.74	0.307
	High	35	30.81		
Family togetherness	Low	30	27.78	−9.69	0.037*
	High	35	37.47		
General EPS	Low	30	26.45	−12.16	0.010*
	High	35	38.61		

**$p<0.01$, *$p<0.05$

At the same time, data also suggest that among the six educational motivation dimensions, low GTE subjects have weaker strength except for social stimulation. It seems that low GTE subjects have more tendencies to participate in in-service training owing to reasons like escaping from complex relationship, overcoming the frustration in work, breaking routine, and avoiding the loneliness.

8.7 Reflections on In-service Training

One of the research purposes for this research is to detect the deficiency of in-service training programs for teachers in Yunnan. Reflections from program developers, trainers and trainees can depict an exclusive image from different perspectives, and consequently help us understand better the gaps between government's expectation and teachers' needs. Questions regarding the efficiency of in-service training programs, especially NTP were asked. According to 12 trainees who were interviewed, NTP is an efficient program offered, though there are still problems which are worth further consideration and discussion. The main debates are focusing on the length of the program, the content of the program and the attendees of the program.

8.7.1 "Long program is better than short one."

Owing to the financial problem, short-term programs are usually offered for saving money and time. However, it seems they do not have better effects as expected. "I joined one before. It was very short, just few days. I sat there in a daze. I didn't remember a thing."① As TS2 said, teachers usually forget what they were trained. TS4 agreed that long-term training is more systematic and works better than the short-term ones.

> I joined other trainings before, but they were short-term and didn't have any effects. Though some foreign teachers came to train us for a week, I still felt inefficient. This time (NTP) was three month. It is much longer than others… All the courses were arranged systematically. I can improve my knowledge profoundly.②

However, in answering whether NTP can help improve teachers' English, PT2

---

① TS2-M1F. (2012, 12, 28). An interview with TS2-M1F. (R. Li, the interviewer & W. Zhong, the translator)
② TS4-M2M. (2012, 12, 30). An interview with TS4-M2M. (R. Li, the interviewer & W. Zhong, the translator)

replied confirmatively, "I don't think the program really does something in this aspect." He explained as the following,

> You know, because it is only a three month program. If there is anything this program can do it is to help to make some changes to those teachers' ideas. To make them realize that there is still a long way to go in terms of language proficiency.[①]

For PT2, compared with four-year degree programs, three-month training is still a short program. However, he stated the significance of changing teachers' ideas or beliefs on English teaching, and believed those ideas would be the stimuli to motivate teachers to change their deeds because action is the only proof of the effectiveness of in-service training, just as he said, "Only if they have this awareness and motivation, even after the program, they want to and they can keep doing that, it would be effective."[②]

PD is more optimistic about responding to the effectiveness of NTP through the comparison with short-term programs.

> I think NTP we are doing is a very good project or model for in-service teacher training, because a short-term program has many problems. Short-term ones usually just touch each point (not study it in a deeper and thorough way). As for the topic training[③], such as teaching reading for this time and teaching speaking next time, it is not offered systematically and sustainably. Our program can include every aspect of training. Trainees will receive as much information as they need in three-month time… They can learn new knowledge in a very relaxed and comfortable way (not like the short-term stuffing the training within one day). Also, they can meet other

---

① PT1. (2012, 8, 14). An interview with PT1. (W. Zhong, the interviewer)
② PT1. (2012, 8, 14). An interview with PT1. (W. Zhong, the interviewer)
③ Topic training is mostly used these years as an effective means for in-service training. Each time the program emphasizes on one aspect of the key skills, such as student-centered teaching methods, and learners have to learn the theoretical background of that skill and some practical way of conducting that skill. Usually, topic training takes one or two days for the maximum. However, most teachers still think time is limited.

teachers from all around the province, which is very helpful to broaden their minds.[①]

8.7.2 "Some techniques are impractical for us."

As stated previously, PT2 believed it is quite necessary to help update those trainees' ideas in teaching, and the thing, however, as to whether they would implement what they have learnt remains questionable. Awareness seems not the only stimuli for triggering actions, and social context also contributes to teachers' hesitance. Though courses in NTP were more systematically arranged, interviewees pointed out some contents or techniques taught are impractical, which prevented them from making changes.

> It's my first time to take a three-month program. This time my strongest impression was I observed many classes taught by some of the best middle school teachers in Yunnan. I was impressed by their ways of teaching and handling the textbook, the strategies of motivating students and their abilities of dealing with group works. They are much more capable than me. However, we are in different context. They used different kinds of materials for teaching, but we can't get access to that. They used multimedia in the classroom to attract students, but we only have cassettes and the tape recorder is so old that the electrician didn't want to fix it. They use whiteboard but we are still using blackboard and chalks. Some of the teachers were sent to learn new technology but we don't have the hardware to run those technology. You learnt the skills to kill the dragon, but we don't have the dragon to kill.[②]

TS3 vividly portrayed the awkward situation of some in-service training programs that some suggestions offered in the training are not suitable for their working context, just as TS4 stated.

---

① PT1. (2012, 8, 14). An interview with PT1. (W. Zhong, the interviewer)
② TS3-H2M. (2012, 12, 30). An interview with TS3-H2M. (R. Li, the interviewer & W. Zhong, the translator)

Chapter 8 Education Participation Motivation of Secondary School English Teachers in Multilingual Areas

> We have to update the theory, like the teaching procedures, to fit our situation. They recommend us to teach English in English, but it's hard for our students. We can just use as much as possible.①

TS11 (referring to Appendix 9) mentioned that if teacher trainers' working environment were similar to the trainees', their suggestions would be easier to conduct.

> I think we also need some detailed guidance. Theories are not practical. It is necessary that someone gave us practical methods or suggestions. I think that would be better. For example, some experts only provide suggestions based on situations in the big cities. I think that is not practical. Some (experts) would relate to the situations in rural areas, like Miss Zhao. She is from rural areas, so what she taught us is easy to conduct, but for the teacher trainer from Yunnan University Secondary School (one of the top 10 middle schools in Yunnan), her suggestions are hard (for us). After all, students' qualities are different, and our own teaching abilities are weak. It would be more challenging (for us).②

To some extent, trainees are critical about what they have learnt and what they can do. The difference between TS4 and TS3 is that TS4 seeks for possibilities of change, but TS3 is less willing to make adjustment, in that they have different beliefs on teaching profession (referring to Section 5.5). As mentioned, TS3 has taught for 20 years and he didn't want to be a teacher for the low salary. The more he devoted, the worse he would feel. On the contrary, TS4 is a student-centered believer who enjoys teaching a lot; moreover, he acknowledges students' motivation for English learning and is willing to try all means to change the situation.

> Contents like IPA, pronunciation, cross-cultural knowledge are helpful for me. I realized the importance of pronunciation and I planned to teach IPA at the beginning. Once they know the way of pronunciation, it will be easier

---

① TS4-M2M. (2012, 12, 30). An interview with TS4-M2M. (R. Li, the interviewer & W. Zhong, the translator)
② TS11-H5F. (2013, 11, 16). An interview with TS11-H5F. (W. Zhong, the interviewer & W. Zhong, the translator)

for me to teach new words to them. I will teach the phonics to build up confidence for my students. I will also integrate cross-cultural knowledge into the text to stimulate their interests.①

Besides teachers' belief, different learning style is another reason to determine their preference for in-service training, such as TS1, "I enjoy watching open class② and hate the theories"③. In TS1's case, open class will benefit her more than lectures, because "open class can show me exactly how they are teaching and it shows that is useful"④. TS6 illustrated that "Though lectures were useful, I prefer open class…I think some of the activities are practical for me, like a teacher suggesting several strategies for remembering the words as a warming-up. However, in another school, the teacher didn't spend time on vocabulary teaching, that is helpless for me"⑤. Opposite to TS1 and TS6, TS7 (referring to Appendix 9) uttered her preference about lectures. "I enjoy having lectures. No matter what the content is, a lecture would offer useful knowledge to us. However, if the students from open classes are at a different language level from my students, their demonstration would be of limited help to me."⑥

To conclude, teachers' assuming that some activities in the training programme

---

① TS4-M2M. (2012, 12, 30). An interview with TS4-M2M. (R. Li, the interviewer & W. Zhong, the translator)

② Open class is a way usually used in China for teacher professionalization. One teaches the class in front of many others as a demonstration of the teaching model. Group of observers or experts will discuss the class right after their observation. The class is usually given in an auditorium and experts will comment on the teaching so that all the audiences will learn together. In some schools, open class is a daily routine that all teachers should present at least once a semester.

③ TS1-H1F. (2012, 12, 28). An interview with TS1-H1F. (R. Li, the interviewer & W. Zhong, the translator)

④ TS1-H1F. (2012, 12, 28). An interview with TS1-H1F. (R. Li, the interviewer & W. Zhong, the translator)

⑤ TS6-M4F. (2013, 11, 8). An interview with TS6-M4F. (W. Zhong, the interviewer & W. Zhong, the translator)

⑥ TS7-H3F. (2013, 11, 16). An interview with TS7-H3F. (W. Zhong, the interviewer & W. Zhong, the translator)

Chapter 8   Education Participation Motivation of Secondary School English Teachers in Multilingual Areas

are impractical is mostly due to diverse teaching contexts, including students' language level and school administrative situations.

8.7.3 "Government should send young teachers to learn more, not just experienced teachers."

Among the twelve trainees in the interview, TS3 is the eldest and most experienced one. Different from others, he is also the only one pointing out the problem of the eligibility of in-service training programs.

> Such programs shouldn't only offer to experienced teachers, but also young teachers. For a teacher, five years can make his way of teaching fixed if he doesn't learn by himself… He will gradually become rigid and fossilized.①

The fossilization phenomenon can be comprehended through the golden doctrine of English learning that "Practice makes perfect". Once one stops practice, one may forget what has already been mastered. Who should come to the in-service training programs? This question is hard to answer because everyone needs training, and each teacher has the equal right. However, the problem is the current resources cannot satisfy the need of every teacher, thus the problem of eligibility comes out.

The large population has been a historical problem for the Chinese Government; hence training the "backbone teachers", the teachers who are academically better than others, is the usual solution. These backbone teachers, so called "seed teachers" are viewed as seeds that are assumed to benefit and contribute more from and after the training. In this way, government can save money because training one teacher can spread the effects to a whole area (Yuan, 2005). However, not each backbone teacher can perform as expected. Some teachers didn't learn well, not to mention teaching others; some learnt well, but couldn't teach others; and some are reluctant to teach others. Most of the teachers still have to learn by themselves with little help or

---

① TS3-H2M. (2012, 12, 30). An interview with TS3-H2M. (R. Li, the interviewer & W. Zhong, the translator)

guidance. Another consequent problem of the "backbone teacher" is that some training is highly competitive, and for others no one wants to attend. Moreover, considering the pressure of the entrance examination, school leaders have other considerations. In one teacher training program I participated in Yongde, an experienced teacher claimed his dilemma in giving an open class.

> Open class can make teachers learn most, and it is also a good way to present ourselves. If you teach well, you get more chances to work in a better school; but if you don't teach well, you may lose your job after this year's contract. I am the best English teacher in my school. My principal doesn't want me to give an open class. He is afraid others will learn from us and we cannot get No. 1, and he is also afraid other schools will offer me a better position. Anyway, he spent too much time and money on cultivating me. (cf. Zhong, 2010: 197)

Hence, in some cases, teachers who attended training are those who had little pedagogic knowledge in language teaching or didn't perform well in the teaching practice.

Chapter 9 Teachers' Professional Development Needs

I set out on this research in order to explore the needs of professional development for English teachers in ethnic minority areas of Yunnan. The research was motivated by my concerns about the efficiency of teacher in-service training programs, NTP in particular (referring to Section 1.1), that I participated in for the past few years, and my personal experience as an English learner as well as an teacher from that particular area. In order to develop the research, questionnaire data were collected from trainees who participated in NTP from one teachers' university in Yunnan in 2012 and 2013, and 12 trainees from the related districts, 2 teacher trainers and 1 program director working in the NTP during the same period were interviewed. In this chapter, the book synthesizes the results from both primary sources of data previously presented from Chapter 6 to Chapter 8, then discusses the implications of the major findings, and answers the one fundamental research question, including implications and further potential areas of the research, as well as making recommendations with regard to the in-service training of English teachers from ethnic minority areas in Yunnan Province.

I did not know at the very beginning of the research what professional development needs of English teachers from ethnic minority areas would be exactly like. Since I myself, as one of the ethnic minority people, was born and grew up in an urban city, and according to social cognitive psychology and constructivist learning theory (referring to Chapters 3, 4 and 5), I thought that teachers' language learning attitudes, teacher efficacy, and their demographic features would influence their motivation in teacher training. NTP is the outcome of central government's original purpose of updating teacher professionalism according to MOE and MOF (2010). It aimed to "develop high quality teacher training resources, innovate teacher training modes and methods, for the sake of carrying a nationwide primary and secondary teacher training into a new stage". Nevertheless, things do not always appear as expected. Through my investigation, I found that not all of the existing teacher professional development theories and the relevant areas of teacher efficacy, as well as statements about language learning attitudes are universally applicable in particular ethnic minority areas in Yunnan. With regard to 12 research questions (referring to Section 1.5) concerning strength of teachers' English learning attitudes, strength of teacher efficacy, and strength of in-service training motivation for each orientation, and related demographic differences, Chapter 6 to Chapter 8 provide detailed results. Three major findings regarding the relationship between language learning attitudes and training motivation, and the relationship between teacher efficacy and in-service training obtained from my research, are presented in the following section.

9.1 Three Major Findings

This section discusses the three major findings derived from Chapter 6 to Chapter 8. Some of the findings are contradictory to the assumptions set in the literature review; some challenge conventional beliefs; and some others just add to our existing assumptions.

9.1.1 AEL contributes most to the motivation in in-service training

Some studies (referring to Chapter 5) claim that attitude consists of an affective reaction. Attitude to the social value of a target language is a determinate cause for subjects' general desire for learning that language (referring to Section 6.3.4). Baker (1992) even proposed that attitude could be used to expound upon the orientation and predict the persistence of human behavior. In this investigation, AEL contributes most to the motivation in teacher training programs, particularly in three orientations of education participation, namely cognitive interests, communication improvement, and professional advancement (referring to Section 8.4).

The reasons for this might be related to the measurement used for testing teachers' education motivation being modified in relation to some distinctive needs of English teachers, such as four items in communication improvement (Items 1, 3, 11, 17, referring to Table 8.2). In the meantime, the three items (Items 1, 3, 4, referring to Table 6.1) chosen to test language-learning attitudes indicate strong individual affection towards the target language. Moreover, teachers' motivation for cognitive interests, communication improvement, and professional advancement were highly correlated to the general strength of education participation; thus like a chain reaction, direct connection from one to anyone else would affect its influence on others. In addition, this result implies the tendency that increasing individuals' feelings about the target language would probably stimulate them more to participate in the in-service training program.

9.1.2 AES has a considerable effect on the motivation for professional advancement and cognitive interests

Gardner's socio-psychological model (referring to Section 5.3) of second language learning suggested that a positive relationship exists between learners' motivation for learning a language and their interests in the target language community, in other words their AES and AEC. Data indicated that the correlation between subjects' feelings about English speakers and their motivational orientation regarding professional advancement and cognitive interest was insignificant (referring to Table 8.9), though data suggested that subjects had similar weak AES and AEC (referring to Section 6.1).

Possible reasons would be that 3 items used to test AES might in fact demonstrate some requirements of *Shide* (referring to Section 2.2.2), the commanding element of the professional teacher in the Chinese concept. "knowledgeable" "(having) great fortune and high status" "respectable" (Items 6, 7, and 8 respectively, Table 6.1) have been necessary characteristics of a professional teacher characterised by Confucian sages. Although teachers' current financial conditions were not particularly sound, they seem to be longing for the ideal position of intellectuals. Thus, their feelings towards English speakers that are "knowledgeable" "(having) great fortune and high status" "respectable" correlated to their needs in cognitive interests and professional advancement; in other words, in the process of pursuing professional development, their beliefs about professional teachers are unintentionally revealed through their AES.

9.1.3 Instrumental attitudes to English lead to pragmatic needs in teacher training

Studies (referring to Chapter 5) show that in foreign language learning contexts, instrumental motivation would be stronger rather than integrative one due to the exposure of learners to the target language community being very limited. Data suggest that subjects have considerably strong attitudes to the social value and particular use of English, which are instrumental-oriented attitudes in nature (referring to Section 5.3). Moreover, their attitudes to the social value of English have significant negative correlation to the social contact orientation of training motivation (γ_s=–0.180, p<0.05, referring to Section 8.4), which implies that the stronger instrumental attitudes to English they hold, the weaker their desire to participate in the training for interpersonal connections is. In addition, similar to their attitudes to the social value of English, AEC presents negative correlation between social contact and social stimulation orientations of in-service training as well (referring to Table 8.9).

The reasons would be, firstly, the training was organized in a Chinese context, thus interpersonal connection would merely be with Chinese people rather than English speakers. In this circumstance, the attitudes to social value of English had little connection to their desire for communicating with Chinese people. For the same reason, their AEC presents a similar tendency to their motivation in interpersonal connections through in-service training.

On the basis of interview data, in fact, my investigation shows that teachers' instrumental-oriented attitudes to English have considerable positive correlation to the practical needs in teachers' training (referring to Section 6.4.1, 6.4.2, 7.3.1 and 8.7.2). They consider English is a "cultural carrier" that enables them to "know people from other culture" "pay more attention to cultural development" and English could be a "medium" used to approach other knowledge (referring to Section 6.4.1). Moreover, interviewees even stated three functions of the social value of English, namely, increasing knowledge, expanding one's vision, and adapting to society (referring to Section 6.4.2). Influenced by this belief, they tried various ways like "using games" "reducing homework" "watching movies" to solve their difficulties in motivating students to learn English in a multilingual context in which Han culture is the mainstream (referring to Section 7.3.1). Consequently, the courses provided in NTP couldn't satisfy their needs in that the suggestions given by experts are not suitable for their teaching context. It seems English teachers from ethnic minority regions focused more on their working context; hence, whatever theories were discussed in a lecture, if that were formulated on the basis of urban cities, they would be considered useless. Even for the open class, the method most trainees favor, some also pointed out the adaptability of "their methods" to "our students" (referring to Section 6.4.2).

One of my research questions is about teacher efficacy. Generally speaking, data show that subjects have strong teacher efficacy (referring to Section 7.1). However, this result does not concur with the PD's comments.

> "Teachers have very low teacher efficacy. They always think about whether their works are meaningful and valuable. They attribute (the low efficacy) to different reasons. Most complained about the income and working environment."[①]

The reason for discrepancy between my data and PD's words is probably that PD offered this comment on the basis of assumptions she received from literature and her experience rather than empirical data.

In addition, in the interview, PD explained that curriculum development was based on her ways of needs analysis, which stated as follows.

> "I have done researches on English pedagogy, so before developing the curriculum, I know I had to do the need analysis first. Firstly, I would enter the middle school to interview with the teachers or do some questionnaire analysis. I also reviewed other literature on post-training reflections. These were the first resource of my needs analysis. The second resource was from the questionnaire I distributed after the trainees arrived. Based on these, I

---

① PD. (2014, 6, 7). An interview with PD. (W. Zhong, the interviewer & W. Zhong, the translator)

could understand what teachers' needs are. Then, according to those needs I separate the courses into several modules. However, there is a national curriculum guideline from the educational administration. Our courses should follow the requirements, like the guideline mentions the training courses should include teachers' moral education (in Chinese *Shide*), teaching beliefs and something relating to teaching practice like students' differences. I develop the whole curriculum based on all these requirements, teachers' needs and my own understandings." ①

It seems that the curriculum development process for NTP was more complicated than imagined. Although PD did the needs analysis on the basis of literature and questionnaire, a national curriculum guideline in which specific requirements, such as teachers' moral education, was offered to make sure the curriculum should follow the guideline. In fact, besides the contents of training, the ways of training, including the timing arrangement, were also clearly stated in the guideline (MOE & MOF, 2010). Moreover, PD had to hand in a training proposal at least three months before the training actually started. In the proposal she was required to provide all courses' names, which meant the results from needs analysis she conducted after the trainees arrived could not be used for the same group of trainees, but would be useful in the next year with different groups of trainees. Usually, the needs analysis on trainees who took the training in 2010 would be beneficial to trainees who came in 2011. However, the national guideline might change because NTP was a pilot program at the beginning and the central government hoped local universities and secondary schools could find out their ways to help teacher development. Thus, new requirements might appear each year. "In 2010 and 2011, the guideline didn't mention about the exact teaching hours requirement, but from 2012, it included that." ② As PD mentioned, in 2014, when I, as the new program director, was writing the training proposal for a new round NTP starting from September of 2014, the guideline clearly stated the general time and curriculum arrangements for each month. As a current program director, my task was only writing a detailed executive plan based on the guideline. I have to admit, there is

---

① PD. (2014, 6, 7). An interview with PD. (W. Zhong, the interviewer & W. Zhong, the translator)
② PD. (2014, 6, 7). An interview with PD. (W. Zhong, the interviewer & W. Zhong, the translator)

little room for me to change the course contents; but I think that making an effective plan as I wished is not a mission impossible. To some extent, this research conducted from 2010 to 2014 offered insight into understanding teachers' needs. As far as I am concerned, for English teachers working in ethnic minority areas, four specific needs are addressed to be satisfied through in-service training.

9.2 Need One: Specific Language Support for Teachers Who Cannot Speak Ethnic Minority Languages

Many research studies (Cummins, 1977; Ellis, 1994; Lin, 1997) have assumed that the ethnic minority students would welcome the use of their mother tongue(s) to teach them a third language, instead of L2. It was also my assumption that ethnic minority languages would be more beneficial for English teachers, because if they could teach English by students' L1 (ethnic minority languages) not their L2 (Chinese or Mandarin), students might learn English better and teachers would have higher teacher efficacy. However, data results (referring to Section 6.1.1 and Section 6.2.1) indicate that, in general, subjects have positive attitudes to English learning but negative attitudes to ethnic minority language learning. It seems applying L1 to L3 instruction is unwelcome, which is in accordance with Hu's (2007a) research findings.

Interviewees explained the reasons from two aspects: firstly, the policy doesn't allow using ethnic minority languages as a medium of instruction in middle school (referring to Section 7.4.2); secondly, Chinese is more convenient than ethnic minority languages in multilingual districts (referring to Section 7.4.1). Hu's (2007a) study provides another explanation that students in China have to pass all kinds of examinations given in standard Chinese, which requires students to reach a high level of Chinese knowledge. Another possible reason would be that students who speak ethnic minority languages are the minority in one classroom. This reflects the data of teachers, where among 186 subjects, only 19 can speak ethnic minority languages (referring to Appendix 9).

Nevertheless, if the teachers are unwilling to learn ethnic minority languages, their help provided for the students would be limited and at the same time teachers would naturally feel helpless confronting those students (referring to Section 7.4). Researchers

(Debi, 1988; Swan et al., 1990) believe that using L1 in teaching and encouraging the minority students to learn their L1 will contribute to the popularization of basic education and the quality of minority education and developing the minority culture because learning occurs if the teacher talks about unknown phenomena in a familiar language (cf. Hu G. W., 2007b). I'm not suggesting that these teachers should be willing to learn ethnic minority languages, and I'm fully in agreement if they are not. However, it is only that these teachers are working in multilingual areas and their students are coming from various ethnic minority groups. Assuming in some districts with lots of immigrants whose mother tongue is not English, it would be natural for teachers to prefer teaching in English to in other languages, and it is also necessary for government to provide language support to those students in the condition that they are required to learn another foreign language. Imagining a Japanese child and a Chinese child learning French in the same classroom in the US, both of them have to learn English well first. Hence, in ethnic minority areas, English teachers who cannot understand ethnic minority languages and ethnic minority students whose mother tongue is not Chinese need special language support. Bilingual teacher's training, for example, might be a good solution to solve the language barrier problem.

However, a valuable issue which needs to be taken into consideration when providing bilingual training is the "proximity principle" (Yuan et al., 2013), which signifies that the linguistic origin of English and the ethnic minority languages should be closer. TS6 claimed that if English were taught in Jingpo language, it would be easier for the similarities between these two languages. "We use English expressions for the twelve months because in our language (Jingpo) we don't have (words for months). It is just that the pronunciation is slightly different."[①] In this case, Jingpo students might benefit more through L1 to L3 than other students.

9.3　Need Two: English Content Knowledge Training

For English and non-English teachers, regarding teacher efficacy, two results

---

① TS6-M4F. (2013, 11, 8). An interview with TS6-M4F. (W. Zhong, the interviewer & W. Zhong, the translator)

(referring to Section 7.1, 7.2.3 and Table 7.2) are worth discussing. Firstly, English teachers have slightly weaker teacher efficacy than non-English teachers (referring to Section 7.1). Secondly, English teachers tend more to believe in the fact that the possibility of increasing their own effort would change students' achievement; however, they do not think their capability improvement can change through time (referring to Section 7.2.3). Another way to understand this is that, in contrast to non-English teachers, for English teachers, personal efforts account more for their professional developments in helping their students than their own teaching experiences. These results are in accordance with my estimation that English teaching is much harder in rural areas than other subjects, if not, teachers would reveal similar teacher efficacy strength. In other words, English teachers think they have to make continuous efforts in learning English as a means to help students. Not like non-English teachers who assume the experience they have got in teaching is more important to help their students.

As mentioned many times, some of these English teachers do not major in English. Among the twelve interviewees in the research, two (TS4 and TS8) are not English majors. This shortcoming on the one hand makes them feel uneasy to teach English, on the other hand it encourages them to make consistent efforts in learning English; otherwise they cannot help the students. As for those teachers who are English majors, owing to different reasons like inefficient pre-service training[①], pronunciation problem caused by mother tongue[②③④], and not enough chances to use English[⑤⑥], they

---

[①] TS5-M3F. (2013, 11, 8). An interview with TS5-M3F. (W. Zhong, the interviewer & W. Zhong, the translator)

[②] TS2-M1F. (2012, 12, 28). An interview with TS2-M1F. (R. Li, the interviewer & W. Zhong, the translator)

[③] TS6-M4F. (2013, 11, 8). An interview with TS6-M4F. (W. Zhong, the interviewer & W. Zhong, the translator)

[④] TS10-M6F. (2013, 11, 16). An interview with TS10-M6F. (W. Zhong, the translator)

[⑤] TS5-M3F. (2013, 11, 8). An interview with TS5-M3F. (W. Zhong, the interviewer & W. Zhong, the translator)

[⑥] TS7-H3F. (2013, 11, 16). An interview with TS7-H3F. (W. Zhong, the interviewer & W. Zhong, the translator)

still consider it is really necessary for them to improve their basic English skills, listening, speaking, reading and writing, which is also revealed by their strong desire in the communication improvement (referring to Section 7.1).

9.4 Need Three: Specific PCK Knowledge Suitable to Ethnic Minority Context

Schulman's (1987) conception of the knowledge base for teaching has focused specifically on 'pedagogical content knowledge' (PCK), or teachers' ability to present subject matter in ways that students can understand and appreciate (referring to section 2.1.4). Trainees argued that teaching methods suggested by the experts are not suitable for them because they are from rural areas and their working environment (including students' abilities, teachers' educational background, school administration, parents' guidance and local educational policy) are totally different to that of urban areas; nevertheless, most of the experts giving lectures were using examples from urban schools, which most trainees think unsuitable for them (referring to Section 5.7.2).

Constructivist educators (Piaget, 1955; Vygotsky, 1986; Bruning et al., 2011) believe that learning happened in certain social and cultural background, which emphasizes the importance of students' learning experience (referring to Section 2.2). If students can't link anything they learn from the textbook or in the classroom to their daily life, reciting the vocabulary and sentence patterns will become the only way for them to remember "dead knowledge" (knowledge that is not personalized or understood by learners). Gong Yafu (2011), one of the well-known English educators and English textbook writers in China, recalled his memory of observing the English class in one secondary school in a rural county of Yunnan. He said,

> When we went to Yunnan to get feedbacks of using our textbooks, we observed one class. It was about discussing the food. The students had to use "I ate or I had" to describe the food they ate. Each student could only say "I ate potato". I was curious that frankly there were many new words like "bread", "pizza", and "cake", but students couldn't use them. I raised my query to the teacher after class and he replied that "(w)e only have potato

Chapter 9 Teachers' Professional Development Needs

here, and students eat them every day. They never saw bread, pizza, and cake before, and some of them might have no chance to see those in their whole life. The New Curriculum Standard requires that we should encourage students to use English relating to their daily life, and this is their daily life. Of course, they also eat other things but those words are not listed in the textbook, and we don't know how to say those in a correct way…" Then, I realized we should provide more help to the teachers in rural areas, such as providing more words close to their lives. (Gong, 2011)

Professor Gong frankly pointed out that they had ignored the actual needs of English teachers from rural areas when they wrote the textbook. However, from the teacher's speech Gong quoted, we can also see that some teachers lack the ability to adapt the material from the textbook to fit the circumstances of their students. This is also a common phenomenon in rural areas.

In China, owing to the national entrance examination, the central government suggests the national standard like the New Curriculum Standard; thus all schools have to use the same textbooks as a means of equality. For English, there are two sets of textbooks recommended by the MOE. However, these two are all designed for urban students who start learning English from primary schools. Although government encourages local schools to design books which are suitable for their students, few schools choose to do so. Firstly, local educational bureaus couldn't find experts helping them to design the textbooks; secondly, the local government doesn't have the special budget for this; thirdly, government leaders are afraid this action may result in low enrolment rate to college in their county; fourthly, new textbook means new training of the teachers, and that will cost money and time, which both administrators and teachers are unwilling to afford. All in all, educational reform takes risks and no one is capable of shouldering the bad consequence. Finally, many reasons lead to the current situation that teachers have little freedom in choosing the best and most suitable textbooks for their students, not to mention the syllabus. Consequently, they are forced to follow a higher standard which is actually not designed for their working environment. Thus, if they can't change the textbooks, or the syllabus, they have to seek solutions from effective teaching methods, because they and their students are facing the same examinations.

Besides effective teaching methods that can improve students' examination scores, motivating students to learn English is one of English teachers' essential needs. English teachers feel frustrated about motivating students (referring to Section 5.2.1), which actually links back to their own attitudes and to learning English. Among the five dimensions of ELA (AEC, AES, AEL, attitudes to social value of English, and attitudes to particular use of English), data show that in general, most participants have negative AEC but positive attitudes to the other four dimensions (referring to Table 6.4). Moreover, more participants have positive attitudes to SVE and PUE (referring to Table 6.4). The results show that teachers' attitudes to English are more for instrumental orientation (referring to Section 6.1.2), which suggests they emphasize more on the instrumental function of English. Hence, they consider English is useful in the examination to further studies (referring to Section 5.6.1), and it might be helpful to find a good job (referring to Section 5.6.2), but they see little function of English in daily life and they believe "most of the students will have little chances to meet the foreigners in their whole life"[①]. This attitude to English is socially constructed and common in areas in which English is taught as a foreign language instead of second language (Gardner, 1985; Dörnyei, 1990; Yuan, 2007). This attitude to English is also reflected in teachers' needs in the in-service training programs.

> They care more on methods which help them improve students' scores. If you don't link this to their training, they consider it (the training) not useful.[②]

Thus, improving students' scores is English teachers' ultimate goal in the training, but methods that help motivating students to learn English is the important key to speed up that goal. "Ways to motivate students to learn English", for example, might be a good topic in teacher training program.

---

① TS11-H5F. (2013, 11, 16). An interview with TS11-H5F. (W. Zhong, the interviewer & W. Zhong, the translator)

② PD. (2014, 6, 7). An interview with PD. (W. Zhong, the interviewer & W. Zhong, the translator)

9.5 Need Four: A Lifelong Support System

Trainees argued about the issue regarding the length of the training (referring to 5.6.1). NTP provides a three-month training that is actually the longest in-service training program in contemporary China. However, most of the interviewees mentioned that though they thought this three-month program was better than other training programs, it was still hard for them to make some changes in their teaching after they returned to work[1][2][3][4][5][6]. Studies of memory performance during the act of learning, usually referred to as working memory, indicate there are three basic stages: sensory memory, short-term memory and long-term memory (Healy & McNamara, 1996; Bruning, Schraw & Norby, 2011). In Healy and McNamara's (1996) modal model, sensory memory is the initial memory component that perceives, recognizes, and assigns meaning to the incoming stimuli. Incoming stimuli are first perceived in visual or auditory form, then matched to a recognizable pattern, and then assigned a meaning to be stored as short-term memory. However, short-term memory needs several information processing strategies like encoding and retrieval processes to become long-term memory, the permanently stored information. Hence, short-term training can only provide information stored as short-term memory, and trainees need more activities to elaborate and enhance the storage of information. Even if training makes the information stored as long-term memory, it still might be forgotten due to lack of continuous stimuli.

---

[1] TS2-M1F. (2012, 12, 28). An interview with TS2-M1F. (R. Li, the interviewer & W. Zhong, the translator)

[2] TS5-M3F. (2013, 11, 8). An interview with TS5-M3F. (W. Zhong, the interviewer & W. Zhong, the translator)

[3] TS7-H3F. (2013, 11, 16). An interview with TS7-H3F. (W. Zhong, the interviewer & W. Zhong, the translator)

[4] TS9-M5F. (2013, 11, 16). An interview with TS9-M5F. (W. Zhong, the interviewer & W. Zhong, the translator)

[5] TS10-M6F. (2013, 11, 16). An interview with TS10-M6F. (W. Zhong, the translator)

[6] TS11-H5F. (2013, 11, 16). An interview with TS11-H5F. (W. Zhong, the interviewer & W. Zhong, the translator)

A better or more effective model should include the following-up support. According to my knowledge, teachers' change can't be successful only through three-month training. After they went back, at the beginning they would meet many difficulties and that is the moment they need guidance and help from experts most. Although the MOE also asks for this now, it is almost impossible if you think about the number of the trainees. If we trained 100 teachers, say one expert will follow up with 2 of them, then we need 50 experts. How can we have so many experts to do this beyond their daily routines? However, I still think this is the most efficient way. Only after cooperating with those teachers side by side to make sure certain kind of teaching method is conducted in a stable and efficient way, is the training actually finished.[①]

As PD suggested, the follow-up support for the teachers is strongly recommended, especially for those who work in rural areas and suffer lack of resources. A lifelong support system regarding their professional development might be more beneficial for all teachers.

9.6 Implications of In-Service Training for Teachers from Ethnic Minority Areas

Teacher training in rural areas has been consistently changing in recent years. Various programs have tried diverse methods to help teachers in secondary schools, but the efficiency of those programs is not always sound. "High investment but low outcomes" "low coverage rate" "not sufficient contents" are usually argued as the shortcomings of in-service teacher training (Yang & Li, 2010; Zhong, 2008, 2010). The two conflicts between "teaching" and "learning", and "learning" and "using" are the major characteristics of less-efficient English teacher training in Yunnan (Zhong, 2008). According to data from this research, the current NTP provides a new model of teacher training and most people consider it is satisfactory, but there are still many

---

① PD. (2014, 6, 7). An interview with PD. (W. Zhong, the interviewer & W. Zhong, the translator)

possibilities to make in-service English teacher training more efficient.

According to social constructivism and cognitive learning theories, learning is socially constructed. Moreover, teacher professionalism is a lifelong process that is continuously changing because the requirements for teachers differ in various eras and also the learning styles are reforming with the development of technology (Hargreaves & Goodson, 1996; M. Tichenor & J. Tichenor, 2005). In today's society, when e-learning and mobile learning become new ways of education, teachers are required to grasp more skills. Hence, as far as I am concerned, there should not be a fixed model for teacher training. Also, seeking out a good model is not teacher trainers' main concern. I think, at least, the future teacher training projects could consider the following aspects.

9.6.1 Creating a PCD system

In teacher training projects, in-service teachers are not only the trainees or learners who need to be educated, but also experienced teacher educators because of their sufficient experiences. At the beginning of Chapter 2, the book quoted a Confucius saying that "Even when walking in a party of no more than three I can always be certain of learning from those I am with". In fact, peer education not only happens between learners but also among teachers. As trainees, in-service teachers' participation in the course development process will make the training focus more on their urgent needs and stick to their problems, which will consequently make the training more efficient. Tayler (2006) suggests the PCD includes five circulated stages—need analysis, syllabus designing, curriculum developing, implementing new curriculum, and developing courses evaluation system. A systematic PCD does not end with evaluation, but evaluation will start a new round of needs analysis. Thus, a public platform in which trainees and trainers can voice their opinions is strongly needed.

9.6.2 Building up an online community including trainees, trainers and experts

With the development of Internet, online resources are cheap and even sometimes free for teachers. In China, teachers can easily download free teaching plans from

Internet and also some websites, like Hujiang English.com, can provide free grammar tests for teachers to use in their daily teaching. However, a major difficulty for teachers in ethnic minority areas is that they cannot simply download, but need to adjust those materials to fit their students. Current online community is the place for teachers to discuss their problems; however, experts' guidance is much more important, especially for novice teachers. As teacher trainers, we should also participate in those online communities to answer trainees' questions. Only in this way can trainees receive sustainable support.

Sometimes, it will be easier for teachers to realize that they are having the same difficulties as others are if they chat online with peers. At the same time, through their discussion, under the guidance from teacher trainers and other experts, they can find out solutions by themselves. Also, being part of an online community will make teachers feel they are not alone, which will encourage them to make more changes in their teaching after the training. Moreover, all the data from discussion in the online community can be used as narrative resources for further study of teacher professional development.

9.6.3 Developing bilingual or trilingual language supporting courses for ethnic minority language speakers

For teachers and learners who speak ethnic minority languages, it is necessary to develop specific courses for them. Teacher trainers or curriculum developers should cooperate more with ethnic minority linguists and ethnic minority culture experts to develop suitable courses. The basic aim for these courses is helping teachers and learners who speak ethnic minority languages to realize the most important phonetic and syntactic similarities and disparities between their mother tongue and English. If it is possible, trilingual materials and courses (ethnic minority languages, Chinese and English) could be offered to teachers and learners. If teachers could receive trilingual courses, they would use the trilingual materials to help ethnic minority language speakers to learn English, and also these teachers would know the equivalent phrases in other languages to help their teaching. If learners have some trilingual materials in hand, they could learn new knowledge with the help from both Chinese speakers and other ethnic minority language speakers.

9.6.4 Scaffolding teachers with cultural knowledge in language teaching

The attitudes towards language learning are greatly influenced by learners' attitudes to the target culture (referring to Section 4.1). This is to say cultural knowledge and cultural recognition will affect learners' language learning efficiency. However, two situations always appear in the classroom of ethnic minority areas owing to poor cultural awareness. Sometimes, teachers lack cultural knowledge of English speaking countries. In this case, they may feel challenged to explain certain texts in the book and would easily feel low efficacy in teaching English. Sometimes, teachers are short of knowledge of ethnic minority culture. In this case, they may violate students' cultural taboos without noticing, and thereby lead to students' low motivation for English learning. In either way, teachers' efficiency on language learning will head to a negative trend. Scaffolding teachers with cultural knowledge of English speaking countries and also ethnic minority groups is of great importance.

Bibliography

陈冰冰，陈坚林 (Chen, B. B. & Chen, J. L.). 2008. 大学英语教学改革环境下教师信念研究 (之一)——大学英语教师信念与实际课堂教学情况分析. 外语电化教学, (2): 14-20.

戴胜 (Dai, S.). 2006. 礼记 (第18篇 学记). 国学导航 http://www.guoxue123.com/jinbu/0201/01lj/017.htm [2019-1-19].

邓文英 (Deng, W. Y.). 2004. 我国外语教育规划初探. 成都信息工程大学学报, 19 (3): 469-471.

段洁云 (Duan, J. Y.). 2011. 外国语学院2010年度"国培计划"项目报告. 云南师范大学，昆明.

高文，徐斌艳，吴刚 (Gao et al). 主编. 2008. 建构主义教育研究. 北京: 教育科学出版社.

顾明远 (Gu, M. Y.). 2001. 课程改革的世纪回顾与瞻望. 教育研究, (7): 15-19.

管培俊 (Guan, P. J.). 2005. 积极进取，锐意创新，推动教师教育和教师队伍建设迈上新台阶//教育部师范教育司主编. 加强与改革教师教育，服务基础教育：教师教育文件、经验材料选编. 北京: 高等教育出版社，13-32.

郭家铨 (Guo, J. Q). 2001. 中国英语教育简论. 佛山科学技术学院学报 (社会科学版), 9(2): 50-56.

国家统计局 (NBSC). 2011. 第六次人口普查公告 (第1号). http://www.stats.gov.cn/tjsj/tjgb/rkpcgb/qgrkpcgb/201104/t20110428_30327.html [2019-2-28].

国家统计局 (NBSC). 2012. 云南省2010年第六次人口普查主要数据公报. http://www.stats.gov.cn/tjsj/tjgb/rkpcgb/dfrkpcgb/201202/t20120228_30408.html [2019-2-28].

国务院 (State Council). 2012. 中华人民共和国义务教育法实施细则. http://edu.wenzhou.gov.cn/art/1992/3/12/art_1324580_7501623.html [2019-1-19].

韩愈 (Han, Y.). 师说.

胡文仲 (Hu, W. Z.). 2001. 我国外语教育规划的得与失. 外语教学与研究, 33 (4): 245-251.

蒋宇红(Jiang, Y. H.) . 2011. 课堂互动情景中的教学效能感水平探究：对西南少数民族地区高校英语教师专业发展的启示. 民族教育研究, 22 (3): 86-90.

教育部 (MOE). 1985. 中共中央关于教育体制改革的决定. https://baike.baidu.com/item/中共中央关于教育体制改革的决定/5496886 [2019-1-19].

教育部 (MOE). 1992. 九年义务教育全日制初级中学英语教学大纲(试用修订版). http://old.pep.com.cn/peixun/xkpx/peixun_1_1/kbjd/jiedu/201009/t20100927_915085.htm [2019-1-15].

教育部 (MOE). 2001a. 基础教育课程改革纲要（试行）. http://www.edu.cn/20010926/3002911.shtml [2018-5-15].

教育部 (MOE). 2001b. 教育部关于积极推进小学开设英语课程的指导意见. 教基〔2001〕2号.
教育部 (MOE). 2003. 2002年全国教育事业发展统计公报. http://www.MOE.gov.cn/srcsite/A10/s7058/201007/t20100713_92861.html [2018-5-15].
教育部 (MOE). 2007. 2006年全国教育事业发展统计公报. http://www.MOE.gov.cn/s78/A03/ghs_left/s182/MOE_633/tnull_23240.html [2018-5-15].
教育部 (MOE). 2012. 2011年全国教育事业发展统计公报. http://old.MOE.gov.cn/publicfiles/business/htmlfiles/MOE/MOE_633/201208/141305.html [2018-5-15].
教育部 (MOE). 2013. 2012年全国教育事业发展统计公报. http://www.MOE.gov.cn/srcsite/A03/s180/MOE_633/201308/t20130816_155798.html [2018-5-15].
教育部, 财政部 (MOE & MOF). 2010. 教育部财政部关于实施"中小学教师国家级培训计划"的通知, 教师〔2010〕4号. http://www.MOE.gov.cn/srcsite/A10/s7034/201006/t20100630_146071.html [2018-5-15].
课程教材研究所教育史研究课题组 (Education History Research Project of Curriculum and Textbook Research Institute). 2008. 20世纪中小学课程标准(教学大纲)英语发展概况. 人教网. http://old.pep.com.cn/ce/czyy/tbjxzy/kcbz/kbjd/201009/t20100908_887044.htm [2019-1-15].
李国钧, 王炳照 (Li, G. J. & Wang, B. Z.). 2000. 中国教育制度通史. 济南: 山东教育出版社.
李岚清 (Li, L. Q.). 2005. 为了13亿人的教育. 北京: 外语教学与研究出版社.
李舒文 (Li, S. W.). 2011. 就业专业对不对口, 农村教师兼任多科专业难发展. http://www.jyb.cn/basc/xw/201112/t20111231_472367.html [2018-5-15].
李想, 陈丽平(Li, X. & Chen, L.P.). 2014. 国家不能在家庭教育中缺席. http://www.legaldaily.com.cn/index/content/2014-06/23/content_5614772.htm?node=20908 [2018-5-15].
林晓 (Lin, X.). 2008. 大学公共英语教师教学效能感: 影响因素及应对策略. 江南大学学报(教育科学版), 28 (4): 32-36.
刘道义 (Liu, D. Y.). 2001-02-15. 小学开外语步子要稳妥. 光明日报, 5.
刘晓萍 (Liu, X. P.). 2007. 农村初中英语教师个人教学效能感调查研究. 中小学外语教学(中学篇), (8): 11-15.
刘雅雯 (Liu, Y. W.). 2010. 大学英语教师的教学效能感与课堂提问行为关系研究. 宁波教育学院学报, 10 (2): 62-76.
刘英杰 (Liu, Y. J.). 1993. 中国教育大事典. 杭州: 浙江教育出版社.
鲁子问 (Lu, Z. W.). 2003. 中国外语教育政策的释然分析与应然设想. 山东师范大学外国语学院学报: 基础英语教育, 16 (1): 6-12.
陆道坤 (Lu, D. K.). 2010. 规避"钟摆现象"实现中国式教师教育体制的新发展. 教育理论与实践, (1): 39-42.
吕枫 (Lü, F.). 2006. 小学英语教师的教学效能感及其影响因素. 中小学外语教学(小学篇), (4): 7-12.
马平 (Ma, P.). 2012. "支架理论"框架下英语专业《英语阅读》教学探讨. 外国语文, (3): 131-134.
马田 (Ma, T.). 2011. 新文化时期外国现代教育思想的传入及其影响. 中南大学硕士学位论文.
彭红兵 (Peng, H. B.). 2008. 农村初中英语教师工作效能感调查研究. 南昌高专学报, (6):

100-102.

覃成强 (Qin, C. Q.). 2007. 论英语教师的教学信念与课堂教学实践的关系——一项基于认知调查和课堂观察的研究. 外语教学, 28 (5): 40-44.

群懿，李馨亭 (Qun, Y. & Li, X. T.). 1991. 外语教育发展战略研究. 成都：四川教育出版社.

施春燕 (Shi, C. Y.). 2009. 高职院校英语教师教学效能感的调查与分析. 高等函授学报（哲学社会科学版），23 (9): 14-16.

施惠萍，高亚利 (Shi, H. P. & Gao, Y. L.). 2010. 大学英语机辅语言教学中教师效能感与教师态度的研究. 长春大学学报, 20 (8): 88-92.

四川外国语学院高等教育研究所 (HERC). 1993. 中国外语教育要事录(1949—1989). 北京：外语教学与研究出版社.

滕婷婷，吴本虎 (Teng, T. T. & Wu, B. H.). 2011. 高职英语教师教学效能感调查研究. 职业教育研究, (4): 66-68.

王立科 (Wang, L. K.). 2009. 我国教师教育政策发展三十年回顾与展望. 国家教育行政学院学报, (1): 30-35.

王诗喏 (Wang, S. R). 2009. 高校外语教师个人教学效能感及其教龄特点研究. 赤峰学院学报, (6): 97-98.

王帅峰 (Wang, S. F.). 2012. 教师工资考察. http://theory.people.com.cn/GB/49157/49166/13530319.html [2018-5-15].

杨东东，周亚东，于泽元 (Yang, D. D. et al). 2016. 教师身份认同的历史流变——从先秦至清末. 教育学术月刊, (8): 3-8.

杨红艳 (Yang, H. Y.). 2004. 白族学生英语习得的有关问题与对策. 云南民族大学学报 (哲学社会科学版), (6): 116-118.

叶澜 (Ye, L.). 2001. 教师角色与教师发展新探. 北京：教育科学出版社.

原一川，钟维，吴建西，饶燿平，范庆江 (Yuan, Y. C. et al.). 2013. 三语背景下云南跨境民族外语教育规划. 云南师范大学学报(哲学社会科学版), 45 (6): 18-25.

云南省教育厅 (Educational Bureau of Yunnan Province). 2005. 尊重实践,发展实践：中小学中青年骨干教师培训的追求//教育部师范教育司主编. 加强与改革教师教育，服务基础教育：教师教育文件、经验材料选编. 北京：高等教育出版社.

云南省教育厅（Educational Bureau of Yunnan Province）. 2008. 云南省 2007—2008 学年初教育事业统计公报. 云南教育, 7: 19-21. http://mall.cnki.net/onlineread/Mall/MallIndex?sourceid=10&fName=YNJS200807017*19-21* [2018-5-15].

云南省人民政府 [PGYNP]. 2002. 云南省教育振兴行动计划. http://news.sina.com.cn/c/2002-09-28/1457749001.html [2019-1-15].

云南省统计局 (Statistic Bureau of Yunnan Province). 2011-5-11. 云南省第六次全国人口普查成果来之不易. 云南日报: 4.

张伟江，陈国良(Zhang, W. J. & Chen, G. L.). 2002. 教育服务产业运行研究. 教育发展研究, (5): 5-11.

郑华 (Zheng, H.). 2001. 小学开设英语课若干问题探讨. 教育实践与研究, (11): 39.

Bibliography

中国教育在线（Eol. Cn）. 2001—2013 年全国高校毕业生人数.

钟维 (Zhong, W.). 2008. "以生为本"：终生教育理念下的教师教育——云南省基础教育教师队伍建设的新思考//中共云南省委宣传部，云南省社会科学界联合会，云南师范大学编，解放思想、科学发展：云南省第二届社会科学学术年会云南师范大学专场文集. 昆明：云南大学出版社，129-135.

中央人民政府 (CPGPRC). 2006a. 中华人民共和国义务教育法 (主席令第 52 号). http://www.gov.cn/ziliao/flfg/2006-06/30/content_323302.htm [2018-5-15].

中央人民政府 (CPGPRC). 2006b. 实行"两免一补"政策. http://www.gov.cn/ztzl/fupin/content_396672.htm [2018-5-15].

中央人民政府 (CPGPRC). 2011. 实行"两免一补"政策. http://www.gov.cn/gongbao/content/2011/content_2020905.htm [2018-5-15].

中央人民政府. 1994. 中华人民共和国教师法. http://www.gov.cn/banshi/2005-05/25/content_937.htm [2018-5-15].

朱熹 (Zhu, X.). 2015. 论语集注. 郭万金编校. 北京：商务印书馆.

朱迎春 (Zhu, Y. C.). 2006. 从教育公平原则看中国城乡教育差距. 河北师范大学学报 (教育科学版), (5): 75-79.

邹为诚 (Zou, W. C.). 2010. 中国基础教育阶段外语教师的职前教育研究报告 //中国基础英语教师教育研究. 上海：华东师范大学出版社.

Adamson, B. & Morris, P. 1997. The English curriculum in the People's Republic of China. *Comparative Education Review*, 41: 3-26.

Alderman, M. K. 2004. *Motivation for Achievement: Possibilities for Teaching and Learning (2nd ed.)*. Mahwah: Lawrence Erlbaum Associates.

Armor, D., Conroy-Oseguera, P., Cox, M., et al. 1976. *Analysis of the School Preferred Reading Programs in Selected Los Angeles Minority Schools, REPORT NO. R-2007-LAUSD*. Santa Mónica: Rand Corporation.

Ashton, P. 1984. Teacher efficacy: A motivational paradigm for effective teacher education. *Journal of Teacher Education*, 35 (5): 28-32.

Ashton, P. T. & Webb, R. B. 1986. *Making a Difference: Teachers' Sense of Efficacy and Student Achievement*. New York: Longman.

Au, S. Y. 1988. A critical appraisal of Gardner's social psychological theory of second-language (L2) learning. *Language Learning*, 38: 75-100.

Baggini, J. 2005. What professionalism means for teachers today? *Education Review*, 18 (2): 5-11.

Bai, S. Y. 2002. *An Outline History of China*. Beijing: Foreign Languages Press.

Baker, C. 1992. *Attitudes and Language*. Adelaide: Multilingual Matters Ltd.

Ball, D. 1990. The mathematical understandings that prospective teachers bring to teacher education. *The Elementary School Journal*, 90: 449-466.

Bandura, A. 1986. *Social Foundations of Thought and Action: A Social Cognitive Theory*. Englewood Cliffs: Prentice-Hall.

Bandura, A. 1993. Perceived self-efficacy in cognitive development and functioning. *Educational Psychologist*, 28: 117-148.

Bandura, A. 1997. *Self-efficacy: The Exercise of Control*. New York: Freeman.

Bandura, A. 2006. Guide for Constructing Self-Efficacy Scales. In: Pajares, F. and Urdan, T.S., Eds., Self-Efficacy Beliefs of Adolescents. Greenwich: Age Information Publishing.

Bao, C. Y. 2006. Policies for compulsory education disparity between urban and rural areas in China. *Frontiers of Education in China*, (1): 40-55.

Beed, P. L., Hawkins, E. M. & Roller, C. M. 1991. Moving learners toward independence: The power of scaffolded instruction. *The Reading Teacher*, 44: 648-655.

Benz, C., Bradley, L., Alderman, M., et al. 1992. Personal teaching efficacy: Developmental relationships in education. *Journal of Educational Research*, 85: 274-286.

Blanz, M., Mummendey, A., Rosemark, M., et al. 1998. Responding to negative social identity: A taxonomy of entity management strategies. *European Journal of Social Psychology*, 28(5). https://doi.org/10.1002/(SICI)1099-0992(199809/10)28:5<697::AID-EJSP889>3.0.CO;2-# [2018-5-15].

Boshier, R. 1971. Motivational orientations of adult education participants: A factor analytic exploration of Houle's typology. *Adult Educational Quarterly*, 2: 3-26.

Boshier, R. 1976. Factor analysts at large: A critical review of the motivational orientation literature. *Adult Education*, 27(1): 24-27.

Boshier, R. 1977. Motivational orientations re-visited: Life-space motives and the education participations scale. *Adult Education*, 27(2): 89-115.

Boshier, R. 1991. Psychometric properties of the alternative form of the education participation scale. *Adult Education Quarterly*, 41(3): 150-167.

Boshier, R., Huang, Y. & Song, L. 2006. Market socialism meets the lost generation: Motivational orientations of adult learners in Shanghai. *Adult Education Quarterly*, 56(3): 201-222.

Bruning, R. H., Schraw, G. J. & Norby, M. M. 2011. *Cognitive Psychology and Instruction (5th ed.)*. Boston: Pearson.

Chamot, A. U., O'Malley, J. M., Barnhardt, S. et al. 1999. *The Learning Strategies Handbook*. New York: Longman.

Chang, J. Y. 2006. Globalization and English in Chinese higher education. *World Englishes*, 25(3): 513-525.

Charles, C. M. & Mertler, C. A. 2004. *Introduction to Educational Research*. Beijing: Foreign Language Teaching and Research Press.

Chen, B. B. & Chen, J. L. 2008. On Teachers' Belief in the Context of College English Teaching Reform—An analysis on College English teachers' belief and their practical classroom teaching behavior. *Journal of Liaoning Medical University (Social Science Edition)*, (2): 14-20.

Chester, M. D. & Beaudin, B. Q. 1996. Efficacy beliefs of newly hired teachers in urban school. *American Educational Research Journal*, 33: 233-257.

Clement, R., Dörnyei, Z. & Noels, K. 1994. Motivation, self-confidence, and group cohesion in the foreign language classroom. *Language Learning*, 44: 417-448.

Clement, R. & Kruidenier, B. G. 1983. Orientations in second language acquisition: 1. The effects of ethnicity, milieu, and target language on their emergence language learning. *Language Learning*, 33(3): 273-291.

Cobb, P. & Bowers, J. 1999. Cognitive and situated learning perspectives in theory and practice. *Educational Researcher*, 28: 4-15.

Confucius. 1998. *The Analects*. A. Waley, trans. Beijing: Foreign Language Teaching and Research Press.

Crookes, G. & Schmidt, R. W. 1991. Motivation: Reopening the research agenda. *Language Learning*, 41(4): 469-512.

Cross, K. P. 1981. Adults as Learners: Increasing Participation and Facilitating Learning. *Journal of Higher Education*, 54(5): 587.

Cummins, J. 1977. Cognitive factors associated with the attainment of intermediate levels of bilingual skills. *Modern Language Journal*, 61(1/2): 3-12.

Debi, P. P. 1988. Monolingual myopia and the petals of the Indian lotus: do many languages divide or unite a nation? In T. Skutnabbi-Kangas & J. Cummings (Eds.), *Minority Education: From Shame to Struggle* (pp. 379-389). London: Minority Rights Group.

Dörnyei, Z. 1990. Conceptualizing motivation in foreign language learning. *Language Learning*, 40(1): 45-78.

Dörnyei, Z. 2001. *Teaching and Researching Motivation*. Harlow: Pearson Education Ltd.

Dörnyei, Z. 2005. *The Psychology of the Language Learner: Individual Differences in Second Language Acquisition*. Mahwah: Lawrence Erlbaum Associates.

Dörnyei, Z. & Clément, R. 2001. Motivational characteristics of learning different target languages: Results of a nationwide survey. In Z. Dörnyei & R. Schmidt (Eds.), *Motivation and Second Language Acquisition* (pp. 399-432). Honolulu: University of Hawaii at Manoa, Second Language Teaching and Curriculum Center.

Duan, J. Y. 2011. *Project Report on "National Training Plan" in 2010*. Yunnan Normal University, Kunming.

Ellis, R. 1994. *The Study of Second Language Acquisition*. Oxford: Oxford University Press.

Englund, T. 1996. Are professional teachers a good thing? In I. Goodson & A. Hargreaves (Eds.), *Teachers' Professional Lives* (pp. 75-87). London: Falmer Press.http://career.eol.cn/kuai_xun_4343/20130129/t20130129_898345.shtml [2018-5-15].

Evans, L. 2008. Professionalism, professionality and the development of education professionals. *British Journal of Educational Studies*, 56(1): 20-38.

Feng, A. W. 2009. English in China: Convergence and divergence in policy and practice. *AILA Review*, 22: 85-102.

Feng, A. W. 2011. *English Language Education Across Greater China*. Clevedon: Multilingual

Matter Ltd.

Fosnot, C. T. 2008. *Constructivism: Theory, Perspective and Practice.* New York: Teachers College Press.

Fradd, S. H. & Lee, O. 1998. Development of a knowledge base for ESOL teacher education. *Teaching and Teacher Education*, 14(7): 761-773.

Gagné, A. 2008. Insights on teacher education and reform. (Sina-Canadian Teacher Education International Conference).

Gall, D. M., Borg, R. W. & Gall, P. J. 1996. *Educational Research: An Introduction (3rd ed.).* New York: Longman.

Gao, W., Xu, B. Y. & Wu, G. 2008. *Constructivism in Education.* Beijing: Educational Science Publishing House.

Gardner, R. C. 1985. *Social Psychology and Second Language Learning: The role of Attitudes and Motivation.* London: Edward Arnold.

Gardner, R. C. 2000. Correlation, causation, motivation, and second language acquisition. *Canadian Psychology*, 41: 10-24.

Gardner, R. C. 2005. *Motivation and Attitudes in Second Language: Encyclopedia of Language and Linguistics (2nd ed.).* Oxford: Elsevier.

Gardner, R. C. 2006. The socio-educational model of second language acquisition: A research paradigm. *Eurosla Yearbook*, 6: 237-260.

Gardner, R. C. & Lambert, W. E. 1972. *Attitudes and Motivation in Second Language Learning.* Rowley: Newbury House.

Gardner, R. C., Tremblay, P. F. & Masgoret, A. M. 1997. Towards a full model of second language learning: An empirical investigation. *The Modern Language Journal*, 81: 344-362.

Garst, W. C. & Ried, L. D. 1999. Motivational orientations: Evaluation of the education participation scale in a nontraditional doctor of pharmacy program. *American Journal of Pharmaceutical Education*, 63: 300-304.

Gay, L. R. 1996. *Educational Research: Competencies for Analysis and Applications.* New York: Merrill/Prentice Hall.

Genesee, F., Rogers, P. & Holobow, N. 1983. The social psychology of second language learning: Another point of view. *Language Learning*, 33: 209-224.

Gibson, S. & Dembo, M. 1984. Teacher efficacy: A construct validation. *Journal of Educational Psychology*, 76: 569-582.

Gong, Y. F. 2011. *Talk in TESOL Symposium in China.* Beijing: Beijing Normal University.

Goodson, I. F. 2000. The principled professional. *Prospects*, XXX(2): 181-188.

Grossman, P. L. 1990. *The Making of a Teacher: Teacher Knowledge and Teacher Education.* New York: Teachers College Press.

Guo, J. Q. 2001. A brief study of the English education in China. *Journal of Foshan University (Social Science)*, 9(2): 50-56.

Han, Y. 768 AD-824 AD. On the Teacher. http://so.gushiwen.org/view_71178.aspx [2018-5-15].

Hansen, M. H. 2010. Lessons in Being Chinese: Minority education and ethnic identity in Southwest China. *China Journal*, 21(45): 389-390.

Hargreaves, A. 2000. Four ages of professionalism and professional learning. *Teachers and Teaching: History and Practice*, 6(2): 151-182.

Hargreaves, A. & Goodson, I. F. 1996. Teachers' professional lives: Aspirations and actualities. In I. F. Goodson & A. Hargreaves (Eds.), *Teachers' Professional Lives*. London: Falmer Press.

Hart, S. P. & Marshall, J. D. 1992. The question of teacher professionalism. https://files.eric.ed.gov/fulltext/ED349291.pdf [2018-5-15].

Hashweh, M. Z. 1996. Effects of science teachers' epistemological beliefs in teaching. *Journal of Research in Science Teaching*, 33: 47-63.

Healy, A. F., & McNamara, D. S. (1996). Verbal Learning and memory: Does the modal model still work? *Annual Review of Psychology*, 47, 143-172.

HERC. 1993. *Chronicle of Foreign Language Education in China*. Beijing: Foreign Language Education Press.

Houle, C. O. 1961. *The Inquiring Mind*. Madison: University of Wisconsin Press.

Hoy, W. K. & Woolfolk, A. E. 1990. Socialization of student teachers. *American Educational Research*, 27: 279-300.

Hoyle, E. 2001. Teaching: Prestige, status and esteem. *Educational Management and Administration*, 29(2): 139-152.

Hu, D. Y. 2007. *Trilingual Education of Members from Ethnic Minority Nationalities in Yunnan*. Kunming: Yunnan University Press.

Hu, G. W. 2005. English language education in China: Policies, progress, and problems. *Language Policy*, (4): 5-24.

Hu, G. W. 2007. The misleading academic discourse on Chinese-English bilingual education in China. *Review of Educational Research*, 78(2): 195-231.

Hu, W. Z. 2001. A matter of balance: Reflections on China's foreign language policy in education. *Foreign Language Teaching and Research*, 33(4): 245-251.

Huang, R. X. 1994. A brief review on Huang Yanpei's theory and practice on vocational education. *Development Research*, (7): 26-30.

Huang, S. C. 2008. Assessing motivation and learning strategies using the motivated strategies for learning questionnaire in a foreign language learning context. *Social Behavior and Personality*, 36(4): 529-534.

Ingersoll, R., & Merrill, L. (2012). *Seven Trends: The Transformation of the Teaching Force*. Philadelphia, PA: University of Pennsylvania, Consortium for Policy Research in Education.

Kagan, D. M. 1992. Implications of research on teacher belief. *Educational Psychologist*, 27: 65-90.

Kruidenier, B. & Clement, R. 1986. *The Effect of Context on the Composition and Role of Orientations in Second Language Acquisition*. Quebec: International Center for Research on

Bilingualism.
Kumar, R. 1997. *Research Methodology: A Step-by-Step Guide for Beginners*. Melbourne: Addison Wesley Longman Australia Pty Limited.
Lemon, N. 1973. *Attitudes and Their Measurement*. London: B. T. Batsford Ltd.
Lewin, K. 1947. Frontiers in group dynamics: concept, method, and reality in social science. *Human Relations*, 1(1): 5-42.
Li, G. J. & Wang, B. Z. 2000. *History of Chinese Education System*. Ji'nan: Shandong Education Press.
Li, L. Q. 2005. *Education for 1.3 Billion*. Beijing: Foreign Language Teaching and Research Press.
Lin, J. 1997. Policies and practices of bilingual education for the minority in China. *Journal of Multilingual and Multicultural Development*, 18(3): 193-205.
Liu, Y. J. 1993. *Book of Major Educational Events in China*. Hangzhou: Zhejiang Educational Press.
Lortie, D. 1969. The balance of control and autonomy in elementary teaching. In Etzioni, Amitai, *The Semi-professions and Their Organization: Teachers, Nurses, Social Workers* (pp.1-53). New York: Free Press.
Lortie, D. 1975. *School Teacher: A Social Study*. Chicago: University of Chicago Press.
Lukmani, Y. M. 1972. Motivation to learn and learning proficiency. *Language Learning*, 22: 261-273.
Lundberg, G. A. 1942. *Social Research: A Study in Methods of Gathering Data (2nd ed.)*. New York: Longmans, Green and Co.
Luszczynska, A. & Schwarzer, R. 2005. Social cognitive theory. In M. Conner & P. Norman (Eds.), *Predicting Health Behavior* (pp. 127-169). Buckingham: Open University Press.
Ma, P. 2012. A study of the teaching of extensive reading for English majors from the perspective of scaffolding theory. *Journal of Sichuan International Studies University*, (3): 131-134.
Maslow, A. H. 1954. *Motivation and Personality*. New York: Harper and Row.
Maslow, A. H. 1970. *Motivation and Personality* (3rd ed.). New York: Harper and Row.
McMillan, J. H. 2008. *Educational Research, Fundamentals for the Consumer (5th ed.)*. New York: Pearson.
Melissa, K. 2004. *The Everything New Teacher Book: Increase Your Confidence, Connect with Your Students, and Deal with the Unexpected*. Canada: Adams Media.
Merriam, S. B. & Caffarella. 1999. *Learning in Adulthood: A Comprehensive Guide*. San Francisco: Jossey-Bass Publishers.
Merriam, S. B., R. S. Caffarella, & L. M. Baumgartner. 1999. *Learning in Adulthood: A Comprehensive Guide*. San Francisco: Jossey Bass.
Merriam-Webster. 2014. Professional. http://www.merriam-webster.com/dictionary/professional [2014-7-15].
Miller, H. L. 1967. Participation of adults in education: A force-field analysis. http://eric.ed.gov/ERIC WebPortal/recordDetail?accno=ED011996 [2018-5-15].

Milner, H. R., & Hoy, A. W. 2003. A case study of an African American teacher's self-efficacy, stereotype threat, and persistence. *Teaching & Teacher Education*, 19(2), 263-276.

MOE. 1992. Nine-year Compulsory Education Full-time Junior Secondary English Syllabus (Pilot). http://old.pep.com.cn/peixun/xkpx/peixun_1_1/kbjd/jiedu/201009/t20100927_915085.htm [2018-5-15].

MOE. 2002. 2002 Statistical Bullentin on National Educational Development in 2002 of China. http://222.edu.cn/jiao_yu_fa_zhan_498/20060323_74584.shtml

Moshman, D. 1982. Jean Piaget meets Jerry Falwell: Genetic epistemology and the anti-humanist movement in education. *Genetic Epistemologist*, 10: 10-13.

NBSC. 2011. Sixth national census major data communique (No. 1). http://www.stats.gov.cn/tjgb/rkpcgb/qgrkpcgb/t20110428_402722232.htm [2018-4-20].

NBSPRC. 2012. 6th national census of Yunnan Province in 2010. http://www.stats.gov.cn/tjsj/tjgb/rkpcgb/dfrkpcgb/201202/t20120228_30408.html [2018-5-15].

Newman, D., Griffin, P. & Cole, M. 1989. *The Construction Zone: Working for Cognitive Change in School*. Cambridge: Cambridge University Press.

Noels, K. A. 2001. New orientations in language learning motivation: Towards a model of intrinsic, extrinsic, and integrative orientations and motivation. In Z. Dörnyei & R. Schmidt (Eds.), *Motivation and Second Language Acquisition*. Honolulu: University of Hawai'i at Manoa.

Noels, K. A., Clement, R. & Pelletier, L. G. 1999. Perceptions of teachers' communicative style and students' intrinsic and extrinsic motivation. *The Modern Language Journal*, 83: 23-34.

Nunan, D. 2001. Is language teaching a profession? http://english.cersp.com/jiaoshi/200509/156.html.

O'Connor, A. B. 1979. Reasons nurses participate in continuing education. *Nursing Research*, 28(6): 354-359.

O'Connor, A. 1982. Reasons nurses participate in self-study continuing education. *Nursing Research*, 31: 371-374.

O'Donnel, A. M. 2006. The role of peers and group learning. In A. M. Alexander & P. H. Winne (Eds.), *Handbook of Educational Psychology* (pp. 781-802). Mahwah: Erlbaum.

Oller, J. W., Baca, L. & Vigil, F. 1977. Attitudes and attained proficiency in ESL: A sociolinguistic study of Mexican Americans in the Southwest. *TESOL Quarterly*, 11: 173-183.

Oxford Dictionaries. 2013. Non-parametric. https://en.oxforddictionaries.com/definition/non-parametric [2018-5-15].

Oxford Dictionaries. 2014. Profession. http://www.oxforddictionaries.com/definition/english/profession [2018-5-15].

Packer, M. & Goicoechea, J. 2000. Sociocultural and constructivist theories of learning: Ontology, not just epistemology. *Educational Psychologist*, 35: 227-241.

Pan, L. 2011. English language ideologies in the Chinese foreign language education policies: A world-system perspective. *Language Policy*, (10): 245-263.

Pang, V. O. & Sablan, V. 1998. Teacher efficacy: Do teachers believe they can be successful with

African American students? In M. Dillsworth (Ed.), *Being Responsive to Cultural Differences: How Teachers Learn* (pp. 36-90). San Francisco: Corwin Press.

Piaget, J. 1955. *The Child's Construction of Reality*. London: Routledge and Kegan Paul.

Postilione, G. A. 1992. The implications of modernization for the education of China's national minorities. In R. Hayhoe (Ed.), *Education and Modernization: The Chinese Experience*. Oxford: Pergamon Press Inc.

PT1. (2012-8-14). Interview with PT1. (W. Zhong, Interviewer & W. Zhong, Translator)

PT2. (2012-8-5). Interview with PT2. (W. Zhong, Interviewer & W. Zhong, Translator)

Qin, C. Q. 2007. The relationship between English teachers' beliefs and classroom practices. *Foreign Language Education*, 28(5): 40-44.

Qin, H. & Bao, Q. 2010. *Empirical Research on Constructivist Teaching Strategies: A Case Study of High School English Teaching in Rural Areas of Yunnan*. Kunming: Yunnan University Press.

Ramage, K. 1990. Motivational factors and persistence in foreign language study. *Language Learning*, 40: 189-219.

Ramey-Gassert, L. & Shroyer, M. G. 1992. Enhancing science teaching self-efficacy in preservice elementary teachers. *Journal of Elementary Science Education*, 4(1): 26-34.

Raudenbush, S. W., Rowen, B. & Cheong, Y. F. 1992. Contextual effects on the self-perceived efficacy of high school teachers. *Sociology of Education*, 65: 150-167.

Research Center for Development, Shanghai Education Science Institute. 2002. Analysis on evolution and problem of popularizing compulsory education in China (In Chinese). *Research in Educational Development*, (5): 5-11.

Roberta, K. 1993. Social psychological factors related to the study of Arabic among Israeli high school students. *Studies in Second Language Acquisition*, 15(1): 23.

Rosenholtz, S. J. 1989. *Teachers' Workplace: The Social Organization of Schools*. New York: Longman.

Ross, J. & Gray, P. 2006. Transformational leadership and teacher commitment to organizational values: The mediating effects of collective teacher efficacy. *School Effectiveness and School Improvement: An International Journal of Research, Policy and Practice*, 17(2): 179-199.

Rubie-Davies, C., Flint, A. & McDonald, L. 2012. Teacher beliefs, teacher characteristics, and school contextual factors: What are the relationship? *British Journal of Educational Psychology*, 82(2): 270-288.

Rubin, J. 2001. Language learner self-management. *Journal of Asian Pacific Communication*, 11(1): 25-37.

Schraw, G. & Olafson, L. 2002. Teachers' epistemological world views and educational practices. *Issues in Education*, 8: 99.

Schunk, D. H. 1991. Self-efficacy and academic motivation. *Educational Psychology*, 26: 207-231.

Schwarzer, R. 1992. *Self-efficacy: Thought Control of Action*. Washington, D. C.: Hemisphere.

Schwarzer, R. & Hallum, S. 2008. Perceived teacher self-efficacy as a predictor of job stress and burnout: Mediation analyses. *Applied Psychology: An International Review*, 57: 152-171.

Schwarzer, R. & Jerusalem, M. 1995. Generalized self-efficacy scale. In J. Weinman, S. Wright & M. Johnston (Eds.), *Measures in Health Psychology: A User's Portfolio, Causal and Control Beliefs* (pp. 35-37). Windsor: NFER-NELSON.

Schwarzer, R., Schmitz, G. S. & Daytner, G. T. 1999. Teacher self-efficacy scale. http://userpage.fu-berlin.de/~health/teacher_se.htm [2018-5-15].

Schwarzer, R., Schmitz, G. S. & Tang, C. 2000. Teacher burnout in Hong Kong and Germany: A cross-cultural validation of the Maslach Burnout Inventory. *Anxiety, Stress, and Coping*, 13: 309-326.

Shulman, L. S. 1986. Those who understand: Knowledge growth in teaching. *Educational Researcher*, 15: 4-14.

Shulman, L. S. 1987. Knowledge and teaching: Foundations of the new reform. *Harvard Educational Review*, 57: 1-22.

Smylie, M. A. 1995. Teacher learning in the workplace: Implications for school reform. In T. R. Guskey & M. Huberman (Eds.), *Professional Development in Education: New Paradigms and Practices* (pp. 92-113). New York: Teachers College Press.

Soodak, L. & Podell, D. 1998. Teacher efficacy and the vulnerability of the difficult-to-teach students. In J. Brophy (Ed.), *Expectations in the Classroom* (pp. 75-109). Greenwich: JAI Press.

Spring, J. 1985. *American Education: An Introduction to Social and Political Aspects*. White Plains: Longman.

Stinnett, T. M. 1962. *The Profession of Teaching*. Washington, D.C.: Center for Applied Research in Education.

Summers, G. F. 1969. *Attitude Measurement* (2nd ed.). Chicago: Rand McNally.

Swan, M., Lapkin, S., Rowren, N., et al. 1990. The role of mother tongue literacy in third language learning. *Language, Culture and Curriculum*, 3(10): 65-81.

Taylor, P. 2006. *How to Design a Training Course*. Beijing: Beijing Normal University Press.

Tichenor, M. & Tichenor, J. 2005. Understanding teachers' perspectives on professionalism. *The Professional Educator*, 27(1&2): 89-95.

Tong, X. M. 2011. Foreign language education policy in China: A national security oriented view. *Social Science Quarterly*, (2): 222-224.

Tschannen-Moran, M., Woolfolk Hoy, A. & Hoy, W. K. 1998. Teacher efficacy: Its meaning and measure. *Review of Educational Research*, 68(2): 202-248.

UNESCO. 1966. The ILO/UNESCO recommendation concerning the status of teachers. http://unesdoc.unesco.org/images/0016/001604/160495e.pdf [2018-5-15].

Vygotsky, L. 1978. *Mind in Society: The Development of Higher Psychological Processes*. Cambridge: Harvard University Press.

Vygotsky, L. S. 1986. *Thought and Language (rev. edn.)*. Cambridge: The MIT Press.

Wang, D. 2011. The new curriculum and the urban-rural literacy gap. *Chinese Education and Society*,

44(6): 87-101.

Wang, G. L. 2013. Review on qualitative studies of English teacher efficacy in China (2006-2012). *English Teacher*, (9): 60-65.

Wang, J. Y. & Li, Y. 2009. Research on the teaching quality of compulsory education in China's west rural schools. *Frontiers of Education in China*, 4(1): 66-93.

Wang, J. Y. & Zhao, Z. C. 2011. Basic education curriculum reform in rural China: Achievements, problems, and solutions. *Chinese Education and Society*, 44(6): 36-46.

Wang, L. K. 2009. Review and expectation of teacher education policy within 30 years in China. *Journal of National Academy of Education Administration*, (1): 30-35.

Warren, L. L. & Payne, B. D. 1997. Impact of middle grades organization of teacher efficacy and environmental perceptions. *Journal of Educational Research*, 90(5): 301-308.

Weisstein, E. W. Pearson's skewness coefficients. http://mathworld.wolfram.com/PearsonsSkewness Coefficients.html [2018-5-15].

Weisstein, E. W. Statistical median. http://mathworld.wolfram.com/StatisticalMedian.html [2018-5-15].

Wen, Q. F. 2004. *Applied Linguistics Research Methods and Thesis Writing*. Beijing: Foreign Language Teaching and Research Press.

Wenden, A. L. 2002. Learner development in language learning. *Applied Linguistics*, 23(1): 32-55.

Wertsch, J. V. 2008. From social interaction to higher psychological processes: A clarification and application of Vygotsky's theory. *Human Development*, 51: 66-79.

Wikipedia. 2014. New Culture Movement. http://en.wikipedia.org/wiki/New_Culture_Movement [2018-5-15].

Wikipedia. 2018. Mathematical Statistics. https://en.wikipedia.org/wiki/Mathematical_statistics [2019-1-15].

Wilson, J. D. 1996. An evaluation of the field experiences of the innovative model for the preparation of elementary teachers for science, mathematics and technology. *Journal of Teacher Education*, 47(1): 53-59.

Wilson, S. M. & Wineburg, S. S. 1993. Wrinkles in time and place: Using performance assessments to understand the knowledge of history teachers. *American Educational Research Journal*, 30: 729-769.

Wise, A. 1989. Professional teaching: A new paradigm for the management of education. In T. J. Sergiovanni & J. H. Moore (Eds.), *Schooling for Tomorrow* (pp. 301-310). Boston: Allyn and Bacon.

Woolfolk, A. & Hoy, W. 1990. Prospective teachers' sense of efficacy and beliefs about control. *Journal of Educational Psychology*, 82(1): 81-91.

Wu, X. 2005. *Teacher Change: Issues in In-Service EFL Teacher Education*. Beijing: Foreign Language Teaching and Research Press.

Xun, K. 313 BC-211 BC. Zhi Shi. http://baike.baidu.com/view/9902015.htm?fr=aladdin [2018-5-15].

Yang, B. & Li, X. C. 2010. Problems of teacher professional development in poor rural areas: A case study of Lincang County in Yunnan Province. In B. Z. Zhou, L. Wang & T. F. Li (Eds.), *Teacher Professional Development in Poverty Areas: Case Study on Lincang County of Yunnan Province* (pp. 98-109). Kunming: Yunnan Art Press.

Yang, H. Y. 2004. Intrinsic and extrinsic factors and English acquisition of English learning of Bai students. *Social Science of Inner Mongolia*, (3): 45-47.

Ye, L. 2001. *New Look on Teacher Roles and Teacher Development.* Beijing: Educational Science Publishing House.

YMJFG. 1992. *Yunnan Provincial Statistics Report of 1992.* Kunming: Statistics Bureau of the Yunnan Provincial Government.

Yuan, G. 2005. Speech in Teacher Education Working Conference of 2005. In Teacher Education Bureau of MOE (Ed.), *Selected Documents of Teacher Training Guidelines and Experiences* (pp. 3-12). Beijing: Higher Education Press.

Yuan, Y. C. 2007. *Attitude and Motivation for English Learning of Ethnic Minority Students in China.* Shanghai: Shanghai Foreign Language Education Press.

Yuan, Y. C., Zhong, W., Wu, J. X., et al. 2013. Trilingual education and foreign language education: Planning of cross-border ethnic minorities in Yunnan, China. *Journal of Yunnan Normal University (Humanities and Social Sciences)*, 45(6): 18-25.

Yunnan Daily. (2002-10-7). Yunnan Daily, 1.

Yunnan Daily. (2011-11-5). Yunnan Daily, 4.

Zeng, X. D. 2012. *Blue Book of Teacher: Annual Report on the Teachers in China 2012.* Beijing: Social Science and Academic Press.

Zhang, D. N. & Fang, K. L. 2004. *Introduction of Chinese Culture.* Beijing: Beijing Normal University Press.

Zhang, G. R. 2004. The application of the theory of scaffolding in the teaching of College English Writing. *Foreign Language and Their Teaching*, (9): 37-39.

Zhang, L. J. 2000. Metacognition in L2 literacy learning: The case of ten Chinese tertiary students learning to read EFL. In A. Brown (Ed.), *Developing Multiliteracies* (pp. 83-96). Singapore: Nanyang Technological University Press.

Zhang, L. J. 2008. Constructivist pedagogy in strategic reading instruction: Exploring pathways to learner development in the English as a second language (ESL) classroom. *Instructional Science*, 36(2): 89-116.

Zhang, T. S., Deng, Y. C., Yang, R. Y., et al. 2007. Balanced development of compulsory education: Cornerstone of education equity. *Frontiers of Education in China*, 2(4): 469-493.

Zheng, W. 2001. A background overview of the development of English education in primary schools. *Zhejiang Teaching and Research*, (3): 19-20.

Zheng, Z. Z. 1987. *Teacher Education.* Hong Kong: Hong Kong Chinese University Press.

Zhong, W. 2010. Case study on English teacher in ethnic minority areas of Lincang. In B. Z. Zhou, L. Wang & T. F. Li (Eds.), *Teacher Professional Development in Poverty Areas: Case Study on*

Lincang County of Yunnan Province (pp. 195-199). Kunming: Yunnan Art Press.

Zhong, W. 2011. *Personal Report on NTP in 2011*. Kunming: Yunnan Normal University.

Zhong, W. & Gan, J. H. 2007. A tentative study on constructing the in-service training Internet platform for secondary school teachers. *Journal of Higher Education Research*, (2): 169-172.

Zhong, W. & Li, P. 2010. *Teacher Working Motivation, Self-Efficacy, and Their Correlation: Modification of WPI and TSES*. Kunming: Yunnan Normal University.

Zhong, W. & Yuan, Y. C. 2012. *Annual Report on NTP of English Teachers in 2012*. Kunming: Yunnan Normal University.

Zou, W. C. 2010. Report on pre-service training of secondary school foreign teacher in China. In W. C. Zou (Ed.), *Secondary School English Teacher Education in China*. Shanghai: East China Normal University Press.

Appendix 1　Questionnaire in English

I. Basic Information (Please tick "√" in the "□").

1. Gender: □A. female　□B. male
2. Age: □A. 21-30　□B. 31-40　□C. 41-50
3. Teaching years: □A. 5 or less than 5　□B. 6-10　□C. 11-20　□D. 21-30
4. Professional title: □A. Advanced level　□B. Intermediate level　□C. Primary level
5. Teaching courses: □A. English　□B. Others　□C. English and others
6. Ethnic groups: □A. Han　□B. Ethnic minorities
7. Mother tongue: □A. Chinese　□B. Ethnic minority languages

II. Language Learning Attitudes (Multiple choice, no more than three answers)

　　　　A. Chinese　　　　B. English　　　C. Ethnic minority languages

1. I want to learn _____ because I want to study it.
2. I want to learn _____ because it has a long history.
3. I want to learn _____ because it is beautiful.
4. I want to learn _____ because I like it.
5. I want to learn _____ because people who speak it are nice and kind.
6. I want to learn _____ because people who speak it are knowledgeable.
7. I want to learn _____ because people who speak it have great fortune and at a high status.
8. I want to learn _____ because people who speak it are respectable.
9. I want to learn _____ because it represents a great culture.
10. I want to learn _____ because it represents the culture I favor.
11. I want to learn _____ because it represents an interesting culture.
12. I want to learn _____ because it represents a civilized culture.

13. I want to learn _____ because the society needs it.
14. I want to learn _____ because it can improve my work.
15. I want to learn _____ because it can let me communicate with people from different cultures.
16. I want to learn _____ because it can make me knowledgeable.
17. I want to learn _____ because it can help me deal with my work better.
18. I want to learn _____ because it can help me improve my teaching proficiency.
19. I want to learn _____ because my leaders arranged it.
20. I want to learn _____ because it can satisfy some of my personal needs.

III. Self-efficacy

Please read each item carefully, tick ("√") the answer in "□" which suits you most. Please tick the answer like "☑".

Items	Not at all true	Barely true	Moderately true	Exactly true
1. I am convinced that I am able to teach successfully all relevant subject content to even the most difficult students.	□	□	□	□
2. I know that I can maintain a positive relationship with parents, even when tensions arise.	□	□	□	□
3. When I try really hard, I am able to teach even the most difficult students.	□	□	□	□
4. I am convinced that, as time goes by, I will continue to become more and more capable of helping to address my students' needs.	□	□	□	□
5. Even if I am disrupted while teaching, I am confident that I can maintain my composure and continue to teach well.	□	□	□	□
6. I am confident in my ability to be responsive to my students' needs, even if I am having a bad day.	□	□	□	□

				Continued
Items	Not at all true	Barely true	Moderately true	Exactly true
7. If I try hard enough, I know that I can exert a positive influence on both the personal and academic development of my students.	☐	☐	☐	☐
8. I am convinced that I can develop creative ways to cope with system constraints (such as budget cuts and other administrative problems) and continue to teach well.	☐	☐	☐	☐
9. I know that I can motivate my students to participate in innovative projects.	☐	☐	☐	☐
10. I know that I can carry out innovative projects, even when I am opposed by skeptical colleagues.	☐	☐	☐	☐

IV. Education Participation Scale

To what extent did these reasons influence you to enrol in the National Training Program? Think back when you enrolled in the National Training Program and indicate the extent to which each of the reasons listed below influenced you to participate in. Tick the answer which best reflects the extent to which each reason influenced you to enroll in. Be frank. There are no right or wrong answers.

Items	No influence	Little influence	Moderate influence	Much influence
1. To improve my English	☐	☐	☐	☐
2. To make new friends	☐	☐	☐	☐
3. To understand Western culture	☐	☐	☐	☐
4. To improve my current working situation	☐	☐	☐	☐

Professional Development Needs of Secondary School English Teacher: An Empirical Study Based on Multilingual Ethnic Areas of Yunnan Province

Continued

Items	No influence	Little influence	Moderate influence	Much influence
5. To escape from complex relationship	☐	☐	☐	☐
6. To satisfy the needs of other family members	☐	☐	☐	☐
7. To acquire more knowledge	☐	☐	☐	☐
8. To become acquainted with friendly people	☐	☐	☐	☐
9. To get something meaningful out of life	☐	☐	☐	☐
10. To find a better job	☐	☐	☐	☐
11. To improve my English reading and writing ability	☐	☐	☐	☐
12. To expand my mind	☐	☐	☐	☐
13. To help me talk with my children	☐	☐	☐	☐
14. To achieve an occupational goal	☐	☐	☐	☐
15. To increase my job competence	☐	☐	☐	☐
16. To answer questions asked by my children	☐	☐	☐	☐
17. To improve my English speaking ability	☐	☐	☐	☐
18. To enjoy learning	☐	☐	☐	☐
19. To keep up with children	☐	☐	☐	☐
20. To make friends	☐	☐	☐	☐
21. To overcome the frustration in the work	☐	☐	☐	☐
22. To break the routine	☐	☐	☐	☐
23. To avoid loneliness	☐	☐	☐	☐
24. To meet new people	☐	☐	☐	☐

Appendix 2　Questionnaire in Chinese

尊敬的老师：

您好！了解语言类教师的文化身份认同情况与其对语言学习的态度能够更好地促进语言类教师和其他教师的差异研究。本问卷为一篇博士论文的一部分内容，问卷采用无记名方式，请您根据自身的实际情况回答相关的问题。在做问卷的过程中如有问题，请向在场人员咨询。

谢谢您的支持！

一、基本信息（请在所选项前的"□"内打"√"）

1. 学校类别：□A. 小学　　□B. 初中　　□C. 高中　　□D. 大学
2. 性别：□A. 女　　□B. 男
3. 教龄：□A. 5 年或 5 年以下　　□B. 6~10 年　　□C. 10 年以上
4. 年龄：□A. 21~30 岁　　□B. 31~40 岁　　□C. 41~50 岁
5. 职称：□A. 高级　　□B. 中级　　□C. 初级
6. 教授科目：□A. 英语　　□B. 其他
7. 民族：□A. 汉族　　□B. 少数民族
8. 母语：□A. 汉语　　□B. 少数民族语言

二、第二语言学习的态度（请根据实际情况选择最符合的项填入，本题为不定项选择，最多 3 项）

　　　　　　　A. 汉语　　　　B. 英语　　　C. 少数民族语言

1. 我想学习 ＿＿＿＿＿＿＿＿ 因为我想研究它。
2. 我想学习 ＿＿＿＿＿＿＿＿ 因为它有悠久的历史。
3. 我想学习 ＿＿＿＿＿＿＿＿ 因为它很优美。
4. 我想学习 ＿＿＿＿＿＿＿＿ 因为我喜欢它。
5. 我想学习 ＿＿＿＿＿＿＿＿ 因为说它的人善良、友好。

6. 我想学习 _____ 因为说它的人有学问。
7. 我想学习 _____ 因为说它的人有地位、有前途。
8. 我想学习 _____ 因为说它的人受他人尊重。
9. 我想学习 _____ 因为它所代表的文化丰富多彩。
10. 我想学习 _____ 因为它所代表的文化是我喜欢的。
11. 我想学习 _____ 因为它所代表的文化很有趣。
12. 我想学习 _____ 因为它所代表的文化体现了一种文明。
13. 我想学习 _____ 因为当今社会很需要它。
14. 我想学习 _____ 因为它能促进我的工作。
15. 我想学习 _____ 因为它能让我和不同文化的人更好地交流。
16. 我想学习 _____ 因为它能让我很有学识。
17. 我想学习 _____ 因为它能让我更好地展现我的个人身份。
18. 我想学习 _____ 因为我是这种文化的一部分。
19. 我想学习 _____ 因为它能给我一种归属感。
20. 我想学习 _____ 因为我想成为这个群体的一部分。
21. 我想学习 _____ 因为它能让我胜任目前的工作。
22. 我想学习 _____ 因为这能提升我的教学效果。
23. 我想学习 _____ 因为这是领导安排的。
24. 我想学习 _____ 因为它能满足我某方面的需要。

三、自我效能

请您认真阅读以下每一道题，并根据自己的实际情况，在题后最符合自身情况描述选项的"□"上画"√"。在每一道题上不需要花过多的时间考虑，凭第一感觉给出答案即可。请您在结束后认真检查是否有漏选的题目。谢谢您的合作！

题目	非常不符合	有一点符合	基本符合	非常符合
1. 我相信即使面对最差的学生，我也能够成功地教他学会与学科相关的所有内容。	□	□	□	□
2. 我认为即使压力增大，我也能和父母维持积极的关系。	□	□	□	□
3. 当我尽力去做的时候，即使是最差的学生我也能教会。	□	□	□	□

续表

题目	非常不符合	有一点符合	基本符合	非常符合
4. 我发现,随着时间的推移,我会越来越有能力去帮助我的学生满足他们的需求。	□	□	□	□
5. 即使教学活动被打断,我也有信心保持镇静,并将教学活动很好地继续下去。	□	□	□	□
6. 即使我的心情很糟,我也相信我有能力去应对学生的需求。	□	□	□	□
7. 如果我尽全力去做,我相信我可以对学生的人格以及学术发展起到积极的作用。	□	□	□	□
8. 我相信我能够采用创新的方法去处理由于体制约束带来的问题(如预算削减和其他管理问题),并将教学活动很好地进行下去。	□	□	□	□
9. 我认为我能鼓励我的学生去参与创新型的课题。	□	□	□	□
10. 即使有同事对我的创新型课题持怀疑态度,我确信自己还是能将其开展下去。	□	□	□	□

四、学习动机

请您认真阅读以下每一道题,它们涉及你来参加本次"国培计划"的原因,请根据自己的实际情况,在题后最符合自身情况描述选项的"□"上画"√"。在每一道题上不需要花过多的时间考虑,凭第一感觉给出答案即可。请您在结束后认真检查是否有漏选的题目。谢谢您的合作!

题目	非常不符合	有一点符合	基本符合	非常符合
1. 我参加本次培训是为了提升我的英语水平。	□	□	□	□
2. 我参加本次培训是为了交新朋友。	□	□	□	□
3. 我参加本次培训是为了能够了解西方文化。	□	□	□	□
4. 我参加本次培训是为了改善我的工作现状。	□	□	□	□
5. 我参加本次培训是为了逃脱复杂的人际关系。	□	□	□	□

续表

题目	非常不符合	有一点符合	基本符合	非常符合
6. 我参加本次培训是因为家里人需要我学习。	☐	☐	☐	☐
7. 我参加本次培训是为了学习更多的知识。	☐	☐	☐	☐
8. 我参加本次培训是为了认识友好的人。	☐	☐	☐	☐
9. 我参加本次培训是为了让我的生活更有意义。	☐	☐	☐	☐
10. 我参加本次培训是为了找到更好的工作。	☐	☐	☐	☐
11. 我参加本次培训是为了提升我的英文读写水平。	☐	☐	☐	☐
12. 我参加本次培训是为了拓展我的思考能力。	☐	☐	☐	☐
13. 我参加本次培训是为了更好地和子女交流。	☐	☐	☐	☐
14. 我参加本次培训是为了达到我的职业发展目标。	☐	☐	☐	☐
15. 我参加本次培训是为了增强我的工作能力。	☐	☐	☐	☐
16. 我参加本次培训是为了能回答子女提出的问题。	☐	☐	☐	☐
17. 我参加本次培训是为了能够更好地用英语表达。	☐	☐	☐	☐
18. 我参加本次培训是因为我喜欢学习。	☐	☐	☐	☐
19. 我参加本次培训是为了能赶上我的孩子。	☐	☐	☐	☐
20. 我参加本次培训是为了交朋友。	☐	☐	☐	☐
21. 我参加本次培训是为了逃避工作中的压力。	☐	☐	☐	☐
22. 我参加本次培训是为了改变以前的生活状态。	☐	☐	☐	☐
23. 我参加本次培训是为了远离孤独和寂寞。	☐	☐	☐	☐
24. 我参加本次培训是为了认识新的人。	☐	☐	☐	☐

Appendix 3   Interview Questions (English)

I. Questions for all teachers

1. Please briefly introduce yourself to us.
2. What are the difficulties for you as an English teacher in rural areas?
3. Do you think you can solve those difficulties by yourself? Why?
4. How do you usually solve those difficulties?
5. Who do you usually ask for help?
6. Have you had any chance for professional training up till now?
7. What kinds of trainings can you receive?
8. How much do you like them?
9. Do you love being a teacher?
10. Do you have ethnic minority students? (If yes, then ask Question 11; If no, go to Question 15.)
11. What ethnic groups do they belong to?
12. Can they speak minority languages?
13. What do you think about the ethnic minority students?
14. Is it more difficult for you to teach English to ethnic minority students?
15. What are the most important things you need for your work?
16. How did English language change you (learning/teaching)?

II. Questions for ethnic minority teachers

1. Can you speak your ethnic minority language? (If yes, then ask Question 2; If no, go to Question 3.)
2. When did you start learning Chinese?

3. When did you start learning English?

4. How did you learn English in the past?

5. What were your English teachers like?

6. Can your English teacher speak your ethnic minority language?

7. As an ethnic minority teacher, do you think it's harder for you to teach English?

8. What are the difficulties for you to teach English contrasting to other teachers?

9. Do you think it's important for ethnic minorities to know their own languages?

10. How did the Chinese language change you?

III. Questions for teacher trainers

1. Please briefly introduce yourself to us.

2. What is your role in the National Training Plan?

3. What do you think about your students in the National Training Plan? (Do they love learning English? Do they love teaching English?)

4. Did you have chances to teach in the rural middle schools? (If yes, please describe your experience.)

5. Do you have ethnic minority students? (If yes, ask Question 6. If no, go to Question 8.)

6. What do you think about ethnic minority students?

7. Is it more difficult for you to teach English to ethnic minority students?

8. Do you think English is useful to you? (Please explain the reasons why you think so.)

9. Do you think English is useful to your students?

10. Do you think it is necessary to teach English in rural areas of Yunnan? Why?

11. How did English change you (learning/teaching)?

Appendix 4 Reliability and Factor Analysis of Language Learning Attitude

Alpha Reliability Statistics

Cronbach's Alpha	0.854
N of items	20

Reliability Statistics

Cronbach's Alpha				Total N of Items	Correlation Between Forms	Spearman-Brown Coefficient		Guttman Split-half coefficient
Part 1		Part 2				Equal length	Unequal length	
Value	N of items①	Value	N of items②		0.621			0.762
0.769	10	0.776	10	20		0.766	0.766	

Notes: ①The items are: C1B, C2B, C3B, C4B, C5B, C6B, C7B, C8B, C9B, C10B; ②The items are: C11B, C12B, C13B, C14B, C15B, C16B, C17B, C18B, C19B, C20B

Item-Total Statistics

Items	Scale mean if item deleted	Scale variance if item deleted	Corrected item-total correlation	Cronbach's Alpha if item deleted
C1B	12.23	18.803	0.393	0.849
C2B	12.60	19.235	0.350	0.850
C3B	12.26	18.528	0.455	0.846
C4B	12.12	18.678	0.468	0.846
C5B	12.54	18.812	0.426	0.848
C6B	12.20	18.809	0.399	0.849
C7B	12.09	18.706	0.482	0.845
C8B	12.24	18.671	0.422	0.848
C9B	12.41	18.470	0.469	0.846
C10B	12.37	18.212	0.527	0.843
C11B	12.28	18.592	0.436	0.847
C12B	12.34	18.722	0.401	0.849
C13B	11.91	19.673	0.413	0.849
C14B	11.98	18.973	0.525	0.845
C15B	11.98	19.437	0.369	0.850
C16B	12.05	18.814	0.484	0.845
C17B	11.98	19.005	0.514	0.845
C18B	12.04	18.566	0.569	0.842
C19B	12.20	19.255	0.288	0.854
C20B	12.04	18.782	0.504	0.845

Appendix 4 Reliability and Factor Analysis of Language Learning Attitude

KMO and Bartlett's Test

Kaiser-Meyer-Olkin Measure of Sampling Adequacy	Bartlett's test of sphericity		
	Approx. Chi-Square	df	p
0.856	1051.917	190	0.000

Total Variance Explained (20 Items)

Components	Initial eigenvalues			Extraction sums of squared loadings			Rotation sums of squared loadings		
	Total	% of Variance	Cumulative %	Total	% of Variance	Cumulative %	Total	% of Variance	Cumulative %
1	5.556	27.780	27.780	5.556	27.780	27.780	2.688	13.440	13.440
2	2.158	10.788	38.568	2.158	10.788	38.568	2.543	12.715	26.156
3	1.214	6.069	44.636	1.214	6.069	44.636	2.141	10.706	36.861
4	1.079	5.395	50.031	1.079	5.395	50.031	2.059	10.293	47.154
5	1.063	5.314	55.345	1.063	5.314	55.345	1.638	8.191	55.345
6	0.929	4.645	59.990						
7	0.890	4.448	64.438						
8	0.840	4.201	68.640						
9	0.766	3.830	72.470						
10	0.731	3.655	76.125						
11	0.707	3.534	79.659						
12	0.646	3.232	82.890						
13	0.567	2.833	85.724						

Continued

Components	Initial eigenvalues			Extraction sums of squared loadings			Rotation sums of squared loadings		
	Total	% of Variance	Cumulative %	Total	% of Variance	Cumulative %	Total	% of Variance	Cumulative %
14	0.537	2.684	88.408						
15	0.487	2.435	90.843						
16	0.439	2.196	93.039						
17	0.410	2.052	95.091						
18	0.382	1.910	97.001						
19	0.341	1.705	98.706						
20	0.259	1.294	100.000						

Note: The extraction method is principal component analysis

Total Variance Explained (16 Items)

Components	Initial eigenvalues			Extraction sums of squared loadings			Rotation sums of squared loadings		
	Total	% of Variance	Cumulative %	Total	% of Variance	Cumulative %	Total	% of Variance	Cumulative %
1	4.525	28.284	28.284	4.525	28.284	28.284	2.138	13.362	13.362
2	1.796	11.223	39.507	1.796	11.223	39.507	1.955	12.218	25.580
3	1.167	7.292	46.799	1.167	7.292	46.799	1.879	11.747	37.327
4	1.043	6.521	53.320	1.043	6.521	53.320	1.871	11.696	49.023
5	1.037	6.478	59.799	1.037	6.478	59.799	1.724	10.776	59.799
6	0.887	5.546	65.345						

Appendix 4 Reliability and Factor Analysis of Language Learning Attitude

Continued

Components	Initial eigenvalues			Extraction sums of squared loadings			Rotation sums of squared loadings		
	Total	% of Variance	Cumulative %	Total	% of Variance	Cumulative %	Total	% of Variance	Cumulative %
7	0.808	5.050	70.395						
8	0.772	4.825	75.220						
9	0.666	4.164	79.384						
10	0.601	3.757	83.141						
11	0.579	3.619	86.759						
12	0.519	3.245	90.005						
13	0.485	3.030	93.034						
14	0.439	2.741	95.775						
15	0.381	2.383	98.158						
16	0.295	1.842	100.000						

Note: The extraction method is principal component analysis

Rotated Component Matrix[a]

Items	Components				
	1	2	3	4	5
C12B	0.779				
C9B	0.702				
C2B	0.621				0.405
C10B	0.588				

Continued

Items	Components				
	1	2	3	4	5
C15B		0.790			
C20B		0.667			
C16B		0.581			
C19B			0.712		
C17B			0.694		
C18B			0.664		
C6B				0.766	
C7B				0.709	
C8B				0.593	
C1B					0.694
C4B					0.661
C3B					0.500

Notes: The extraction method is principal component analysis; the rotation method is varimax with Kaiser normalization

a. Rotation converged in 7 iterations

Appendix 5   Reliability Analysis of Chinese Teacher Self-Efficacy

Reliability Statistics

Cronbach's Alpha	N of items
0.812	10

Item-Total Statistics

No.	Items	Scale mean if item deleted	Scale variance if item deleted	Corrected item-total correlation	Cronbach's Alpha if item deleted
1	I am convinced that I am able to teach successfully all relevant subject content to even the most difficult students.	26.15	17.425	0.460	0.799
2	I know that I can maintain a positive relationship with parents, even when tensions arise.	24.90	18.615	0.359	0.809
3	When I try really hard, I am able to teach even the most difficult students.	26.05	17.748	0.442	0.801
4	I am convinced that, as time goes by, I will continue to become more and more capable of helping to address my students' needs.	25.39	17.376	0.577	0.785

Continued

No.	Items	Scale mean if item deleted	Scale variance if item deleted	Corrected item-total correlation	Cronbach's Alpha if item deleted
5	Even if I am disrupted while teaching, I am confident that I can maintain my composure and continue to teach well.	25.34	17.784	0.518	0.792
6	I am confident in my ability to be responsive to my students' needs, even if I am having a bad day.	25.47	18.023	0.507	0.793
7	If I try hard enough, I know that I can exert a positive influence on both the personal and academic development of my students.	25.10	18.081	0.474	0.797
8	I am convinced that I can develop creative ways to cope with system constraints (such as budget cuts and other administrative problems) and continue to teach well.	25.60	17.184	0.554	0.787
9	I know that I can motivate my students to participate in innovative projects.	25.45	17.624	0.547	0.789
10	I know that I can carry out innovative projects, even when I am opposed by skeptical colleagues.	25.54	18.000	0.482	0.796

Appendix 6   Factor Analysis of Chinese Teacher Self-Efficacy

KMO and Bartlett's Test

Kaiser-Meyer-Olkin Measure of Sampling Adequacy	Bartlett's test of sphericity		
	Approx. Chi-Square	df	p
0.830	446.892	45	0.000

Total Variance Explained

Factors	Initial eigenvalues			Extraction sums of squared loadings		
	Total	% of Variance	Cumulative %	Total	% of Variance	Cumulative %
1	3.769	37.692	37.692	3.097	30.966	30.966
2	1.145	11.448	49.140			
3	1.100	11.004	60.144			
4	0.814	8.145	68.289			
5	0.692	6.916	75.205			
6	0.600	6.000	81.205			
7	0.580	5.798	87.003			

Continued

Factors	Initial eigenvalues			Extraction sums of squared loadings		
	Total	% of Variance	Cumulative %	Total	% of Variance	Cumulative %
8	0.492	4.919	91.921			
9	0.435	4.353	96.274			
10	0.373	3.726	100.000			

Note: The extraction method is Maximum Likelihood

Goodness-of-Fit Test

Chi-Square	df	p
96.742	35	0.000

Appendix 7 Reliability Analysis of Modified EPS (Chinese)

Reliability Statistics

Cronbach's Alpha	N of items
0.859	24

Item-Total Statistics

No.	Items	Scale mean if item deleted	Scale variance if item deleted	Corrected item-total correlation	Cronbach's Alpha if item deleted
1	I joined this training for improving my English.	53.54	102.448	0.443	0.853
2	I joined this training for making new friends.	55.08	107.505	0.338	0.856
3	I joined this training for understanding Western culture.	53.92	102.110	0.539	0.850
4	I joined this training for improving my current working situation.	53.62	106.202	0.318	0.858
5	I joined this training for escaping from complex relationship.	55.22	110.056	0.220	0.859
6	I joined this training because my family members want me to do so.	55.23	108.853	0.293	0.858
7	I joined this training for more knowledge.	53.10	108.229	0.319	0.857

Continued

No.	Items	Scale mean if item deleted	Scale variance if item deleted	Corrected item-total correlation	Cronbach's Alpha if item deleted
8	I joined this training because people who participate in this program are kind.	54.68	104.406	0.447	0.853
9	I joined this training for a meaningful life.	53.54	104.366	0.467	0.852
10	I joined this training for finding a better job.	54.74	106.426	0.311	0.858
11	I joined this training for improving my English reading and writing ability.	53.66	101.294	0.504	0.851
12	I joined this training for expanding my mind.	53.36	104.419	0.539	0.851
13	I joined this training for being able to talk with my children.	54.54	105.017	0.378	0.855
14	I joined this training for my professional development.	53.47	104.553	0.464	0.853
15	I joined this training for strengthening my working ability.	53.11	107.145	0.401	0.855
16	I joined this training for being able to answer my children's questions.	54.84	103.962	0.453	0.853
17	I joined this training for improving my English speaking ability.	53.48	100.379	0.537	0.850
18	I joined this training because I love learning.	53.68	104.695	0.452	0.853
19	I joined this training for keeping up with my children.	55.00	105.744	0.381	0.855
20	I joined this training for making different kinds of friends.	54.73	100.362	0.641	0.846

Appendix 7   Reliability Analysis of Modified EPS (Chinese)

Continued

No.	Items	Scale mean if item deleted	Scale variance if item deleted	Corrected item-total correlation	Cronbach's Alpha if item deleted
21	I joined this training for overcoming frustration in my work.	55.09	109.056	0.211	0.860
22	I joined this training for breaking my routine.	54.46	103.587	0.432	0.854
23	I joined this training for avoiding loneliness.	55.31	108.239	0.336	0.856
24	I joined this training for getting to know new people.	54.82	102.729	0.534	0.850

Reliability Statistics

Cronbach's Alpha				Total N of items	Correlation between forms	Spearman-Brown coefficient		Guttman Split-Half coefficient
Part 1		Part 2				Equal length	Unequal length	
Value	N of items	Value	N of items		0.715			0.832
0.738	12①	0.781	12②	24		0.834	0.834	

Notes: ① The items are as follows. I joined this training for improving my English. I joined this training for making new friends. I joined this training for understanding Western culture. I joined this training for improving my current working situation. I joined this training for escaping from complex relationship. I joined this training because my family members want me to. I joined this training for more knowledge. I joined this training because people who participate in this program are kind. I joined this training for a meaningful life. I joined this training for finding a better job. I joined this training for improving my English reading and writing ability. I joined this training for expanding my mind. ② The items are as follows. I joined this training for being able to talk with my children. I joined this training for my professional development. I joined this training for strengthening my working ability. I joined this training for being able to answer my children's questions. I joined this training for improving my English speaking ability. I joined this training because I love learning. I joined this training for keeping up with my children. I joined this training for making different kinds of friends. I joined this training for overcoming frustration in my work. I joined this training for breaking my routine. I joined this training for avoiding loneliness. I joined this training for getting to know new people

Appendix 8 Exploratory Factor Analysis of EPS (Yunnan)

KMO and Bartlett's Test

Kaiser-Meyer-Olkin measure of sampling adequacy	Bartlett's test of sphericity		
	Approx. Chi-Square	df	p
0.835	1466.567	153	0.000

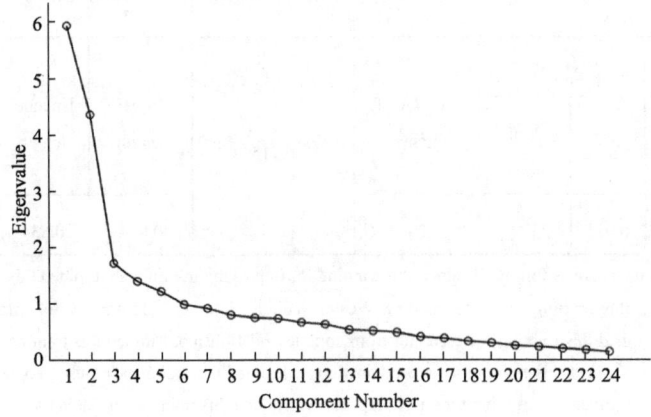

Appendix 8 Exploratory Factor Analysis of EPS (Yunnan)

Communalities

Items	Initial	Extraction
1. To improve my English	1.000	0.796
2. To make new friends	1.000	0.567
3. To understand Western culture	1.000	0.651
4. To improve my current working situation	1.000	0.664
5. To escape from complex relationship	1.000	0.711
6. To satisfy the needs of other family members	1.000	0.622
7. To acquire more knowledge	1.000	0.576
8. To become acquainted with friendly people	1.000	0.581
9. To get something meaningful out of life	1.000	0.604
10. To find a better job	1.000	0.408
11. To improve my English reading and writing ability	1.000	0.818
12. To expand my mind	1.000	0.625
13. To help me talk with my children	1.000	0.592
14. To achieve an occupational goal	1.000	0.632
15. To increase my job competence	1.000	0.684
16. To answer questions asked by my children	1.000	0.775
17. To improve my English speaking ability	1.000	0.831
18. To enjoy learning	1.000	0.383
19. To keep up with children	1.000	0.761
20. To make friends	1.000	0.735
21. To overcome the frustration in work	1.000	0.669
22. To break routine	1.000	0.642
23. To avoid loneliness	1.000	0.438
24. To meet new people	1.000	0.781

Note: The extraction method is principal component analysis

Total Variance Explained

Components	Initial eigenvalues			Extraction sums of squared loadings			Rotation sums of squared loadings		
	Total	% of Variance	Cumulative %	Total	% of Variance	Cumulative %	Total	% of Variance	Cumulative %
1	5.904	24.601	24.601	5.904	24.601	24.601	3.277	13.653	13.653
2	4.342	18.091	42.692	4.342	18.091	42.692	3.220	13.418	27.071
3	1.714	7.143	49.836	1.714	7.143	49.836	2.761	11.505	38.576
4	1.390	5.794	55.629	1.390	5.794	55.629	2.474	10.306	48.882
5	1.212	5.052	60.681	1.212	5.052	60.681	2.265	9.436	58.318
6	0.982	4.094	64.775	0.982	4.094	64.775	1.550	6.457	64.775
7	0.915	3.814	68.588						
8	0.795	3.314	71.903						
9	0.745	3.104	75.007						
10	0.730	3.043	78.050						
11	0.661	2.753	80.803						
12	0.627	2.614	83.416						
13	0.530	2.209	85.625						
14	0.511	2.129	87.754						
15	0.484	2.015	89.769						
16	0.408	1.699	91.468						
17	0.383	1.594	93.062						
18	0.331	1.380	94.442						

Appendix 8 Exploratory Factor Analysis of EPS (Yunnan)

Continued

Components	Initial eigenvalues			Extraction sums of squared loadings			Rotation sums of squared loadings		
	Total	% of Variance	Cumulative %	Total	% of Variance	Cumulative %	Total	% of Variance	Cumulative %
19	0.304	1.265	95.707						
20	0.256	1.067	96.774						
21	0.237	0.986	97.760						
22	0.207	0.861	98.622						
23	0.182	0.756	99.378						
24	0.149	0.622	100.000						

Note: The extraction method is principal component analysis

Appendix 9 General Profile of the Interviewees

As the following table shows, interviews were conducted with twelve trainees drawn from the samples being surveyed, two trainers and one program director from the NTP. The two trainers, one male and one female, from the NTP, were interviewed to talk about their impression of teacher students and their attitudes toward language education in ethnic minority or rural areas. One of them is an ethinic minority teacher and the other is a Han teacher. The twelve trainees, two males and ten females, are from the NTP from 2011 to 2013. Six of them are ethnic minority teachers and the other six are Han teachers working in ethnic minority areas. The program director interviewed is the one who is in charge of the NTP of other interviewees. They have different experiences of English learning and are presumed to offer various conceptions on English education and English teacher training. They were chosen based on purposive sampling (referring to Section 3.3). To begin with, I will give a brief introduction about each interviewee under different code names.

Demographic Information of Interviewees

Items		Roles in NTP		
		Teacher trainer	Trainee	Program director
Ethnicity	Han	1	6	1
	Ethnic minorities	1	6	0
Gender	Male	1	2	0
	Female	1	10	1

Appendix 9　General Profile of the Interviewees

Continued

	Items	Roles in NTP		
		Teacher trainer	Trainee	Program director
Educational background	English majors	2	10	1
	Non-English majors	0	2	0
Language ability	Chinese & English	1	8	1
	Chinese, English & ethnic minority language(s)	1	4	0
Teaching years	Less than 10 years	1	5	0
	11 to 20 years	1	4	1
	More than 20 years	0	3	0

A. Program Trainer 1 (PT1)

PT1 started learning English from her middle school with a group of Han students from a Han teacher. She loves learning English from the moment she started to learn. The reason was simply that she loved her English teacher. PT1 studied English Education in college. She participated in a joint part-time MA program at one university in Yunnan and an Australian university and received her MA in Applied Linguistics in Kunming in 2003.

After graduating from her undergraduate studies, she has been teaching College English in a university in Yunnan for more than 12 years. Most of the time, her students are non-English majors. From 2010 to 2013, she was the teacher trainer in NTP. She taught Classroom English to primary school teachers in 2010 and middle school teachers in 2011 (actually she also taught the same course in 2012 and 2013 after the interview was conducted).

Both of her parents are from ethnic minorities. Her father's ethnicity is Wa (or Va) but her mother is Bulang. According to traditional Chinese culture, if parents got married from different minorities, children should follow the father's nationality. PT1 is not the exception. Following her parents' example, she has a mixed nationalities marriage also. Being one of Wa people by herself, she married a Bai and gave birth to a son. Again, her son followed her husband's nationality, Bai.

Being a little girl, she started to speak Wa language to her grandpa and grandma because "they only know their minority language"[①]. She maintained this cultural heritage though she received her education in urban schools with groups of Han students. Because of lacking school education in her minority language, she knows what the written language looks like but she cannot write a single word of Wa and never tried to write it. She cannot even picture the written language of Wa in her mind. Different from PT1, her son, who cannot speak any minority language, can understand his parents and grandparents when they are speaking in minority language. Moreover, he can understand both Bai language from his father's side and Wa language from PT1's side because he spends one month each year during the Spring Festival with his grandparents who seldom speak Mandarin.

B. Program Trainer 2 (PT2)

PT2 started working at one university after his undergraduate study. Up till now, he has been teaching for 17 years. Most of the time, he teaches English Listening to English majors. Different from PT1, PT2's job requires higher English proficiency. While he was an undergraduate student, PT2 participated in a three-month student teacher program in a middle school at one of the rural areas in Yunnan. During that time, his major achievement was helping students to improve their English pronunciation.

Like most of people in China, PT2 belongs to the Han group. Also, he came from rural areas. It is because of education that his life changed. PT2 majored in English Education for BA. Same as PT1, he received his MA in Applied Linguistics in 2003 from the joint part-time program.

From 2010 to 2012, PT2 was the teacher trainer in NTP. He taught Classroom English to middle school English teachers. Also, he participated in NGO programs at the spring or summer break as a volunteer to train English teachers in mountainous areas.

---

① PT1. (2012, 8, 14). An interview with PT1. (W. Zhong, the interviewer)

C. Teacher Student 1 (TS1)

TS1 is from a county in Tibetan Autonomous Prefecture of Deqen, Yunnan. She was born in that area and has been teaching for 24 years in a middle school in ethnic minority areas. She felt lucky that she has been always teaching in the downtown areas but not the mountainous areas.

TS1 is one of the Han people. However, same as most of the teachers working in ethnic minority areas, due to the inhabitants, TS1 can speak more than one ethnic minority languages. In her case, she can speak Naxi, Lisu and Tibetan. English, as for many local people, is usually the third or the fourth language to them.

Satisfied with her teacher status, TS1 still feels sorry for her family because she engages more energy in her work than family members. Being an English teacher in an ethnic minority areas, she admits that teaching English is not important; nevertheless, in her words, "Teaching students how to behave as a real human being is more important"[①].

TS1 was the student of NTP in 2012. Before NTP, she joined other kinds of teacher training programs, such as the continuing teacher training programs offered by Educational Bureau of Yunnan Province. Among all the activities, she loves watching the Teaching Samples most. It is a commonly used peer education training method for in-service teachers in China. Through presenting videoed classroom teaching by some good teachers, teacher students can visualize their own classroom, and more importantly, they serve as models that others can try to achieve.

D. Teacher Student 2 (TS2)

TS2 is from Yulong County in Lijiang Prefecture, Yunnan. Yulong is one of the 128 National Poorest Counties in China. She has 10 years of teaching experience, but started her current job from 2011. The school where she is working now is located in the mountainous areas. Eighty percent of her students are minorities. She loves her job but sometimes feels helpless. She thinks her area is too undeveloped. She hopes she can learn more teaching methodologies, especially some updated ones, to help her

---

① TS1-H1F. (2012, 12, 28). An interview with TS1-H1F. (R. Li, the interviewer & W. Zhong, the translator)

teaching.

Like her students, TS2 learnt her mother tongue at home from her parents. In the first year of primary school, she started to learn Mandarin. English came to her life six years later than Mandarin. She was lucky that her teachers in her primary school and middle school can speak Naxi language, her mother tongue. It helped a lot for her language education.

TS2 is a three-year-old son's mother now. Both TS2 and her husband are Naxi people. Hence, they speak their minority language at home with their parents and son. However, she realized that her mother tongue has a negative influence on her Mandarin and English pronunciation, and affect her teaching as well. She assumed learning Mandarin at a young age would be beneficial to her son, so she decided to teach Mandarin only to her son. However, because her mother-in-law cannot speak Mandarin, after struggling for days, she agreed to teach her son Naxi instead of Mandarin. Still, this decision made her son suffer a lot in his first kindergarten year.

E. Teacher Student 3 (TS3)

TS3 is an ambitious young man who wanted to go out of the little town and do something "big"; however, his parents needed him to have a stable job. In order to help the family in raising his younger brothers, TS3 gave up his dream and became an English teacher. With 20 years of English teaching experience, TS3 is working in a boarding middle school from a rural county in Dehong Dai and Jingpo Autonomous Prefecture, Yunnan. TS3 is luckier than other teachers in his district, because his school has a better working environment, consequently, better students in talking exams. Facing the pervasive social belief that "education is useless" in local areas, TS3, as well as most teachers working in rural areas in Yunnan, shoulders more pressure. On the one hand, the school regulation needs to keep every student finishing the three-year studies of the Secondary level. If the teacher fails to maintain the students, he will receive fewer bonuses at the end of the year. TS3 has to try his best to encourage students staying in the school, though he realizes some of them will never go on with their studies. On the other hand, with a salary that merely fits the need of a basic living standard, and in the light of seeing capable teachers transferred to government or better schools, TS3 has been struggling to judge whether the price he paid really worth the income he got.

TS3 is eager for success. He thinks if he were ten years younger now, he will quit the job to fulfil his dream. Nevertheless, the complex cultural pressure makes him hesitate. Though he keeps complaining a lot about the low income of teachers, he has to do this job till his retirement with a hope that the government can change the policy and bring him a better life.

F. Teacher Student 4 (TS4)

As one of the Bai people, TS4 directly learnt his mother tongue from his parents. Same as many other ethnic minorities living in the autonomous areas, TS4 started learning English from his secondary school. TS4 was not an English teacher originally. He majored in Chinese at college. However, it was his passion for English that made him to be one. His love of English traced back from his high school English teacher who was close to students and even made TS4 and his pals think "we have to learn English well; otherwise we are doing no good to him"[①].

TS4 has students from other ethnic minorities like Lisu and Yi. He always needs help from his students to be the interpreters because he cannot speak other ethnic minority languages and also it is forbidden to use bilingual approaches (Mandarin and ethnic minority language) to teach in the classroom from the 7th grade. He struggles most with students' motivation for English learning. He and his colleagues tried their best to create a beautiful image of "going out" and "experiencing different things"; however, weak guidance from parents made their efforts useless. Very few students went to the college in the town where he is working now. Some of the local residents have never gone to other towns nearby, let alone big cities.

The eight-year working experience gives TS4 a positive attitude towards his career. He believes that teachers self-development can solve all the difficulties. He refused to join many short-term teacher training programs but volunteered to the NTP this time, because long-term training is more systematic and gives him more chance to learn.

---

① TS4-M2M. (2012, 12, 30). An interview with TS4-M2M. (R. Li, the interviewer & W. Zhong, the translator)

TS4 has not been a father yet, but he wishes that his child will learn English and also ethnic minority languages. He holds the conception that expertise in more languages can equip his child with stronger ability to achieve a blessed future.

G. Teacher Student 5 (TS5)

TS5 is a novice teacher who just has one year teaching experience and she majored in English Education. She is teaching in a middle school at a small village in Lincang. Her father is Bai and her mother is Bulang. Following her mother, she is a Bulang, but she cannot speak Bulang language, neither can her parents. She has grown up in the village not far away from her parents' home which is actually a Han culture district. Her classmates in primary and middle schools were mostly Han people.

She loved English when she was a child, which was also the reason that she pursued her degree in English. She did not feel English learning was difficult when she was young. However, lacking in experience and receiving little guidance from pre-service training, she felt frustrated when she started teaching English. "I didn't understood what the procedure of English teaching would be and no one could help me with that."[1] At the beginning, she felt isolated by the experienced teachers because she tried to teach English in a relaxed atmosphere which was quite opposite to other teachers. After three months' training, she seemed satisfied with the program. "I felt lucky I could receive the training only after one year (of working)… I used to follow other experienced teachers' words, but after the training now I know how I can organize my class."[2]

H. Teacher Student 6 (TS6)

TS6 is an experienced ethnic minority teacher with eleven years teaching experience. She has to teach at least 16 periods (about 12 hours) each week. She is one of Jingpo people and can speak Jingpo language and some Dai language. Her students usually include Dai, Jingpo and Han, so she can only use Chinese to teach English.

---

[1] TS5-M3F. (2013, 11, 8). An interview with TS5-M3F. (W. Zhong, the interviewer & W. Zhong, the translator).

[2] TS5-M3F. (2013, 11, 8). An interview with TS5-M3F. (W. Zhong, the interviewer & W. Zhong, the translator).

The biggest challenge for her is that most of her students do not want to learn English. "In one class, if I can have five students who pass the English test, that would be great for me!"① Normally, she has more than 50 students in Grade 1 in the secondary school, but students will become less and less in Grade 2 and Grade 3. "Some students don't want to study. Some quit the school in Grade 2 and some in Grade 3. They prefer working in other places."②

I. Teacher Student 7 (TS7)

TS7 has been teaching in the secondary school in Simao for more than 20 years since 1993. She mostly taught English in the middle school, but one year for Politics. She has worked in two middle schools. The one in which she is currently working is located in an urban area with few ethnic minority students, but the one where she worked before had many Dai students. She feels that motivation plays an important role in learning. "If the students like to learn and want to learn, they can learn it well, no matter whether Han or minorities."③

She was born in an rural area and getting a job with stable income was her dream. She wanted to participate in a finance business but she was poor in mathematics which held her back. She adored teachers when she was a student. "I think teacher is the God. No matter what he says is right. Whatever he does is a model."④ Being a teacher, she believes a good teacher should have profound knowledge. For her current job, she has the confidence that she can handle it well, but she admits she needs to learn more teaching approaches through the use of computer or multimedia to help English teaching.

---

① TS6-M4F. (2013, 11, 8). An interview with TS6-M4F. (W. Zhong, the interviewer & W. Zhong, the translator)
② TS6-M4F. (2013, 11, 8). An interview with TS6-M4F. (W. Zhong, the interviewer & W. Zhong, the translator)
③ TS7-H3F. (2013, 11, 16). An interview with TS7-H3F. (W. Zhong, the interviewer & W. Zhong, the translator)
④ TS7-H3F. (2013, 11, 16). An interview with TS7-H3F. (W. Zhong, the interviewer & W. Zhong, the translator)

J. Teacher Student 8 (TS8)

TS8 has been working as a secondary school English teacher since 2000 in Cangyuan, an autonomous county of the Wa. Her students are mostly stay-at-home children or left-behind children whose parents are working in other cities and only grandparents or other relatives are taking care of them. Some of her students are Miao people with high dropout rate because "Miao people get married too early. Some (students) were married in Grade 2 of secondary school". She thinks students' parents cannot help her to encourage students to learn.

TS8 didn't major in English, but Chinese. She was assigned to teach English because her score in English was good. She feels her oral English is not good enough which has negative influence on her teaching. Also, she thinks her vocabulary is another defect.

K. Teacher Student 9 (TS9)

TS9 is from a middle school which is only for ethnic minority students and allows bilingual education. Two thirds of her students are Wa people, and others are Dai and Lahu. She is from another ethnic minority group, Bai. She cannot speak any of her students' languages, though she can guess some of them. Mandarin is the only language she uses to teach and communicate with her students. She was not an English major student but she loves English very much. She thinks she lacks disciplinary knowledge in English teaching but doesn't know how she can improve her English. Being a mother who can speak Bai language, TS9 hopes her child can learn more languages like Bai, Chinese, English and some other ethnic minority languages.

L. Teacher Student 10 (TS10)

TS10 has two years working experience. Her ethnicity is Naxi but she can only speak a few words of Naxi language. Her mother is Naxi and her father is Han. In her village, only the aged ones speak Naxi. She never thought about learning Naxi language. All the Naxi language she knows is from others' conversation.

TS10 is teaching in an autonomous district of Lisu people but her students are Lisu, Naxi and Tibetan people. Her students will chat in their own ethnic minority languages but when they talk to the teacher, they will speak in Chinese. She loved

Appendix 9 General Profile of the Interviewees

learning English when she was a child though her English teacher used Chinese to teach her. She is satisfied that her students love her and are willing to learn English though they don't learn it well. She thinks English is useful for her students for external reasons like passing the exams and looking for better jobs. "The tourism business is very important in our district. If they can learn some English, they will have the advantages after graduation, such as being a tour guide, and (English) will help them to get more opportunities."[①]

M. Teacher Student 11 (TS11)

TS11 is teaching in an autonomous county of Dai and Wa people. She has been working for ten years. After she received her degree in English Education, she became an English teacher in a secondary school in a small town. She feels lucky because most of her students are Han people. "Dai students don't want to learn because their families have good income and studying is useless for them…Wa students speak another language and have problems of learning English."[②] TS11 has participated in many teacher training programs but feels most programs she had participated in were short and had little function to her practice. She is eager for specific guidance or suggestions which can be used to enhance her own situation. She feels it is hard to be an English teacher especially when students are not cooperative. She thinks that English is useless for her students except for taking the examinations. "Chinese is enough for them!"[③]

N. Teacher Student 12 (TS12)

TS12 was born in 1975 and received her degree in English at a teachers' college in Dali. In 1997 she volunteered to teach in a secondary school in a rural town. After 11 years, she was transferred to another secondary school in an urban county. In total, she has taught English for 17 years. She is a Han, but 90% of her students are Lisu people since she started working in that rural town. Some of them still could not speak

---

① TS10-M6F. (2013, 11, 16). An interview with TS10-M6F. (W. Zhong, the translator)
② TS11-H5F. (2013, 11, 16). An interview with TS11-H5F. (W. Zhong, the interviewer & W. Zhong, the translator)
③ TS11-H5F. (2013, 11, 16). An interview with TS11-H5F. (W. Zhong, the interviewer & W. Zhong, the translator)

Chinese when she met them in the secondary school. At that time, she tried to learn Lisu language with the aim of helping her students, but after she transferred to the school in the urban county, most students can speak Chinese and she stopped learning Lisu language.

TS12 remembers her mathematics was better than her English but she chose to learn English "without conscious consideration"[①]. She thinks if she did not learn English, she could not become a teacher. Her experience of being an English teacher is merely a dream to her.

O. Program Director (PD)

The PD I interviewed has been working in one normal university for 19 years. She has been the program director or the Chief Expert of NTP for English teachers in her university from 2010 to 2014. She has been teaching courses like English Teaching Pedagogy and English Teaching Skills. Her research area is pre-service and in-service teacher professional development. The PD is in charge of curriculum design and implementation of NTP.

---

① TS12-H6F. (2013, 11, 16). An interview with TS12-H6F. (W. Zhong, the interviewer & W. Zhong, the translator)

Epilogue

This research aimed to undertake study around a professional development need analysis of English teachers from ethnic minority areas. Part of the research aims have been achieved, but some new issues have cropped up and remain unanswered in this research. Hence, the future research could possibly probe the following three issues.

Firstly, some interviewees indicated that their preference for English stimulated them to become English teachers, but also claimed that being in favor of the language seems different to the capacity of teaching the language. The quantitative research on the connection between teachers' attitudes to English learning and teacher efficacy should be invested in the future.

Secondly, many interviewees mentioned that the contents of the NTP didn't match their working context, which implies the research focusing on knowledge base of English teachers (the knowledge necessary to become English teachers) in ethnic minority areas is not enough. Detailed research on this topic should be undertaken in the future to provide fundamental theoretical guidance around English teacher training.

Thirdly, poor family guidance was stated by most interviewees because of parents' reluctance to support their children's education, which might lead to weak teacher efficacy in ethnic minority areas. As this research didn't intend to include parents at the beginning of the research, it is hard to decide whether putting the blame on them is fair or unfair, and also whether their poor guidance could be an obstacle that teachers are facing. Since parents are one of the determinants of their children's success in English learning, which contributes most to teacher efficacy, specific investigation of parents' attitudes is needed in the future.

What this research aimed to do was a correlation and cause-and-effect study. My profession as an English teacher trainer shapes the research design in investigating the trainees' needs in teacher training programs, especially English teachers from ethnic minority areas in Chinese settings. Yunnan is the only province that has 52 ethnic minority groups within a single province in China, and ethnic minority education is a widespread issue, especially in China; in addition, teacher education or training is a fundamental issue regarding the quality of world education; hence, the English teachers' in-service training became my research domain. I narrowed down my research targets and focused the study on one NTP program in a teachers' university in Yunnan, a program which I participated in. Thus the research topics were fixed around a professional development needs analysis of English teachers from ethnic minority areas in relation to their language learning attitudes and teacher efficacy. Then three research questions were set.

To fulfil the research questions, questionnaire and interview instruments were adopted. Data were collected from 186 trainees who played the roles of questionnaire subjects, and 12 trainees, 2 trainers and 1 program director who acted as interviewees. Both qualitative and quantitative methods were involved in the data analyses.

This research has found that:

(1) Attitudes to English contribute most to the motivation to participate in in-service training;

(2) AES has a considerable effect on the motivation in relation to professional advancement and cognitive interest;

(3) Instrumental attitudes to English lead to pragmatic needs in teacher training;

(4) Demographic features are insignificant to differentiate the strength of general teacher efficacy;

(5) Teacher efficacy only determines cognitive interest and professional advancement orientations in NTP.

Issues of teachers' language learning attitudes, teacher efficacy strength and in-service training motivation orientations are that on average, teachers have positive attitudes to English learning but negative attitudes to ethnic minority language learning. AEC and English language are more related to the general strength of ELA. It is noticeable that AC plays a crucial role in determining general language learning attitudes.

The strength of teacher efficacy is strong but not to a significant level. Teaching year and teaching subject relate more to some significant differences of certain items asked. It is worth mentioning that Han teachers present lower teacher efficacy than ethnic minority teachers do.

Regarding in-service training motivation, in general, English teachers have weak motivation. Professional advancement plays the most important role in determining the general educational participation strength. English and non-English teachers present significant differences in their motivation for communication improvement. Teachers from various age groups and teaching-year groups indicate diverse motivation for family togetherness. It seems the elder they grow and the longer they have been working, the more they tend to yearn for family togetherness.

The difficulties in English teaching mainly focus on 1) students' motivation, 2) school management, and 3) family guidance. Language barrier is the most serious obstacle for ethnic minority students and English teachers in English education. The multilingual context and educational policy led to unpopularity of teaching English from L1 to L3. Interviewees confirm the efficiency of NTP; however, the length of the program, contents of the curriculum, ways of training and eligibility of trainees need further consideration.

Professional development needs of secondary school English teachers from ethnic minority areas involve:

(1) Specific language support for teachers who cannot speak minority languages;

(2) English content knowledge training;

(3) Specific PCK knowledge suitable to ethnic-minority context;

(4) A lifelong support system.

This research implies that teachers' attitudes to English and strength of teacher efficacy are correlated to their motivation in in-service training; moreover, their professional development needs are rooted in their special working environment. Given the conditions, teachers would probably have stronger efficacy and in-service training motivation, which might consequently result in more efficient in-service training, if the training is offered on the basis of the ethnic minority context. The main problem lies in that curriculum developed should meet the needs of these teachers, especially those whose mother tongue is not an ethnic minority language, and whose English academic level requires urgently to be upgraded. In this sense, the tasks of the teacher trainers and program directors are much heavier than the trainees because they are not merely teacher educators; they must first become good language learners and researchers.

This is only a pilot research on professional development of English teachers in ethnic minority areas. From the experience of this research, I have learned that there remains a gap between the theoretical knowledge and its application. Through the research practice, the gap might be narrowed to revise or update theories concerning teacher professional development, especially teacher efficacy and teacher beliefs. During the research, I was convinced that teachers' attitudes to language, teacher efficacy and teachers' training motivation are interrelated; moreover, I realized that the representations and causes of teacher efficacy are so complicated that quantitative research could only reveal part of the reality. For complex issue like need analysis, though I take three aspects (i.e., language learning attitudes, teacher efficacy and learning motivation) into account, the quantitative data are still limited in providing a profound answer, due to the measurement designed, in which TE and EPS specifically, are used to test the general tendency of a larger population. In this circumstance, qualitative analysis would offer clearer findings. However, the function of quantitative data is to provide me with a specific area to dig into. Taking the instrumental attitudes to English as an example, quantitative data implied teachers have stronger attitudes to the social value of English and particular use of English, which are both instrumental attitudes; thus, in the interview, my questions regarding teachers' attitudes to English, teaching methods and training needs revealed a link between instrumental attitudes and pragmatic training needs. In this sense, I have to admit, qualitative study would probably be a better solution in exploring the cause-effect relationship of complexity.